Assessment and Evaluation
for
Student Centered Learning
Second Edition

Expanded Professional Version

Assessment and Evaluation
for
Student Centered Learning

Second Edition

Expanded Professional Version

Edited by
Bill Harp
University of Massachusetts Lowell

Christopher-Gordon Publishers, Inc.
Norwood, MA

Credits

Chapter 1

Excerpt from "Questions we ask of ourselves and our students," Becky L. Reimer and Leslie Warshow, *The Reading Teacher,* April 1989. Reprinted with permission of the International Reading Association.

Figure 1.1, "Summary of Quantitative, Comparative Studies for Whole Language vs. Traditional Instruction," from *The Effects of Whole Language Instruction on the Literacy Outcomes of Navajo Students,* unpublished doctoral dissertation. Used with permission of Dr. Dan Garner.

Chapter 3

Figure 3.1, from "Reading Assessment: Time for a Change," Sheila Valencia and P. David Pearson, *The Reading Teacher,* April 1987. Reprinted with permission of Sheila Valencia and the International Reading Association.

Chapter 7

Excerpt from work of Lucas Albrighton used with permission.
Excerpt from work of Silas Bowler used with permission.
Excerpt from work of Daniel J. Eipper used with permission.

Chapter 11

"Knowledge" by Eloise Greenfield, from *Nathaniel Talking* copyright © 1988. Reprinted with permission of Marie Brown Associates. All Rights Reserved.

Chapter 13

Figure 13.1, "Coaching/Evaluation Distinctions," from *Cognitive Coaching: A Foundation For Renaissance Schools* copyright © 1994 by Christopher-Gordon Publishers, Inc. Reprinted with permission.

The first edition of this book was published with the title *Assessment and Evaluation in Whole Language Programs.*

Every effort has been made to contact copyright holders for permission to reprint borrowed material where necessary. We apologize for any oversights and would be happy to rectify them in future printings.

Christopher-Gordon Publishers, Inc.

480 Washington Street

Norwood, MA 02062

Printed in the United States of America

10 9 8 7 6 5 4 3 2 1   99 98 97 96 95 94
ISBN: 0-926842-40-4

Table of Contents

Chapter 13: Effective Inservice: The Key to Change

Epilogue: Applying the Research-Driven Model of Inservice Education

Table of Contents

Chapter 4
Reading Evaluation — Miscue Analysis

Chapter 9

Assessment and Evaluation in Bilingual and Multicultural Classrooms

Chapter 10

Record Keeping in Whole Language Classrooms

Preface

When this book was published in 1991, I opened the preface with the following statement: "The whole language movement is in a very real sense at a crossroads."

That statement, reconsidered in 1994, is an even more accurate description of the situation than it was four years ago. We have made progress, but there are nagging questions remaining about how to bring assessment and evaluation processes into congruence with changed classroom practice. The success we attain in answering these questions may well foretell the future of the whole language movement. We are at a critical point. The wide acceptance of the first edition of this book is a measure of the intense interest in assessment and evaluation issues.

The second edition, now entitled *Assessment and Evaluation for Student Centered Learning,* answers many of the pressing questions about how the collection of data on student learning and the interpretation of those data should be handled. We changed the title of the second edition because of the widespread confusion surrounding the term *whole language.* We still embrace the tenets of whole language instruction and seek to become the finest whole language teachers possible. We have dropped the term *whole language* because it has become both controversial and confused. The mythology shrouding "whole language" is discussed in Chapter 3.

The book begins with an examination of the basic principles of whole language instruction, assessment, and evaluation. Here we have provided a backdrop for the rest of the book, worked at dispelling the myths surrounding whole language instruction, and provided an update on the research base supporting the efficacy of student-centered instruction.

Chapters 2 and 3 examine past assessment and evaluation practices and offer guiding principles for future practice. John Bertrand offers valuable insights on assessment and evaluation by examining the traditional philosophy and methods of testing and evaluation through to present-day needs. He calls for change that will bring assessment and evaluation in line with whole language instruction practice. Bill Harp then offers thirteen principles of assessment and evaluation in whole language. The key here is that assessment and evaluation must be rethought for appropriate use in whole language classrooms. Traditional practices are incongruent with contemporary classroom practice.

Nowhere has assessment and evaluation changed more than in reading education. Our view of the reading process has changed. From seeing reading as a product that can be measured by grade scores on norm-referenced measures, we now look at how children use the reading process — how they draw on the cueing systems to create meaning. In Chapter 4 Janice Henson and Dorothy Watson offer practical suggestions for using miscue analysis in ways that lead to specific strategies for helping children. A new section of this chapter offers the reader numerous vignettes showing miscue analysis in action. These examples will be particularly helpful to teachers in understanding how the procedure works. The practical suggestions offered in Chapter 4 are extended in Chapter 5 by Ward Cockrum and Maggie Castillo, who show how teachers can develop their own assessment and evaluation strategies. New examples have been added to this chapter.

Chapters 6 through 9 present holistic assessment and evaluation in a number of settings. In Chapter 6, Jeanne Reardon invites you into her classroom where she and her primary-grade students collaborate in the evaluation process. Here, assessment is the teacher's discovery and understanding of a child's learning from the child's perspective. New material on the use of portfolios has been added to this chapter.

In Chapter 7, Yvonne Siu-Runyan illustrates ways in which whole language instruction works in intermediate settings by focusing on dialoguing with students about their progress. She carefully shows how talking with students about their progress can be used in combination with anecdotal records and student portfolios. New material points out how students who write tend to read differently (the material shows how literature informs their reading), and includes a list of useful resources and more on how to get students to talk honestly about how the teacher is teaching.

Hilary Sumner Gahagan has totally revised Chapter 8. This chapter shows how authentic assessment, with its emphasis on learners' abilities rather than their deficits, can fit into special education programs. With many examples and checklists, plus two working scenarios, it offers readers much useful and ready-to-use classroom know-how. You will find this chapter helpful because of the move in schools to the inclusionary model in special education.

In Chapter 9, Dorothy King examines the complexities of multicultural classrooms and suggests that observation and analysis are critical to assessment and evaluation in these settings. She underscores the important point that an understanding of cultures is needed to deal with learners appropriately. There are new student assessment/evaluation examples (retellings in first language) that demonstrate literacy learning as compared to apparent language deficits in English.

In Chapter 10, Jean Church focuses on record keeping. This very practical chapter will give you sound rationales for instructional/record-keeping decisions. There are many useful forms and checklists, with new ones focusing on student and parent inclusion in the assessment process.

The book ends with a provocative and challenging chapter from Bill Bintz and Jerry Harste that stretches our thinking about assessment and evaluation to new limits. The authors look at the assumptions underlying current assessment reform and argue that the changes being made are inadequate because they are based on an outmoded model of education. This chapter underscores my opening thesis that assessment and evaluation is very much at a crossroads — a critical crossroads.

I'd like to take this opportunity to thank those many readers who responded so favorably to the first edition of this book. I hope you will approve of the many revisions you will find here. My sincere appreciation goes to the talented contributors who have worked to make the second edition an even better version of an already very good book. Next, my heart-felt thanks to Sue Canavan of Christopher-Gordon Publishers, who had the vision to start this project and has carefully nurtured the revision. And finally, my thanks to the reviewers, Nancy Bolger, Douglas Decker, Jan Kristo, Linda Payne and Virginia Stanley. They carefully examined the first edition and made extremely helpful suggestions for the second edition. The book has benefited from their care and insight.

B.H.
February 1994

Chapter 1

The Whole Language Movement

Bill Harp

The whole language movement is no longer new. In fact, interest in whole language has permeated the entire profession, from the elementary classroom to teacher education programs. Some (Mather, 1992) argue that teacher educators are leading the profession astray by offering teachers-in-training a whole language view of teaching when that view is inappropriate for some learners. Others would argue that whole language makes such good sense that it should be the instructional model for all children (Goodman, 1989). Yet others assert that whole language works against poor children, immigrants, and students with learning disabilities (Kantrowitz, 1990). Much of the debate about the strengths and weaknesses of whole language centers on misunderstandings about the true nature of whole language. The whole language movement may well survive or fail as the result of the profession's response to two very critical needs. The first need is that of bringing assessment and evaluation into congruence with the whole language model. The second need is for the training and retraining of teachers so that they operate from a solid knowledge base that is consistent with the whole language philosophy. If these two needs are not addressed well, the whole language movement will fail. This book is designed to help teachers bring assessment and evaluation into congruence with whole language classroom practice and to develop the knowledge base from which whole language teachers operate.

I have encountered hundreds of teachers during summer whole language workshops and school-year in-service sessions. From what has been said in these encounters, one would have to conclude that the current state of whole language is one of confusion and misunderstanding. The breadth of *interpretations* of the meaning of *whole language* is stunning. In part, the confusion and misunderstanding has led to the acceptance of a mythology about whole language that must be dispelled.

The Whole Language Mythology

Judith Newman and Susan Church (1990, p. 20) published a list of whole language myths in *The Reading Teacher* in 1990. In that article they stated, "These myths are widespread. We've met them head-on all over the continent — here at home in Nova Scotia, in Alberta and Ontario, in Texas, Maine, and California."

The myths defined by Newman and Church have been quoted by many authors. Four of their myths are paraphrased and the accompanying responses are mine. This is followed by six myths observed by this author. Like Newman and Church, I have encountered the following myths from coast to coast in the United States.

Myth One: Whole language is an approach to teaching reading.

Response: Whole language is not an *approach* to anything. It is a mind-set, a philosophy about how children learn that informs our teaching of all things, not just reading. The whole language philosophy, the nature of whole language, will be described presently. For now, let's simply recognize that whole language is a philosophy that drives instruction — a philosophy that says learning in school should be like learning out of school. Learning should be realistic, relevant, authentic, child-centered.

Myth Two: Whole language teachers don't test; they don't really know what kids are learning.

Response: Assessment is the collection of data. Evaluation is the interpretation of that data. Whole language teachers are constantly collecting data on learners and interpreting those data. These activities take a myriad of forms, including observation and anecdotal records, running records or other forms of miscue analysis, collection and evaluation of work samples, conferences, test data, pupil self-evaluation, and teacher's use of developmental checklists, and increasing parent/student/teacher conferences. Whole language teachers KNOW their learners far better than the traditional teacher who can, for example, only describe a reader's progress in terms of instructional grade level.

Myth Three: Whole language teachers don't teach phonics. Phonics is a four-letter word.

Response: Whole language teachers understand that the reading process involves four cueing systems: semantic, syntactic, schematic, and graphophonic. They teach children to skillfully use all four cueing systems as the children *need the instruction* within the context *of meaningful literacy events.* Further, these same teachers can describe where each child is in terms of using the cueing systems, what his or her strengths are, and what the child needs to learn next. A great deal of phonics is taught as part of writing instruction. Phonics is learned by children as they engage in shared reading activities, guided reading activities, writing activities and mini-lessons designed to meet specific needs.

Myth Four: Whole language teachers don't teach, they just fill the room full of books and let the kids have at it.

Response: High quality whole language classrooms are the most structured, thoughtfully planned, and carefully engineered learning environments possible. The structure isn't always instantly visible to the observer, but it definitely is there. Whole language teachers TEACH! But the teaching looks different from traditional practice because the teacher is seldom "center stage." The child's learning needs are center stage. Instructional design is dependent on the teacher's ongoing observation of each learner's strengths and needs.

Myth Five: Whole language teachers don't teach skills, they just teach what they call "strategies" whatever that is.

Response: Just as whole language teachers understand they would be cutting one leg off a three-legged stool if they didn't teach phonics, they understand the importance of teaching skills. They know that children need to learn skills in order to become life-long learners and communicators. Examples are using the references and data sources in the library and spelling conventionally. But strategies, ways to handle processes, are important too. The ability to monitor one's own creation of meaning when reading and having several strategies for doing something about it when meaning fails are critically important as well. These factors constitute the whole language teacher's use of miscue analysis and running records.

Myth Six: Children in whole language classrooms do not do well on norm-referenced tests.

Response: As I have traveled the country doing inservice training during the academic year and summer workshops teachers have frequently reported to me that within a year or two after implementing whole language instruction test scores go up. It stands to reason that if the test has construct validity — that is, that it actually tests reading — than in classrooms where children are reading, reading, reading, scores will improve. It helps, too, if children are taught to deal with the test by understanding that the small texts and multiple-choice questions are foreign to regular classroom practice.

Myth Seven: Whole language is something you can do on Tuesday and Thursday.

Response: Whole language is not something you DO. Implementing whole language instruction requires a thorough understanding of the philosophy and knowledge base. Once this happens, all instruction — every day and for every child — is informed by these factors.

Myth Eight: Whole language instruction requires that you do portfolio assessment, which is nothing more than collecting work samples.

Response: There are really two myths involved here. First, whole language instruction does not require portfolio assessment. Portfolio assessment has been embraced by many whole language teachers because of the fundamental changes in assessment and evaluation. The second myth involves the nature of portfolio assessment itself. Portfolio assessment is only effective if it involves evaluation as well. The contents of the portfolio must be evaluated (interpreted) in terms of children's strengths and their next learning needs.

Myth Nine: Whole language teachers don't know whether or not children have comprehended because they don't ask comprehension questions.

Response: Whole language teachers believe that reading is the creation or re-creation of meaning based on the background knowledge the reader brings to the text. They "measure" comprehension by examining the predictions a reader makes and by asking children to retell what they have read as interpreted by the reader's unique background knowledge. Asking comprehension questions which have predetermined answers means that only the meaning created by the person writing the key to the questions is the possible, acceptable meaning. Whole language teachers reject this view of comprehension but certainly know how well a reader has comprehended a text. Skillful whole language teachers use questions in important ways. Stimulating questions are used to guide wonderful discussions of the literature children have read. Whole language teachers often view the child's understanding of how to use text to answer questions as more important than the answers, themselves.

Myth Ten: Everyone understands what I mean when I say I'm whole language teacher.

Response: Impressions and interpretations differ widely as to what constitute *whole language instruction* and even more confused is the concept of *high quality whole language instruction.* Some view whole language teaching as full of magic and mystery - a "cult-like" activity to which only few can aspire. Nonsense. Nonsense! High quality whole language teaching is carefully planned, professionally executed teaching that holds the learning needs of the child paramount over tests or texts. It is meaning focused, integrated and moves from what the child knows to what the child wants and needs to know next. It is carefully assessed and evaluated. This myth could be dispelled by whole language teachers describing what they do instead of embracing the *whole language* label.

What is Whole Language Instruction?

The teacher is reading an enlarged text of *Greedy Cat* (1988) to a group of first graders. It is a wonderful New Zealand story about a greedy cat who looks in the shopping bag and eats whatever Mum has brought from the store. The predictable text follows a pattern of "Mum went shopping and bought some XXXX. Along came Greedy Cat. He looked in the shopping bag. Gobble, gobble, gobble, and that was the end of that." After the first episode the children are eagerly reading along with the teacher, usually needing support for only the names of the things Mum buys at the store.

The teacher reads "…and that was the end of that!" And asks, "What would you like to do with this story now?" The responses from the children are eagerly offered and extremely varied. One child suggests that they could write about Greedy Cat. Another adds that they could write about Greedy Cat. Some want to make shopping lists for their mother. One child quietly offers the possibility of reading the books to a partner or by one's self. When several children say that's what they want to do, the teacher poses the question of how they can arrange for everyone who might want to reread the book to get a turn. One child suggests a sign-up sheet and busily finds paper and a paper clip to put the sign-up sheet on the cover of the big book. Another child suggests that they could make a game about Greedy Cat and he is instantly joined by two other classmates who want to do that, too.

The teacher then allows each child to choose how to respond to *Greedy Cat* and facilitates his or her other work. A few children return to activities they were engaged in before the reading of *Greedy Cat*, but most of them initiate one of the choices of activities suggested by the group.

Grant, Eric, and Julie have their heads together on the creation of a game. They make several trips to the game cupboard to get ideas for their game board. Olivia goes to the teacher with a writing problem. She wants to write "Greedy cat is too hungry." But she isn't sure which spelling of "to," "two," or "too" is right. The teacher seizes that moment to spend a little time with Olivia on a lesson on "too," and then enters an anecdotal note about Olivia's growth in her record book.

As children complete their chosen activities they share with each other and some move on to the library corner, activity centers, or to complete work started earlier. The teacher calls a group of six to the large table to engage in a guided reading activity with small copies of *Greedy Cat*.

In this classroom, as in other whole language classrooms, the children are viewed as experimenters — each hypothesizing and testing his or her theories. The teacher is the director of the laboratory. The teacher sets the stage for the children to explore, experiment, and grow. The teacher then observes carefully for ways to lead from behind by providing additional experiences that will take the children toward greater literacy.

The scenario above gives us some insight into what is meant by whole language. Consider the important features of what happened in this classroom.

- Children were exposed to literature that confirmed what they know about how language works. The predictable text of *Greedy Cat* allowed even the emergent readers in the group to join in the reading, feel success, and find a way to respond to the selection.

- Whole language teachers think differently about readers'

development and the nature of texts. In traditional classrooms the readability of *Greedy Cat* would have been determined and only children reading instructionally at that level would have been exposed to the text. Because whole language teachers think of readers developmentally, the same text can be used with all children, but the expectations for response from the children will vary. The emergent readers in the classroom benefited from the shared reading of the text with the voice support of the teacher. Other children will be able to engage in guided reading activities with the text with limited support from the teacher and peers. Still others will be able to read the text independently.

- Whole language teachers engage in assessment as an ongoing part of instruction. The teacher noticed each child's participation in the shared reading of *Greedy Cat* and decided which children would benefit from a follow-up guided reading activity. The teacher made an instantaneous decision to engage Olivia in a lesson on writing "to," "two," and "too." That objective was not planned in advance, but became important as Olivia exhibited a need for the instruction.

- Whole language teachers empower children to make choices about what they learn and how they demonstrate that learning. Notice that the question at the end of the shared reading was "What could we do with this story now?" This opened the situation to the wide variety of responses the children chose. Whole language teachers believe that literacy develops naturally through meaningful, functional use of language. The literacy activities the children chose were meaningful and functional to them.

- Whole language teachers value risk-taking and see it as both a tool of evaluation and a form of growth for children. Again, Olivia is an example. She took a risk in spelling "too," and the teacher used that risk-taking as a tool of evaluation and as a way to help Olivia grow.

- Whole language teachers create learning activities that are language rich, success-oriented, and carried out in a noncompetitive environment. In whole language classrooms the *process* is often of greater importance than the *product*.

- Whole language teachers create environments in which children use print in a variety of forms for a variety of important purposes.

Other Characteristics of Whole Language Instruction

Whole language is not an approach to the teaching of reading and writing. It is not a method that can be spelled out in a teacher's guide with a defined set of instructional strategies. Instead, whole language is a mind-set about instruction. It is a mind-set that draws on what we know about the importance of child-centered instruction.

Whole language instruction is not text or test driven. Instead, it is driven by what teachers know about the developmental nature of literacy and the development of children. Whole language teachers are knowledgeable about language and child development. They are knowledgeable about literature as well as other content fields. Whole language teachers arrange rich classroom environments that invite students to use language in meaningful, purposeful ways — and to take risks in doing so. Whole language teachers facilitate this growth in literacy by observing and interacting with children.

Whole language instruction is a total literacy immersion program. Children read, read, read, and read. They write, write, write, and write. They are exposed to whole selections of literature that confirm what they know about how language works. The focus is first and foremost on the creation of meaning. Only after children understand that reading and writing are meaning-creating processes are they exposed to the sub-skills. And then, as they can benefit from that instruction.

Whole language instruction empowers both teachers and learners. It empowers teachers to be true professionals who plan and execute the best in instruction for children. Teachers are empowered to be accountable for their work through documentation in child development and research in instruction and literacy. Children are empowered to take responsibility and ownership for their learning. With choice comes responsibility. In the process children learn self-evaluation, self-confidence and self-appreciation.

Whole language teachers have very strong beliefs about language and how it is learned. Language is used to comprehend the meaning of others, to create meaning, and to share meaning. Language is used for real purposes and to solve real problems. Language is used to get things done, for interpersonal relations, to solve problems, to pretend and imagine, to explain to others, and to re-create past experiences.

Whole language teachers use integrated, thematic units that build bridges between literacy events and a variety of subject areas. Thematic units are defined more broadly than traditional units. They have a focus or topic that cuts across subject matter areas. Themes are often developed during most of the school day. Only those subjects not covered in the theme are scheduled separately. Many literacy goals can best be achieved through thematic units. Interesting activities in which reading, writing, listening, and speaking are required in order to accomplish the content goals serve as dynamic methods for meeting literacy goals.

Whole language teachers operate from a well-defined philosophical base. The probable reason so many of them are so articulate about their beliefs is that they have had to carefully examine their beliefs and defend them. Whole language teachers are so knowledgeable because they keep reading, studying, and going to conferences so they can cope with the tough questions they get from parents, colleagues, and administrators (Goodman, 1989).

The Philosophical Bases of Whole Language

The philosophical bases of whole language are the beliefs teachers hold about how children learn, the role of the teacher and the nature of curriculum.

How Children Learn

Much of what whole language teachers believe about the development of literacy is born of our understanding about how children learn oral language in natural, developmental ways. Strong parallels exist between learning oral language and learning literacy.

The Development of Language

The fundamental philosophical base for whole language is what we know about how children learn language. As parents, we have often been amazed at the wonder of language development, while at the same time being eternally grateful that it wasn't our job to *teach* language to our children. We sometimes forget that the process is not a magical one; children do have to learn to use language and it does take time and effort. Observations of young children learning language have produced several principles of language acquisition.

Language learning is self-generated. Learning to use language is controlled by the learner and does not require external motivation. Children in situations where language is used will learn to use it without reward for each word learned. Communication with significant others is enough to keep the child learning. The best motivation for learning oral language is the same as for learning to read and to write — to communicate with others.

Language learning is informal. Parents do not have language lessons for their children. They play with them, sing with them, make cookies with them, show them the world and supply words to label the environment. Language is learned through its use in meaningful contexts, not through talking about it or analyzing it. Children learn language in the process of living in a social situation and participating in activities with others. They learn literacy in much the same way. This is not to suggest that children learning to read and write will never have instruction, but that instruction should be in a context that is meaningful to the learner. The instruction should be focused on accomplishing communication rather than isolating the forms of language.

Language learning is active. Children learn language as they actively engage in language with others. If a child says "cat" to an approaching the cat the caregiver is likely to respond, "Yes, that is a cat." If the child said "dog" the caregiver would likely say, "No, that is a cat." The child must actively take the label "cat" and decide what it is about this particular animal that makes it not a dog. Children are continually engaging in such active learning processes in learning to communicate. They need the same kind of active learning opportunities in developing literacy.

Language learning is a holistic process. Children learn about the forms and functions of language at the same time. They learn the phonetics (sounds), the pragmatics (rules for using language), the semantics (meanings), and the syntax (word order) all at once. No one would suggest that language be broken into artificial, discrete units to make it easier to learn. If we know that language is not learned by practicing its components outside the process of using it, then it follows that the learning of reading and writing must also be a holistic process that involves children in actual experiences that require reading and writing.

Language learning is variable. Each child has a unique set of experiences and a personal environment that differs somewhat from that of others. Even though children acquiring language pass through very predictable stages and most children in the world acquire language on a similar schedule, there are individual differences. The schedule varies somewhat for each person, but almost all will achieve competence in communicating and will have mastered most of the skills required for communication by the age of five or six.

The Development of Literacy

Whole language teachers draw on what we know about the development of oral language to undergrid our beliefs about the teaching and learning of literacy. We believe that the key principles of language acquisition apply to the development of literacy.

Literacy learning is self-generated. From the time children first scribble a line and "read" it to themselves or someone else, we see the self-generating nature of literacy development. Children want to communicate in written form, and those efforts will grow in environments where adults respond favorably to their reading and writing efforts.

Literacy learning is informal. Much of the real learning about reading and writing occurs outside the context of formal lessons in school. As children write more accurately through successive approximations to adult writing, they receive feedback on their writing. This feedback is then used to confirm their growing beliefs about how writing works. The same is true of reading. Children who understand from the beginning that reading is creating meaning, work through successive approximations to become more and more accurate in their reading. In a sense, each reading activity becomes a lesson for the next reading activity.

Literacy learning is active. Children learn literacy best in situations where they are using reading and writing continually — both in dramatic play and in real communicative contexts. Children, in fact, learn to read and write as they read and write. Whole language teachers find ways to involve reading and writing in virtually all curriculum areas. It is not uncommon to walk into a whole language classroom and have a child greet you with "Do you want to see what I am writing?"

Literacy learning is a holistic process. Children learn about the forms and functions of reading and writing at the same time. Just as learning oral language began with a desire to communicate meaning, so writing and reading begin the same way. Reading and writing need not be learned (in fact, are more difficult to learn) by practicing their components outside the process of using them. Whole language teachers believe that literacy moves from wholes to parts. Children are exposed to whole stories, whole paragraphs, whole sentences before they are ever asked to deal with the component parts, the sounds and letters.

Literacy learning is variable. Each child develops at his or her own pace, but virtually all will achieve competence if the focus is on communication, that is, meaning. Children acquire mastery of literacy through repeated practice with frequent constructive feedback. The practice of reading and writing must always to be in real communicative contexts — not forced, artificial situations.

Reading and writing are inverse processes. The writer begins with ideas and transforms those ideas into print to be shared with and responded to by a reader. The reader begins with the print and ends with ideas that are similar to the ideas of the writer. A transaction occurs between the ideas of the author and the ideas of the reader.

Reading is a very complex process. Both the reader's knowledge of how language works and the ability to draw on background experiences are crucial to using the reading process successfully. Children need opportunities to generate and test hypotheses about print, and to read printed material that is meaningful and predictable. Children also need teachers and parents who stress meaning more than mechanics.

Learning to write is very much like learning to speak and read. It is a developmental process that moves through observable stages. Classroom environments may be structured to foster writing development. In such classrooms oral language is encouraged and celebrated, children engage in activities that invite thinking, talking, reading, and writing, and literature is shared frequently. In such classrooms children value each other's work and the teachers value the work of children.

Composition is not a single act, but a sequence of activities that is described as a process. This process involves prewriting activities, rough drafting, revision, editing, final drafting, and presentation. The process is more important than any one writing piece. Working through the process, frequently with positive feedback from others, results in improved writing.

The Role of the Teacher

The best definition of whole language teachers has been offered by Ken Goodman (1986) when he wrote:

> They believe in kids, respect them as learners, cherish them in all their diversity, and treat them with love and dignity. That's a lot better than regarding children as empty pots that need filling, as blobs of clay that need molding, or worse, as evil little troublemakers forever

battling teachers. Whole language teachers believe that school exists for kids, not that kids are to be filled and molded by behavior modification or assertive discipline into look-alike, act-alike, Barbie and Ken dolls.

Whole language teachers believe there is something special about human learning and human language. They believe all children have language and the ability to learn language, and they reject negative, elitist, racist views of linguistic purity that would limit children to arbitrary "proper" language. Instead, they view their role as helping children to expand on the marvelous language they already use. They expect them to learn and they are there to help them do it. (p. 25)

Teacher as Learner

The role of the whole language teacher is foremost one of learner. Teaching from a strong philosophical and research base about the primacy of language requires constant study, reflection, and planning. Whole language teachers know that the more they know about language and learning, the better teachers they will be. They know that when they keep language whole and meaningful, it will be easier for children to learn because it makes sense. Trust is an important part of the role of the whole language teacher. Whole language teachers trust that all of their children will be capable language learners. Just as parents trust that children will learn oral language, so teachers trust that children will become literate. Whole language teachers surround their students with print the same way parents surround young children with conversation. In both instances the significant adults *trust* that learning will occur.

Teacher as Facilitator

Part of the whole language teacher's role is that of facilitator. The teacher's job is to create a language-rich classroom environment in which children are encouraged to explore, to experiment, and to take risks. Teachers arrange time so that it is flexible enough to permit children long periods of time for reading, writing, exploring, and pursuing personal interests. Some critics of whole language are aghast that the whole language teacher admittedly cannot specify all of the instructional objectives for a day *in advance*. Certainly, the whole language teacher is *responsible* for the learning of the children, but in a child-centered classroom the teacher *structures* the environment so that children can take the lead. And it isn't always possible to know in advance where the lead will take the children and the teacher!

Teacher as Observer and Evaluator

Whole language teachers are observers and evaluators. In traditional programs where the focus of instruction is texts, materials, and a prepackaged curriculum, the evaluation is primarily in the form of tests — a kind of product evaluation. In whole language classrooms the focus is on children, their interests, their need to use language, and the ways in which they use language as they explore, experiment, and communicate. Here the evaluation is primarily process-oriented. Teachers use samples of children's work to assess the ways in which children are growing in their use of the reading and writing processes. In whole language classrooms, teachers more often ask questions intended to challenge children than give answers.

The Nature of Curriculum

The curriculum is everything we want children to know, do, or feel as a result of their educational experience. One of the truly distinguishing traits of whole language classrooms is the curriculum. Whole language curriculum is characterized by ownership on the part of children, choice for children, and activities and materials that are authentic.

Ownership

Whole language teachers believe that the more learning in school can be like learning out of school, the more effective and enjoyable that learning will be. Gordon Wells (1986) encapsulated this belief in his book about children learning language and using language to learn. He said,

> From observation outside school, we know that children are innately predisposed to make sense of their experience, to pose problems for themselves, and actively to search for and achieve solutions. There is every reason to believe, therefore, that, given the opportunity, they will continue to bring these characteristics to bear inside the school as well, provided that the tasks that they engage in are ones that they have been able to make their own. All of us, adults and children alike, function most effectively when we are working on a task or problem to which we have a personal commitment, either because the goal is one that we are determined to achieve . . . or because the activity is one that we find intrinsically satisfying, or both. (p. 120)

In order for children to have ownership of their learning they must have choice and direction in that learning. Through joint teacher/ student planning each day whole language teachers find ways to give children responsibility for deciding what task to undertake and how to get them done. The teacher then supports that effort through careful observation, questioning, guiding, and inviting. In effect, the curriculum is then negotiated between teacher and pupil, with the teacher always having ultimate responsibility.

When children have ownership of the curriculum, teachers discover that many management and motivation problems disappear. When children have agreed to the day's agenda, they behave responsibly, moving from one important task to another with little guidance from the teacher. In fact, children in this environment ask for the teacher's help only when all other resources have been exhausted. Consequently, teachers are freed from many of the mundane classroom management tasks and can give much greater attention to individual children. Creating this kind of classroom environment takes a great deal of hard work and imagination on the part of the teacher. It requires experimentation, too. There is no magic formula. The organization of time, space, and resources is an important element. Whole language classrooms are usually organized around flexible activity centers. The classroom contains a rich assortment of objects and creatures for children to study, chart, graph, and write about. Children have ready access to the myriad of materials necessary to accomplish the task (Bird, 1987).

Choice for Children

Remember the episode with *Greedy Cat* in which the teacher finished reading the book and then asked the children what they could do with the book after that? In this situation the teacher was opening up the range of activities to the imaginations and interests of the children. In whole language classrooms children have choice in the literature they will read and in the topics they will write about. This is not to say that in all situations they will have choice, but in every situation in which it makes sense for children to have choices they will have them. Whole language teachers challenge themselves not to teach as they were taught, but to draw on the best educational thinking in designing instruction.

Authentic Materials and Activities

In the April 1989 issue of *The Reading Teacher,* Becky Reimer and Leslie Warshow published the individual narratives of experienced teachers who were attempting to resolve issues related to whole language. JoAnne Swindle poignantly described her struggle with the meaning of reading ability. Swindle wrote:

> Little Bridget in my kindergarten class three years ago forced me to rethink what I valued as markers of reading ability. Bridget passed all my skills assessment and also all the readiness tests I could find. I could hand her any book in my classroom and she would proceed to sound out each word and blend it into something that sounded like a word.
>
> She made me feel very uneasy, though, because she seemed to only go through the motions of reading without really understanding why she was reading or what she was reading. I felt insecure about recommending her for 1st grade but I had no hard data to justify my feelings. Back then, I thought reading consisted of skills for learners to learn and that my role, as a kindergarten teacher, was to teach one sound a week and by mid-February begin to introduce one word at a time for the students to learn to sound out. By mid-March I introduced my students to reading very carefully controlled sentences.
>
> I was in a quandary, though. Bridget met all my criteria but yet I still knew she wasn't a reader. I sat down with her one day with a book and asked her to read it. She methodically proceeded to sound out each word. I stopped her at one point and asked her about what she had read up until that point. She shrugged her shoulders. I closed the book and asked her what she thought this book was about. She shrugged her shoulders.
>
> I was screaming inside. This child didn't have the foggiest idea about the purposes for print and I hadn't helped her make any of those connections. I had only been asking my students about the sound of particular letters and how they could sound out the words I gave them. I wonder what they thought were the purposes of what I was doing with these letters, sound blending, and words. I never thought about asking them for what it meant to them. I had actually discouraged them from bringing books to school that didn't fit my carefully controlled reading scheme of letters, sound blending and CVC words.
>
> For the past two years I have been consciously trying to orchestrate my curriculum so that reading and writing have real life connections. I start the year with questions which will help me learn about what they know and how they think about reading and writing and also help them to begin to think about the bigger picture for reading and writing: Why do people need to read/write? What is reading/writing for? How do you think you will learn to read/write? What could you do if you knew how to read/write? What do you already know about reading/writing?

> I no longer assume that reading is only skills. I support my kindergarten children by reading books to them and allowing them free reading time for choosing books. (p. 597)

What do whole language teachers mean by authentic texts? The best way to answer that question is to look at the language in texts that are labeled preprimer by one of the basal publishers. One that readily comes to mind went something similar to the following:

Sam and Sally went to the lake.
"Good morning, Frog," said Sam.
"Good morning, Frog," said Sally.
Sam and Sally went down to the lake.
"Duck, Frog," said Sam.
"Good, Frog," said Sally.

Like so many stories controlled for vocabulary and certain phonic elements, the story above is incomprehensible. Whole language teachers reject giving children the kind of texts that fail to confirm what they know about how language works. Children know that stories are supposed to be understandable. They know that language works to create meaning. They expect the same things from print that they expect from oral language. Whole language teachers make sure that the texts they give children confirm what children know about how language works. When basal authors write meaningless stories such as the one above, there is no recognition that readers bring a great deal of knowledge to the reading act.

Teachers must make an initial curriculum choice. They choose a fixed curriculum and demand that learners adjust to it, or they start where learners are and build the curriculum around the needs and interests of the learners. Whole language teachers have chosen the latter. Critics who suggest that such curricular changes can't be made are well served when reminded that curriculum has changed dramatically over the history of American public education. It hasn't always been what it is — and it can still change.

The Research Bases of Whole Language

The true research base for whole language is the vast body of research that informs us regarding how students learn, how students learn to read and write, and what constitutes effective instructional strategies in literacy.

The whole language teacher's assertion that children must be active learners and that learning must be based on students' experiences is based on the work of Bateson (1972), Dewey (1938), and Eisner (1982), to name just a few. The work of these researchers reveals that children's learning needs to be reality-based rather than abstract and removed from experience. Whole language teachers use this body of work to justify the belief that literacy is best learned in a whole, meaningful context.

Our knowledge of language development is at the center of the whole language curriculum. We know that literacy develops along lines parallel to oral language development. Just as children move from producing very immature oral language to highly-developed oral language, so they move from scribbles to complete texts. We appreciate the importance of adult models and adult interaction in both oral language and literacy acquisition. The research base on which these beliefs are founded is made up, in part, by the work of Courtney Cazden (1986), Carol Chomsky (1969 and 1972), Jerome Harste (1984), and Lev Vygotsky (1986).

Reading and writing are processes that have much in common. Both readers and writers begin the process by using previous knowledge about the topic, the way language works, and about our alphabetic writing system. Both readers and writers bring certain expectations to the task. These expectations are based on previous reading and writing experiences, knowledge about the purposes of reading and writing, and knowledge about audiences (Butler and Turbill, 1984). Teachers who understand the development of language, reading, and writing provide activities that involve the children in all these processes. They know that these experiences must also be relevant to the children. Taylor et al. (1986) describes the characteristics of classrooms that implement a whole language view of reading instruction. These characteristics include: multiple and varied stimuli for reading, multiple and varied stimuli for writing, accessible and functional display of children's language products, integrative print, explicit classroom routines, and child-centered activities and instruction.

Whole language classrooms contain many books, directions, schedules, messages, and other materials for reading. Such classrooms stress functional reasons for writing, such as message centers, sign-up lists, and well-stocked writing centers. Print is used to take care of such tasks as attendance taking. Classroom chores and materials produced by the children are used for ongoing activities. Teachers also use print in typical projects such as hatching eggs, so that their students can keep records, check off activities, produce charts, and use reference materials. The daily classroom routines are real opportunities for using print to keep records, make and record choices, and keep track of how many participants are involved in an activity at one time. Finally, the print is child-centered in that most of it is produced by children and reflects their activities and interests.

The research base that informs whole language teachers about the reading process rests, in part, on the work of Marie Clay (1979), Kenneth Goodman (1970 and 1984), Frank Smith (1989), David Rumelhart (1984), Yetta Goodman (1980 and 1983), and William Teale and Elizabeth Sulzby (1986).

The research base that informs whole language teachers about the writing process rests, in part, on the work of Donald Graves (1975 and 1983), Nancy Shanklin (1982), Lucy Calkins (1986), and Marie Clay (1982).

The research base on which whole language teachers build their views of how literacy develops includes the work of Carol Chomsky (1972), Marie Clay (1982), Dolores Durkin (1966), Carol Edelsky (1982), Don Holdaway (1979), Elizabeth Sulzby (1985), and Constance Weaver (1982).

The whole language research base is moving in a new direction. There is a small, growing body of research that looks at the effectiveness of whole language instruction or compares whole language instruction with traditional instruction. Such research is riddled with possibilities for error and misinterpretation, and whole language teachers do not look to this research to justify their work. However, it may be instructive to examine some of the work reported to date.

Hans Grundin (1985) revisited the data reported by Bond and Dykstra (1967) in the USOE First Grade Studies. While there were not true whole language classrooms in the studies, Grundin concluded that those approaches that came closest to being whole language actually produced the best results of the various approaches compared.

Donald Graves and Virginia Stuart (1985) report the results of a two-year extensive study of the writing of 16 children. Major findings included that children write more and produce better writing when they are given control of topics and are encouraged to use their own developmental spelling. Children in the study learned to revise their writing and to assist each other in revision. They discovered that every child in the study had behavioral characteristics in the writing process that applied to that child alone. This led the researchers to conclude that children need a waiting, responsive type of teaching.

Lois Bird (1987) reports that when a resource teacher established a psycholinguistic reading laboratory in which children read and discussed fine children's literature daily, reading grade scores on the California Test of Basic Skills increased dramatically. In one year, fourth, fifth and sixth graders made between 13 and 21 months growth in reading in a nine-month period.

Norman Smith was Principal of Fair Oaks School at the time the school moved from traditional instruction to whole language (Bird, 1989). He reports that interesting changes occurred after the move to whole language. First, student attendance increased. Second, the whole atmosphere of the school improved. He tells the story of one parent who came to Back to School Night to investigate why his daughter was suddenly so positive about school. After a year of whole language, third grade bilingual students began to achieve at nearly the same level on both the CTBS Español and the CTBS English test in the spring. Finally, Smith reports that historically only 10 to 20 percent of Fair Oaks students passed the Redwood City District sixth grade writing proficiency test each fall. After three years of students being immersed in process writing, the passing rate increased to 82 percent.

Carbo (1988), in theorizing that whole language instruction just might dramatically improve literacy levels in the United States, refers to a study done in the Portland, Oregon, Public Schools. In a study of 18,126 students, the Portland public schools reported significantly higher reading achievement after one year of implementing a whole language program, compared to achievement during the previous five years when typical basal reader instruction was used.

A word of caution is in order in looking at this newer research base that compares the effectiveness of whole language instruction with other modes of instruction. Typically the comparison is based on norm-referenced test performance, which whole language teachers do not value. It is paradoxical that even when measures that whole language teachers reject are used, whole language instruction is superior to traditional instruction.

Garner (1993) conducted an extensive review of the quantitative, comparative research that examined the efficacy of whole language in contrast to other forms of instruction. The comparisons of the studies surveyed are presented in Figure 1.1.

Figure 1.1   Summary of Quantitative, Comparative Studies
for Whole Language versus Traditional Instruction

Researchers	Year	Grades	Traditional Measures	Wholistic Measures
1. Gunderson & Shapiro	1987	1st	n.s. (phonics) n.s. (vocabulary)	
2. Hagerty, Hiebert & Owens	1989	2nd, 4th, 6th	W.L. (comprehension) n.s. (writing)	W.L. (reading interview)
3. Ribowsky	1986	K		W.L. (linguistic) W.L. (orthographic) W.L. (graphophonic)
4. Stice & Bertrand	1990	1st, 2nd	n.s. (SRAT) n.s. (writing)	W.L. (retelling) W.L. (CAP) W.L. (interest)
5. Phinney (Weaver)	1986	K	W.L. (normed tests)	
6. Taylor, Blum & Logsdon	1986	K	n.s. (readiness) W.L. (letter recognition & language)	W.L. (print concepts)
7. Stewart	1986	K		W.L. (print concepts)
8. Reutzel & Cooter	1990	1st	W.L. (total reading) W.L. (comprehension) W.L. (vocabulary)	
9. Schafer	1989	2nd	n.s. (vocabulary) n.s. (comprehension)	
10. Kasten	1989	PreK, K	W.L. (ESI test C—for preK) W.L. (tests B,C,E,F—for K)	W.L. (book handling) W.L. (retell—preK)
11. Antonelli	1991	1st, 2nd, 4th, 5th	n.s. (decoding automaticity)	
12. Miller & Milligan	1989	1st	n.s. (decoding nonsense words)	W.L. (deletion test)
13. Azwell	1989	3rd, 4th, 5th	n.s. (reading achievement) W.L. (reading achievement—for high ability & analytic)	
14. Klesius, Griffith & Zielonka	1991	1st	n.s. (comprehension) n.s. (vocabulary) n.s. (phonemic & decoding) n.s. (spelling)	
15. Eldredge	1991	1st	W.L. (phonics) W.L. (vocabulary) W.L. (reading comprehension) W.L. (reading achievement)	W.L. (attitude)
16. Chen	1991	8th (ESL)	W.L. (English reading ability)	W.L. (holistic writing)
17. Dornbos	1991	K	n.s. (reading comprehension)	
18. Shearer	1992	2nd-6th	n.s. (writing composition)	

Findings: Traditional Measures   W.L. = 14, T = 0, n.s. = 17
Wholistic Measures   W.L. = 14, T = 0, n.s. = 0

Key: W.L. = whole language superior, T = traditional superior, n.s. = no significant difference

In summarizing these data, Garner (1993) pointed out a clear pattern of results favoring whole language instruction over traditional instructional practices. He wrote that

> Even on measures more directly related to traditional practices (such as word recognition, decoding and letter names) whole language is equivalent or superior to traditional methods. Not one quantitative, comparative study contrasting these two approaches was located which concluded that traditional approaches were better. (p. 71)

The research base supporting whole language is rapidly growing. When authentic whole language practice is instituted, there are two striking results: children learn and the mythology of whole language is debunked.

References

Antonelli, J. (1991). Decoding abilities of elementary students receiving rule-based instruction and whole language instruction. Unpublished master's thesis, Kean College of New Jersey.

Azwell, T. (1989). An investigation of the effects of a whole language approach on the reading achievement of intermediate grade students who differ in scholastic ability and cognitive style. Unpublished doctoral dissertation, Kansas State University.

Bateson, G. (1972). Effects of conscious purpose on human adaptation. In G. Bateson (Ed.), *Steps to an ecology of mind.* New York: Bantam Books.

Bird, L. (1989). *Becoming a whole language school: The Fair Oaks story.* Katonah, NY: Richard C. Owen.

Bird, L. (1987). *What is whole language?* Paper presented at Whole Language Conference II, Lethbridge, Alberta, Canada.

Bond, G.L. & Dykstra, R. (1967). The cooperative research program in first-grade reading instruction. *Reading Research Quarterly, 2,* 5–142.

Butler, A., & Turbill, J. (1984). *Towards a reading-writing classroom.* Rozell, New South Wales: Primary English Teaching Association.

Calkins, L. (1986). *The art of teaching writing.* Portsmouth, NH: Heinemann Educational Books.

Cazden, C. (1986). Classroom discourse. In M.L. Wittrock (Ed.), *Handbook of research on teaching* (3rd ed.). New York: Macmillan.

Chen, J. (1991). An experimental study of whole language instruction and basal reader instruction for the junior high English as a second language (ESL) students in Taiwan, Republic of China. Unpublished doctoral dissertation, University of Northern Colorado.

Chomsky, C. (1972). Stages in language development and reading exposure. *Harvard Educational Review, 42,* 1–33.

Chomsky, C. (1969). *The acquisition of syntax from 5–10.* Cambridge, MA: MIT Press.

Clay, M. (1982). *Observing young readers.* Portsmouth, NH: Heinemann Educational Books.

Clay, M. (1979). *Reading: The patterning of complex behavior.* Portsmouth, NH: Heinemann Educational Books.

Clay, M. (1982). *What did I write? Beginning writing behavior.* Exeter, NH: Heinemann Educational Books.

Cowley, J. (1988). *Greedy cat.* Wellington, New Zealand: School Publications Branch, Department of Education.

Dewey, J. (1938). *Experience and education.* New York: Macmillan.

Dornbos, K. (1991). The long-term effect of whole language instruction on kindergarten students' reading comprehension after a two-year period, as measured by standardized reading comprehension scores. Unpublished doctoral dissertation, Michigan State University.

Durkin, D. (1966). *Children who read early: Two longitudinal studies.* New York: Teachers College Press.

Edelsky, C. (1983). Segmentation and punctuation: Developmental data from young writers in a bilingual program. *Research in the Teaching of English, 17,* 135–156.

Eisner, E. (1982). *Cognition and curriculum.* New York: Longman.

Eldredge, L. (1991). An experiment with a modified whole language approach in first-grade classrooms. *Reading Research and Instruction, 30* (3), 21–38.

Garner, D. (1993, August). The effects of whole language instruction on the literacy outcomes of Navajo students. Unpublished doctoral dissertation, Center for Excellence in Education, Northern Arizona University, Flagstaff, AZ.

Goodman, K.S. (1989, Spring). Do whole language teachers have to suffer? *Teachers Networking — The Whole Language Newsletter, 9,* 3. Katonah, NY: Richard C. Owen.

Goodman, K. (1970). Behind the eye: What happens in reading. In K. Goodman & O. Niles (Eds.), *Reading: Process and program* (pp. 3–38). Urbana, IL: National Council of Teachers of English.

Goodman, K. (1984). Unity in reading. In A. Purves & O. Niles (Eds.), *Becoming readers in a complex society.* 83rd yearbook of the National Society of the Study of Education: Part I. Chicago, IL: University of Chicago Press.

Goodman, K. (1986). *What's whole in whole language?* Portsmouth, NH: Heinemann Educational Books.

Goodman, K. (1989). Whole language is whole: A response to Heymsfeld. *Educational Leadership, 46* (6), 69–70.

Goodman, Y. (1983). Language, cognitive development and reading behavior. *Claremont Reading Conference Yearbook* (pp. 10–16). Claremont, CA: Claremont Graduate School.

Goodman, Y. (1980). The roots of literacy. *Claremont Reading Conference Yearbook* (pp. 1–32). Claremont, CA: Claremont Graduate School.

Graves, D. (1975). An examination of the writing processes of seven year old children. *Research in the Teaching of English, 9,* 227–241.

Graves, D. (1983). *Writing: Teachers and children at work.* Portsmouth, NH: Heinemann Educational Books.

Graves, D. & Stuart, V. (1985). *Write from the start: Tapping your child's natural writing ability.* New York: New American Library.

Grundin, H.U. (1985). A commission of selective readers: A critique of *Becoming a nation of readers. The Reading Teacher, 39,* 262–266.

Gunderson, L. & Shapiro, J. (1987). Some preliminary findings on whole language instruction. *Reading Canada Lecture, 5,* 22–26.

Hagerty, P., Hiebert, E. & Owens, M. (1989). Student's comprehension, writing and perceptions in two approaches to literacy instruction. In S. McCormick & J. Zutell (Eds.), *Thirty–Eighth Yearbook of the National Reading Conference.* Rochester, NY: National Reading Conference.

Harste, J., Woodward, V. & Burke, C. (1984). Examining our assumptions: A transactional view of literacy and learning. *Research in the Teaching of English, 18,* 84–108.

Holdaway, D. (1979). *The foundations of literacy.* Portsmouth, NH: Heinemann Educational Books.

Kantrowitz, B. (1990, Fall/Winter). The reading wars. *Newsweek* (Special Edition), 8–9, 12, 14.

Kasten, W. & Clarke, B. (1989). Reading/writing readiness for preschool and kindergarten children: A whole language approach. Research Report. ED 312 041.

Klesius, J., Griffith, P. & Zielonka, P. (1991). A whole language and traditional instruction comparison: Overall effectiveness and development of the alphabetic principle. *Reading Research and Instruction, 30* (2), 47–61.

Mather, N. (1992). Whole language reading instruction for students with learning disabilities: Caught in the cross fire. *Learning Disabilities Research and Practice, 7,* 87–95.

Miller, J. & Milligan, J. (1989). Comparison of the whole language approach with a basal reader approach on the decoding and comprehending ability of beginning readers. A paper presented at the European Conference on Reading (6th, Berlin, West Germany, July 31–August 3, 1989). ED 313 693.

Phinney, M. (1986). Cited as personal communication in Weaver, C. (1988). *Reading process and practice: From socio-psycholinguistics to whole language* (pp. 213–215). Portsmouth, NH: Heinemann Educational Books.

Reimer, B.L. & Warshow, L. (1989). Questions we ask of ourselves and our students. *The Reading Teacher, 42,* (8), 596–606.

Reutzel, D. & Cooter, R. (1990, May/June). Whole language: Comparative effects on first-grade reading achievement. *Journal of Educational Research, 83* (5), 252–257.

Ribowsky, H. (1986). The comparative effects of a code emphasis approach and a whole language approach upon emergent literacy of kindergarten children. Unpublished doctoral dissertation, New York University. ERIC reference: ED 269 720.

Rumelhart, D. (1989). Understanding understanding. In James Flood (Ed.), *Understanding reading comprehension.* Newark, DE: International Reading Association.

Schafer, V. (1989). The effects of teaching a whole language philosophy to second grade students. Research Project Report. ED 309 400.

Shanklin, N. (1982). *Relating reading and writing: Developing a transactional model of the writing process.* Monographs in Teaching and Learning. Bloomington, IN: Indiana University School of Education.

Shearer, B. (1992). The long-term effects of whole language instruction on children's written composition. Unpublished doctoral dissertation, University of Minnesota.

Smith, Frank. (1989). *Understanding reading* (4th ed.). New York: Holt, Rinehart and Winston.

Stewart, J. (1986). A study of kindergarten children's awareness of how they are learning to read: Home and school perspectives. Unpublished doctoral dissertation, University of Illinois at Urbana-Champaign.

Stice, C. & Bertrand, N. Research report, Nashville, TN: Tennessee State University Center of Excellence, June 1990. ED 324 636.

Sulzby, E. (1985). Children's emergent reading of favorite story books: A developmental study. *Reading Research Quarterly, 20,* 458–481.

Taylor, N., Blum, I.H. & Logsdon, D.M. (1986). The development of written language awareness: Environmental aspects and program characteristics. *Reading Research Quarterly, 21,* 132–149.

Teale, W.H. & Sulzby, E. (1986). Introduction. In W. Teal & E. Sulzby (Eds.), *Emergent literacy: Writing and reading.* Norwood, NJ: Ablex.

Vygotsky, Lev. (1986). *Thought and language.* Cambridge, MA: MIT Press. (Original work published 1934.)

Weaver, C. (1982). Welcoming errors as signs of growth. *Language Arts, 59,* 438–444.

Wells, G. (1986). *The meaning makers: Children learning language and using language to learn.* Portsmouth, NH: Heinemann Educational Books.

Chapter 2

Student Assessment and Evaluation

John E. Bertrand

This chapter addresses the history of traditional evaluation and assessment in an attempt to chronicle how we have arrived at the present state of affairs. We'll look at the philosophy of traditional evaluation, along with the assumptions on which traditional assessment and evaluation have been based. We'll then identify and contrast the philosophy and assumptions on which whole language evaluation rests with those of traditional forms. The chapter concludes with a review of sources of data and insight for the whole language teacher.

Distinction Between Assessment and Evaluation

Evaluation usually refers to the process whereby a teacher collects, analyzes, and interprets data to determine the extent to which students are achieving instructional objectives (Gronlund, 1985). Assessment is the gathering of data, usually quantitative in nature and based on testing, that provide the information for evaluation to take place. Though technically one is a subset of the other, assessment and evaluation are terms that have often been used interchangeably in traditional classrooms. The measurement of student knowledge or performance is usually accomplished by quantifying some aspect of student output through testing and separating students into categories based on scores. This has led to a blurring of the distinctions between evaluation and assessment or testing (Gronlund, 1985; Mager, 1973). In classrooms, it is nearly always the scores that pupils generate in testing that are used exclusively to evaluate students.

Background

Testing is a very old concept. In the Old Testament, Jephthah (Judg. 12:5) ordered that all those who approached the Jordan River fords and were unable to pronounce the word "shibboleth" should be killed. By doing so, he distinguished between his own men and those of the enemy, who could not say the sound "sh." Thus, those who came and pronounced the password as "sibboleth" failed a very effective, early, criterion-referenced achievement test and received immediate feedback (Micheels & Karnes, 1950). The ancient Chinese used an examination that tested knowledge of the classics to determine who would be admitted to civil service (Phillips, 1968), and students were given performance tests on spelling, composition, grammar, and handwriting as early as Colonial times in the United States (Hodges, 1977).

Students in the United States have always been asked to provide evidence of their learning in structured ways, either by recitation or in writing. Even at beginning levels of schooling, kindergarten and below, the belief that learning can and should be tested has not historically been given much challenge. Teachers have always been expected to give grades and to differentiate between students based on periodic checks of performance, and these checks of performance have been and still are nearly always based on tests of some sort.

The controversies surrounding testing as the principal means of assessment and evaluation have centered around the types of testing to be used, not whether or not testing should exist. The Testing Movement began near the turn of the century with teachers learning how to make objective tests. It changed rapidly to published tests developed by psychometricians who were associated with the rise of statistics in the social sciences. Phillips (1968) reported a study conducted in 1900 wherein copies of the same geometry paper were shown to 116 teachers for grading. The teachers' marks ranged from 28 to 92, leading to criticisms of teachers' ability to grade accurately and objectively. Hulten (1925) gave 28 English teachers a paper to grade and found that 15 of the teachers who passed the paper the first time failed it when they were asked to grade it again two months later. Furthermore, 11 of those who initially failed it passed the paper on the second grading opportunity.

These and other similar reports helped popularize demands for more objective forms of testing.

In this country, calls for testing not open to interpretations by teachers are as old as public education. Horace Mann himself suggested the use of written examinations as early as 1845, calling for large numbers of questions and the standardization of answers. By 1878, the Regents' Examinations were in place in New York. The College Entrance Examination Board was organized in 1900 to provide questions used by about 1,000 colleges as part of entrance requirements.

Nearly as soon as they were in common use, standardized tests began to be criticized. Many people of the day felt that they were undemocratic, and those in the growing scientific movement in education were unhappy with the tests' validity and reliability. As a result, what Micheels and Karnes (1950) called the "Testing Movement in Education" was born. They reported that the first standardized tests born out of the statistical work begun by Thorndike and his students came into being in the field of arithmetic in 1908 and in handwriting in 1910. By 1928, over 1,300 published tests were in existence, with statistically calculated validity and reliability. By 1944, over 60 million standardized tests were administered to over 20 million people. Today, of course, it is virtually impossible to take part in schooling at any level without submitting to periodic standardized tests.

Closely related to the development of statistically reliable standardized tests was the rise of state and private testing bureaus, whose function was to prepare and distribute tests. By the end of World War I, over 100 test bureaus were in operation. In the late 1920s, state-wide testing was introduced. The University of Iowa Every-Pupil Scholarship Testing Program, begun in 1929, was one of the first. By 1939, twenty-six states had similar projects. Coincident to, and to some extent because of, the development of modern-style tests, the statistical concepts and techniques necessary to handle such a huge mass of data were invented. Today, every state in the United States maintains departments of educational testing.

It is important to remember that traditional teacher-made tests and standardized tests vary only in degree of rigor and statistical control. The intent of both is the same, to measure quantitatively a student's attainment of the information and skills specified by the curriculum. In fact, several books urge teachers to use statistical methods to ensure the validity and reliability of teacher-made tests (Gronlund, 1985; Phillips, 1968; Storey, 1970). It is this reliance on quantification that has made testing and evaluation nearly synonymous.

Standardized Testing

In practice, traditional evaluation has evolved as a dual system. Teacher-made tests are usually used to provide grades, while results of standardized tests are used to make or assist in making larger decisions about the pupil, the school, and even the school system. Standardized achievement tests usually share a number of common attributes. For instance, nearly all of them fall into one of two classifications: norm referenced or criterion referenced.

Norm-referenced tests are intended to provide a measure of performance that is interpretable in terms of an individual's relative standing in some known group (Gronlund, 1985). Usually, the comparison group is large (such as all the 12th grade students in a state), and the norms for the test have been established using a large sample representative of that group. Thus, we might say that a student scoring at the 76th percentile in mathematics earned a score that exceeded that of 76 percent of the students in the comparison group.

Norm-referenced tests usually share the following characteristics: They cover a large domain, with a few items measuring each learning task. They are used to discriminate between students for the purpose of rank ordering. They are designed to include items of average difficulty and avoid easy items, in an effort to stimulate a wide range of scores. Interpretation of a score requires a clearly defined population whose norms are well described.

Criterion-referenced tests, on the other hand, usually attempt to provide a measure of performance that is interpretable in terms of clearly defined and relatively narrow domains of learning. That is, specific skills and knowledge are tested, to which the test-giver knows for certain the student has been exposed. These tests are intended to identify strengths and weaknesses in individual students in terms of knowledge and task performance. They are used primarily to test relative mastery and require, for interpretation, a clearly stated level of desired performance. This level of performance may be stated in terms of time, number correct, or a combination of requirements. An example might be: "The students in the third grade at Countwell School will be able to correctly identify at least eight out of ten correct answers on a multiple choice test covering 'Helpers in our Community' each Friday during Social Studies class."

Both criterion and normed tests use the same kinds of questions, and both require a relevant sample of items representing the domain. The quality of the items is judged by the same standards of validity and reliability, and both are usually constructed so that the scores are amenable to statistical manipulation and interpretation.

The Philosophy of Traditional Testing and Evaluation

The above description of traditional testing practices rests on a set of assumptions that had, according to Micheels and Karnes, already taken on the status of articles of faith when their book was published in 1950. The most basic of these assumptions is: "Anything that exists at all exists in some quantity, and anything that exists in some quantity is capable of being measured" (p. 2). They went on to say that achievement certainly exists, both as a concept and a quantity; and therefore, achievement can be measured. The problem, according to Micheels and Karnes (1950) is only in developing instruments that discriminate sufficiently well enough to rank pupils. They said, "Our present instruments for measuring achievement are crude in comparison with the various electronic devices used in physical measurements, but definite improvements are being made continuously. In the years ahead, we shall be able to place more and more faith in the results of such tests" (p. 19).

Little has changed since the 1950s among authorities who accept traditional assumptions about testing and evaluation (Bloom, Madaus, and Hasting, 1981; Gronlund, 1985; Mager, 1973; Payne, 1974; Storey, 1970). All of them generally accept the same set of purposes for evaluation and the same set of assumptions, that is, that objective assessment (testing) is the most appropriate and reliable means of arriving at an evaluation of student performance.

Little seems to have changed in classrooms, as well. Tests are still by far the tool of choice used in grading, and most tests are of the traditional types. Implicit in traditional tests is another, less well articulated set of assumptions that is, nonetheless, quite powerful. This set follows a logical progression that might be stated as follows: Knowledge of facts is the most important goal in grading and evaluation, and this knowledge can be broken down into its component parts. These individual facts can be tested using traditional methods. These traditional methods are valid and reliable in producing a profile of the student's learning. This profile is all that is appropriate to know about a student when assigning a grade.

This logical progression, long accepted, is now beginning to be questioned. Simple observation in most public school classrooms leads to the conclusion that too few students know how to engage in acts of synthesis and higher-order analysis. Glasser (1990) reports that the situation has reached crisis proportions, with less than ten percent of present high school students able to deal with even simple tasks of integrative learning, such as summarizing a 1,000-word theme or calculating the cost of a family meal from a menu. Rather, the average test in public school classes reflects the type of lower-order thinking most students are comfortable with (Shanker, 1990), and measurement is nearly always done by using fill-in-the-blank, true-false, multiple choice, or some other "objective" measure. Critics often point to the lack of context or purpose in this process for students as the reason for many of the present ills in education (Glasser, 1990).

Another assumption upon which traditional testing rests is that teachers should not be allowed to depend on their own judgment in evaluating students. Because there did not historically exist a research-based, commonly accepted theory of language and learning, teacher-assigned grades therefore varied enormously (Hulten, 1925; Phillips, 1968). Only in the last twenty-five or thirty years has a coherent, research-based theory of cognitive acquisition and learning been developed. For this reason, teachers have been urged over the decades to engage in "objective" testing that does not allow them much professional participation in the process of evaluation. Storey (1970) puts it as simply as possible: "The most valid and reliable data available to the classroom teacher is that resulting from his own well-designed, item-analyzed, multiple choice tests" (p. xiv). Storey (1970) stated that these tests yielded student achievement profiles that were easy to produce and revealed all that was needed in evaluation of performance. Implicit in his statement is that teachers' judgments are not valid and reliable enough to produce student achievement profiles.

Embedded in the notion of "objective" testing is the assumption that the outcome of instruction is learning and that learning is testable in some objective fashion. The results of these tests are supposed to provide the type of information that allows the teacher to grade student performance. For these reasons, assessment and evaluation have become synonymous, and teachers have found themselves removed, over the years, farther and farther from the evaluation process. The reality today is that school personnel make life-altering judgments about children with little or no input from those who know the children best, teachers and parents, much less the children themselves. Instead, team meetings of school personnel consider grades, standardized-test scores, and observed behavior as the criteria for the labeling and placement for children.

In many places, standardized tests have "become" the curriculum. The paramount consideration concerning what is taught in many schools is aimed at good test scores (accompanied by the assumption that good scores accurately reflect real learning), and the paramount consideration in evaluation and assessment is to produce numbers by which children can be ranked, labeled, and compared (Smith, 1986; Stice & Call, 1987).

Calls for Change

For several reasons, however, this status quo is changing. First, many educators are dissatisfied with the value of present evaluation/assessment methods as a means of arriving at any true understanding of how well a student can perform. If, in fact, the original assumption underpinning standardized testing — that is, that all students in any given referenced group begin as potential equals — is being violated by teaching to the test, then standardized testing is losing its ability to differentiate between students either individually or in groups with validity and reliability (Stice & Call, 1987).

Some believe that failure of standardized tests to differentiate between students fairly on the basis of what they really know is both undemocratic and potentially racist. Evangelauf (1990), citing a recent report entitled "From Gatekeeper to Gateway: Transforming Testing in America," quoted Bernard R. Gifford, Chairman of the National Commission on Testing and Public Policy, who pointed out that

> There is ample evidence that the testing enterprise has in many instances gone haywire and is driving our educational system in the wrong direction... Current testing, predominately multiple choice in format, is over-relied on, lacks adequate public accountability, sometimes leads to unfairness in the allocation of opportunities, and too often undermines social policies... (p. A1)

It may be seen from the above that more recent judgments of standardized testing are not as genially uncritical as they have been in the past.

Second, the definition of what constitutes education is changing. It is no longer enough, for instance, for workers to be merely able to read simple directions. They must be capable of higher-level kinds of comprehension and synthesis (Mikulecky, 1987). Inability to function in these ways carries with it a strong risk of unemployment. Bertrand

(1987) found that as companies struggled for survival, they tended to lay off up to two-thirds of their workers and gain added productivity from those remaining through the use of robotics and computerization. The employees who retained their jobs were ones who had the literacy skills that allowed them to be trained quickly in radically new ways.

This is a relatively new phenomenon. Shanker (1990) reports the situation as both good news and bad news. The good news is that "...everybody has mastered the basics. Students can read basic material, and they can add, subtract, multiply, and divide whole numbers. But from there on, the news is all bad" (p. 346). Fifty years ago, for everyone to read and do basic math would have been more than a single bright spot in an otherwise dismal picture; it would have been victory itself. As society has become more complex, the requirements for basic participation have risen. Thus, traditional evaluations of such phenomena as worker productivity are being discarded or substantially added to. We in education are likewise faced with finding new ways to determine what pupils can and cannot do that reflect the kinds of learning people need so that they can prosper today.

Lastly, as schools and classrooms are restructured and as philosophies of what constitutes appropriate instruction change, new means to evaluate learning are called for. Standardized tests, designed to assess learning, are being charged with doing no more than labeling learners. Many are calling for site-based management with empowerment to parents and teachers (Cawelti, 1989; Finn, 1987) as a means to establish meaningful evaluation without the constraints of what they see as a bankrupt assessment process.

Rethinking Evaluation

As we have seen, traditional evaluation has evolved from (1) time-honored practices, (2) a view of desirable educational outcomes as products (knowledge of facts), (3) the desire to make evaluation "objective," (4) a belief that it is good to discriminate and separate learners as early as kindergarten, and (5) a belief in the accuracy and reliability of scientific measurement. Smith (1983) points out another aspect of the development of present-day schooling that has served as an additional spur to evaluation and which is spun together with "objective" assessment. He comments on the fact that classrooms today appear to be driven more by programs than by the judgments and expectations of teachers, and that students and teachers alike are often the victims of curricula that do not fit their needs or context. He says:

Programs appear in a number of educational guises — as sets of materials, workbooks, activity kits, guidelines, manuals, record sheets, objectives, television series, and computer-based instructional sequences. The history of instructional programs is probably as long as that of education itself, but they began proliferating during the present century as experts in other fields (such as linguistics, psychology, computer science, and test construction) and other external agents increasingly asserted views about what and how teachers should teach. The assumption that programs could achieve educational ends beyond the capacity of autonomous teachers grew rapidly in North America with the educational panic that followed Sputnik in 1957 and the coincidental development of management systems and operational techniques for the solution of such logistical problems as sending people to the moon... Despite their manifold variety in education, programs have a number of common elements, the most critical being that they transfer instructional decision making from the teacher (and children) in the classroom to procedures laid down by people removed from the teaching situation by time and distance. (pp. 108–109)

Smith (1983) goes on to say that such programs, removed as they are from the instructional setting, are by necessity based on fact and "sub-skill" knowledge and the expectation that children will by their very natures synthesize the facts and "sub-skills" into working practices of reading, writing, and problem solving. Smith (1983) strongly disagrees with this assumption and the sorts of evaluation that are supplied with programs, such as tests of the ability to perform some feat of memory, or mastery of a "sub-skill."

Smith (1983) makes an extremely important point. When knowledge is seen as the memorization of facts and success for the student as the ability to make only lower-level, recognition-style use of those facts, then the types of assessment and related evaluations we have today are a logical outcome of these curricula. For instance, when using traditional basal instructional modes for reading instruction, it is common to assign children worksheets that drill identification of phonic letter patterns and protocols. Such worksheets have no way to provide a context that allows children to have a purpose for their work (other than receiving a grade or going out for recess). Usually, these tasks do not even relate to the story in the basal reader. To make the circle complete, schools often then test these "sub-skills" on standardized tests of what are called "basic skills."

When prepackaged programs are the driving factors in curricula and the focus is surface-level identification of facts, then the unconnected, no-context (and to the children utterly meaningless) sort of assessment previously described can seem logical and reasonable to those who authored the materials. For example, the authors of the basal readers may know that the skill being addressed is recognition of three ways to spell words with the long "a" sound. They know that the story contains long "a" words, four each with three different spellings, repeated five times throughout the text. The fact that the children never make the connection or that the connection is meaningless to children does not seem to matter (Goodman, Shannon, Freeman, & Murphy, 1987). After all, the authors and publishers of the series will never see the students or teachers and must therefore construct assessments that are unconnected with anything else going on in the class. Prepackaged, program-driven curricula are increasingly coming under fire for failing to meet the needs of children. Influential commentators (Glasser, 1990; Finn, 1990; Shanker, 1990) are calling for schools that empower teachers and students and that give them context and meaning in daily activities. Their feeling is that evaluation needs to be contextually meaningful and under the control of teachers and students.

Whole Language Evaluation Philosophy

There are wide differences between whole language and traditional evaluation. Just as traditional evaluation is based on a philosophy and a set of assumptions, so is whole language evaluation. Before it was a curriculum or a means of instruction, whole language was a philosophy about how children learn most effectively and easily, with its origins in the Progressive Era and the period when humanism was emphasized in education (Goodman, 1986b). As an instructional paradigm, it draws from a more recent research base in socio-psycholinguistics.

Some of the main tenets of whole language include:

1. Whole language teachers believe that language is integrative, that it cannot be broken down into fragments and retain meaning. For whole language teachers, meaning is paramount over all other priorities.

2. Whole language teachers define teaching in terms of learning and learners.

3. Whole language teachers want children to become efficient users of language and structure the classroom to help them do so.

4. Whole language classroom activities focus on meaningful

events for children and the authentic learning of language in context; they do not focus on language itself.

5. Whole language learners are encouraged to use language in all its manifold ways, to take risks in using language for their own purposes.

6. Whole language teachers structure classrooms to facilitate the use of a variety of oral and written forms of language. (Goodman, 1986; Watson, 1987)

Because whole language classrooms are structured around authentic literacy events for children, each takes on the distinctive forms and activities brought to the situation by the teacher and the children. What actually happens in classrooms is therefore extremely varied, though whole language teachers, by definition, integrate language and content. For example, whole language teachers tend to agree that spoken and written language forms are only superficially different and that the process of learning each is the same (Cambourne, 1988). As a logical extension of this point, whole language teachers try to create and nurture the natural conditions that make language learning both possible and easy. They do not become prisoners of a prepackaged curriculum that dictates their every move, but rather constantly try to conceive of innovative ways to make learners responsible for their own learning, recognizing that all people must have ownership of their learning and have their own purposes for learning in order to participate with enthusiasm and carryover (Cambourne, 1988).

The logical extension of this principle is that evaluation should be a natural outcome of the process of creating meaning, used by the learner to improve performance and by the teacher to gauge the student's overall progress. In other words, evaluation in the whole language classroom should be as authentic as the instruction, making children partially responsible for evaluating their work, giving teachers responsibility for professional judgment, and arising from the contextual and real events of the class activities.

Evaluation conceived of in this way is not the measurement of the learner's ability to score at a certain level of mastery on a number of criteria. This distinction is at the heart of the difference between whole language and traditional evaluation. Whole language teachers assume that children learn best by doing and that the outcomes of these linguistic, intellectual endeavors are often visible in the processes of creating responses to the environment set up in the classroom. Traditional teachers are required by the very nature of the instructional system they use to engage in assessment that is largely divorced from meaning, no matter how well-intentioned they may be.

An example will help clarify this distinction. One curricular goal of a traditional teacher may be to instruct the children in writing thank-you letters. The teacher therefore would usually conduct a lesson on the proper ways to write a personal letter, emphasizing form, punctuation, and syntax. She or he would then usually require several practice letters, using topics assigned to all the children. At the end of the unit, the teacher would test the children's ability to perform on a criterion-referenced test by grading their performances in emulating as closely as possible the "approved" form of writing a thank-you letter. Children could then be assigned a grade, allowing winners (A's) and losers (F's) to be identified, and those who fell in between to be differentiated by D's, C's, and B's. In addition, the grading process is said to allow "diagnosis" (Bloom et al., 1981; Gronlund, 1985; Storey, 1970). For consistent failures over a wide scale of tasks, the diagnosis is often banishment (at least from the child's point of view) to a "special" class set up to deal with children who cannot make the grade.

The whole language teacher, by contrast, sees letter writing as one of a myriad of functions for language and is reluctant to assign writing for which the student sees no purpose. In this class, children write letters for their own purposes. For example, let us suppose that a child has read four books by Eric Carle. In response to his or her enthusiasm for the books, a teacher might suggest letting the author know how much the child likes his books, by writing a "thank you" for the pleasure the books have given. "You know, I have heard that Eric Carle tries to answer all the letters he gets from children. Would you like to write him and tell him how much you liked his books?" If the child answers positively, the teacher might then ask, "What do you need to know to be able to do that?" This might include looking at other letters, collecting books together to refer to, and talking about what to say in the letter with friends or the teacher. The teacher meanwhile can be satisfied that this activity fits within the parameters of desirable language development and be pleased because a child is busy on a task that is personally meaningful and exciting.

Later, he or she would evaluate the letter with the writer, using information gained from a variety of sources: a peer critique session in which the letter is shared with peers for their responses; a one-on-one conference with the writer to help him or her think through the process;

the writer's own comments that reveal the level of metacognitive awareness of the purposes of the letter; and finally the writing process itself, consisting of drafting, criticism, reconception, rewriting, and so on, addressing syntax and spelling at appropriate times. Notice that successive approximations of this task are evaluated, allowing the child to present to the teacher both the internal details of his or her learning process and his or her ability to perform the task as a complete operation at the end.

The teacher would look at this process from two points of view. First, from the child's point of view, does the feedback they collaboratively develop give the child support and encourage improvement? Second, from the teacher's point of view, does the evaluation illuminate the child's internal processes and provide evidence of the child's intentions, interests, strengths, weaknesses, and growth? Evaluation in the whole language classroom should also enable the teacher to guide future development of the child by providing the teacher with information and insight for informed judgments of the child's progress relative, not to others, but to the child.

Ken Goodman (1986) put it very well.

> ...whole language teachers are concerned with helping learners build underlying competence. They have no interest in getting them to behave in predetermined ways in class and on tests. For example, spelling competence is not a matter of memorizing words for the Friday spelling test, but a matter of first trying out words as they are needed in writing and then learning the limits of invented spelling against social convention. The basic competence of children who can comprehend when they read English is not reflected in tests of word recognition or phonics "skills." Moreover, pupils can give right answers on tests for wrong reasons, and wrong answers for right reasons. Whole language teachers know that the language miscues pupils make often show their underlying competence, the strengths they are developing and testing the limits of. (p. 41)

Just as the whole language classroom centers on process, rather than product, so does whole language evaluation. Learners (students and teachers as learners) engage in an ongoing process of evaluation of their own work and that of others, generating feedback that leads to improvement and development. This process, like everything else in the whole language classroom, is in a state of constant change and adjustment to reflect new knowledge and abilities as they develop.

Sources of Insight for Children and Teachers

What Yetta Goodman (1989a) calls the "double agenda of evaluation" is the underlying issue in all whole language evaluation. Students are learning, and they need feedback that gives them the means to evaluate their own work and to use that work for their own purposes. Simultaneously, teachers are learning about students through reflecting, teaching, conferencing, consulting, facilitating, and demonstrating. Good evaluation of students allows teachers to gauge what students might be ready to learn next and to shape the curriculum of the classroom to support the child's interests as well as the teacher's own purposes. At the same time, a teacher's evaluation of his or her own performance allows opportunities for professional learning and growth.

Goodman (1989a) see this double agenda as simultaneous evaluation of language development, cognitive development, and curriculum in a continuous, ongoing, integral process. Students are learning about their world, answering their own questions, solving their own problems, and evaluating their own learning. Not incidentally, language is the medium in which this process is conducted. Therefore, children are learning language even as they are involved in evaluating their own work and that of others.

For the teacher, this means having knowledge of how children learn, how they learn language, and how they use language in learning. It also means having knowledge of how individual children learn, what specific children are doing (or not doing), and how specific children are developing. Theory, research, and observational reflection form the knowledge base that provides teachers with a general framework and the specific information they need to guide their transactions with children (Bird, 1989). Theory and experience lead to a vision of what good learning looks and sounds like, and the teacher uses this vision to constantly facilitate and structure the experiences children have.

This point is important. Whole language classrooms are often described as being "child driven." Teachers in whole language classrooms believe that children must have a great deal of choice in terms of what subject matter will be addressed, and they provide a variety of options for activities in which the children may engage. This is by no means a laissez-faire process of management. Whole language teachers use an interaction of informed, intentional decision making with reflection, observation, and process evaluation to structure classroom experiences for optimum learning. The whole language teacher's ability to create an environment which "hooks the learner and inspires children to own their own curiosity, intelligence, and learning may be hard to describe, but it is there" (Edelsky, Draper, & Smith, 1983). Such an interaction is the process of synthesis that brings beliefs, goals, observation, reflection, theory, and practice together to produce classroom programs that truly reflect the ideas of whole language. The curriculum pivots around continual feedback to the teacher of how the children's efforts and his or her own are going. Evaluation of children and self is what makes the continually renewing process of whole language instruction possible.

As with language itself, it is the simultaneous nature of all the above that has made whole language curriculum and instruction so difficult to develop. Yetta Goodman (1989a) describes it as a three-dimensional interaction between three axes: (1) interaction, observation, and analysis; (2) formal and informal ways of interacting, observing, and analyzing; and (3) incidental and intrinsic modes of interaction, observation, and analysis. In the course of a day or a week, the typical whole language teacher does interact, observe, and analyze on most or all of these axes, using information, experience, knowledge, and vision to arrive at an informed judgment about each child's development.

This sounds like a difficult task for the teacher, and it is. However, it is the soul of the whole language classroom. A teacher who is not able to judge what is going on in the class must either invent instruction with no basis for judging its effectiveness or follow a prepackaged plan of some sort. Only a realistic and informed analysis of what is happening leads to realistic and informed guidance for what should happen next. Only with true feedback can the teacher match what is happening with a vision of what should be.

Sources of Data for the Whole Language Teacher

Whole language teachers evaluate all the time and constantly use the results to guide and to plan for what happens in class curriculum and instruction. Traditional teachers take only periodic checks of how children are doing and usually require blocks of valuable time to both give tests and provide feedback to children. A whole language teacher who constantly works collaboratively with children also has the intimate knowledge of each child to inform and guide her evaluation of that child. The traditional teacher, hemmed in by "objective" measures, finds that she or he is eventually involved in a process that becomes dehumanizing, in that it insulates her or him from intellectual intimacy with the students.

Engaging children in discussion (either group or individually), facilitating children's work, and planning and evaluating with children is how most whole language teachers spend the day. Traditional teachers tend to spend their time orchestrating classroom events, directing children through activities, moving children and materials through time and space, and correcting children's behavior and their academic work (Stice, Thompson, & Bertrand, 1991). Please notice the distinction here. Traditional teachers spend little time dealing with individuals or small groups in collaborative endeavors. Because of the way traditional classrooms are structured, with a reliance on separate subjects and subject-related blocks of time, there is little time for the kinds of observation, interaction, and analysis in which whole language teachers engage.

Yetta Goodman (1989a) offers the example of a child apparently lost in thought. From this, the teacher may conclude that the child is concentrating or she or he may decide the child is daydreaming. Goodman (1989a) says about this scenario, "Of course, the professional verifies such observational judgments through interacting, by engaging the student in conversation or asking a question, or through more formal evaluation, if warranted" (p. 9). It is easy to visualize this as a positive interchange between student and teacher, with the teacher leaning down and saying, "Hi, what are you thinking?" It is equally easy to visualize this same interchange in a traditional classroom wherein students have a directed task given them for each minute of the class and part of the teacher's job is to demand and ensure "on-task" compliance. Since a large part of the traditional teacher's role is to be an enforcer of task and a warden of time, there will exist a buffer that makes collaboration with students more difficult. Real personal knowledge and real intellectual intimacy with students tends not to exist to nearly the same extent in such programs. Students always know that there will be a test at the end and that they will be in an adversarial position relative to other students and the teacher.

Summary

Testing has existed as a means of either opening up or denying opportunities for many years. In the 20th century, two movements have emerged in traditional classrooms. First, teachers have relinquished, for a number of reasons, most claims to the use of judgment and qualitative evaluation of students in favor of measures based on objective testing methods. Second, standardized tests, both norm- and criterion-referenced, have made huge gains in importance as they relate to the evaluation of both individuals and groups of students. However, both these movements have come under examination and attack recently.

Whole language teachers, by contrast, embrace the ideas of process evaluation based on their own observations, judgments, knowledge of how children learn, and interactions with the children. They usually find standardized tests inappropriate for the goals and ambitions they have for children. These teachers typically spend more time and effort in evaluation than traditional teachers, because evaluation of student performance and teacher performance is the linchpin of the whole language classroom. In the traditional classroom, curriculum is usually program driven, and therefore is set in advance with little attention to the individual interests and abilities of students. They whole language classroom is defined by the teacher's ability to marry theory and practice, constantly reflecting on and responding to the learner, as well as reflecting on and altering teaching as necessary. Evaluation is one of the most essential components of the whole language classroom. Without thoughtful, informed, and collaborative evaluation, whole language classrooms have no rudder to provide direction.

References

Barnes, D., Britton, J., & Rosen, H. (1969). *Language, the learner, and the school.* Middlesex, England: Penguin.

Bertrand, J. (1987). The changing corporate concepts of literacy. In D. Lumpkin (Ed.), *Changing conceptions of reading: Literacy learning instruction.* Muncie, IN: Seventh Yearbook of the American Reading Forum.

Bird, L. (1989). The art of teaching: Evaluation and revision. In K. Goodman, Y. Goodman, & W. Hood (Eds.), *The whole language evaluation book.* Portsmouth, NH: Heinemann Educational Books.

Bloom, B., Madaus, G., & Hastings, J.T. (1981). *Evaluation to improve learning.* New York: McGraw-Hill Book Company.

Cambourne, B. (1988). *The whole story: Natural learning and the acquisition of literacy in the classroom.* Auckland, NZ: Ashton Scholastic.

Cawelti, G. (1989). Key elements of site-based management. *Educational Leadership, 46*(8), 46.

Clay, M. (1990). Research current: What is and what might be in evaluation. *Language Arts, 67*(3), 288–298.

Edelsky, C., Draper, K., & Smith, K. (1983). Hookin' 'em in at the start of school in a "whole language" classroom. *Anthropology and Education Quarterly, 14*(4), 257–281.

Evangelauf, J. (1990). Reliance on multiple-choice tests said to harm minorities and hinder reform; panel seeks a new regulatory agency. *The Chronicle of Higher Education, XXXVI*(37), A1.

Finn, Jr., C. (1990). The biggest reform of all. *Phi Delta Kappan, 71*(8), 584–592.

Finn, Jr., C. (1987). A call for radical change in educational delivery. *Education Digest, 52*(1), 2.

Glasser, W. (1990). The quality school. *Phi Delta Kappan, 71*(6), 425–435.

Goodman, K., Shannon, P., Freeman, Y., & Murphy, S. (1987). *Report on basal readers.* Katonah, NY: Richard C. Owen Publishers.

Goodman, K. (1986). *What's whole in whole language?* Portsmouth, NH: Heinemann Educational Books.

Goodman, Y. (1989a). Evaluation of students. In K. Goodman, Y. Goodman, & W. Hood (Eds.), *The whole language evaluation book.* Portsmouth, NH: Heinemann Educational Books.

Goodman, Y. (1989b). Roots of the whole language movement. *Elementary Education Journal, 90*(2), 113–127.

Goodman, Y. (1985). Kidwatching: Observing children in the classroom. In A. Jaggar & M.T. Smith-Burke (Eds.), *Observing the language learner.* Newark, DE: International Reading Association.

Gronlund, N. (1985). *Measurement and evaluation in teaching* (5th edition). New York: Macmillan Publishing Company.

Hodges, R. (1977). In Adam's fall: A brief history of spelling instruction in the United States. In H. Robinson (Ed.), *Reading and writing instruction in the United States: Historical trends* (pp. 1–16). Newark, DE: International Reading Association.

Hulten, C. (1925). The personal element in teachers' marks. *Journal of Educational Research, 12,* 49–55.

Mager, R. (1973). *Measuring instructional intent.* Belmont, CA: Fearon Pitman Publishers, Inc.

McKenna, M. & Robinson, R. (1980). *An introduction to the cloze procedure.* Newark, DE: International Reading Association.

Micheels, W. & Karnes, M.R. (1950). *Measuring educational achievement.* New York: McGraw-Hill Book Company.

Mikulecky, L. (1987). The status of literacy in our society. A paper presented at Reading Symposium on Factors Related to Reading

Performance IV, Milwaukee, WI: The University of Wisconsin at Milwaukee.

Payne, D. (1974). *The assessment of learning: Cognitive and affective.* Lexington, MA: D. C. Heath and Company.

Phillips, R. (1968). *Evaluation in education.* Columbus, OH: Charles E. Merrill Publishing Company.

Shanker, A. (1990). A proposal for using incentives to restructure our public schools. *Phi Delta Kappan, 71*(5), 345–357.

Smith, F. (1986). *Insult to intelligence.* New York: Arbor House.

Smith, F. (1983). *Essays into literacy.* Exeter, NH: Heinemann Educational Books.

Stice, C. & Call, T. (1987). The test may have become the curriculum. *Tennessee Reading Teacher, 2,* 11–16.

Stice, C., Thompson, D., & Bertrand, J. (1991). *Emergent literacy in two contrasting classrooms: Building models of practice toward a theory of practice.* Nashville, TN: Tennessee State University Press.

Storey, A. (1970). *The measurement of classroom learning.* Chicago: SRA.

Watson, D. (1989). Defining and describing whole language. *The Elementary School Journal, 90*(2), 129–141.

Weaver, C. (1988). *Reading process and practice.* Portsmouth, NH: Heinemann Educational Books.

Chapter 3

Principles of Assessment and Evaluation in Whole Language Classrooms

Bill Harp

In the first edition of this book this chapter opened with the following sentence: "The whole language movement has swept the nation." What was true in 1991 is even more true today. Three years ago we estimated that 20 percent of American classrooms were places where teachers were applying the principles of whole language. Four years later that estimate is easily placed at 40 percent.

The revolution in literacy education we recognized four years ago continues at a rapid pace and is accompanied by both criticism and peril. The criticism is often directed at *whole language* because of the myths we identified in Chapter 1. The peril is a result of the tremendous misunderstandings about *whole language* in the minds of many teachers, administrators, and parents. One of the greatest perils to the whole language movement is the potential failure that will result if we do not come to grips with critical issues in assessment and evaluation. In fact, we are at a critical crossroads in the whole language movement. We have clearly defined (though admittedly there is misunderstanding) the classroom practices that constitute *whole language instruction*. If we do not equally clearly define the classroom practices that constitute *whole language assessment and evaluation*, the chances are very great that "whole language" will fail, our critics will rejoice, and we will be left wondering if it was all just a passing trend, as many have suggested.

Certainly, we must continue to work diligently to dispel the myths of whole language. Simultaneously, we must work with equal diligence to bring assessment and evaluation practices in line with the principles of whole language instruction and learning.

Assessment and evaluation in whole language classrooms requires a new look at the purposes of evaluation. Dorothy Watson set the tone for evaluation in the future at a Whole Language Special Interest Group meeting. She said that we must ask ourselves who evaluation is for. The answer in whole language classrooms is that evaluation is first for students so that they may watch and understand their own progress. Second, evaluation is for teachers. Third, it is for the school, to let administrators, other teachers, and parents know how a child is doing. Finally, evaluation is for the general public and legislators. These various audiences concerned about evaluation processes have their own special interests and needs. The data that will help a child become a better writer may not be the evaluation data that is of interest to the school board member. Whole language teachers recognize that multiple forms of assessment and evaluation are needed, and that they take an important departure from traditional practice when they put the assessment and evaluation needs and interests of the individual learner ahead of all others.

Just as whole language instruction has demanded a fresh new look at teaching and learning, so it now demands a more critical look at assessment and evaluation. Whole language teachers reject assessment and evaluation strategies based in tradition and turn instead to a set of principles that guide their work.

Principle One: Assessment and Evaluation is first and foremost for the individual learner.

We know that in order for real learning to occur the individual child must take responsibility for his or her learning (Cambourne, 1989). For many years in American education, the learner has been left out of the assessment and evaluation process. Many of us can recall being handed a report card in a sealed envelope and admonished to let only our parents open it. The parent often was asked to sign the card, maybe write a comment, and have the child return the card to school. The child stood in the shadows of the process.

Whole language teachers have come to the realization that the child must be involved in assessment (the collection of data on his or her performance) and evaluation (the interpretation of those data for further instructional direction). It is not unusual to find a highly skilled whole language teacher sitting down with a child to review a running record and analyze the results, then asking the child to collaborate in setting the next learning goals. It is common to find this teacher reviewing a piece of writing in light of criteria understood by the child as the child is asked to identify the next learning goal as a writer. The involvement of children in the assessment and evaluation process is critical if they are to take responsibility for their learning. The learner must be a key player in the process, not a disengaged observer of the assessment and evaluation process.

Principle Two: Assessment and Evaluation Strategies Must Honor the Wholeness of Language

We know that children learn to read and write in the same developmental ways that they learn to speak. Our use of language is always driven by a need and desire to communicate. Assessment strategies that attempt to determine what children know and need to learn next and evaluation strategies that measure the effectiveness of instruction must honor the communicative nature of language in all of its forms. Teachers assess what children know about language as they watch children use language in real communicative situations — writing stories and poems, writing lists of plans in activity centers, writing self-evaluations, keeping reading logs, and writing in journals. Teachers watch children read for pleasure, for information and for self-selected purposes. Reading ability is evaluated as children respond in a variety of ways to whole texts, not to fill-in-the-blank activities following the reading of a short, excerpted piece.

Principle Three: Reading and Writing Are Viewed as Processes

Teachers with ten or more years of teaching experience remember well the reading skills checklist that they were asked to complete on a regular basis. The extensive lists of reading subskills were to be kept as each skill was tested, taught, mastered, and in some instances retaught and retested. Many school districts created sets of such tests and ways in which these data could be recorded on computer. Management by objective, it was called. Each objective specified a behavior related to a subskill, e.g., "Given ten unfamiliar words, children will be able to decode initial consonant *d* with 80 percent accuracy." Countless hours were spent creating the tests, administering the tests, and recording the data. When the system worked as intended, a group of teachers could agree that Tuesday morning was skills time, each teacher would select a skill or set of skills to be taught during skill time, and the computer would produce a list of the children across several classrooms who had failed the pretest on those particular skills.

We now know that such skills-based instruction ignores what we know about literacy development. Reading and writing are now viewed as processes, rather than accumulations of small skills. How children are handling the processes is the teacher's focus, rather than the acquisition of discrete skills. In whole language classrooms children are asked to respond first to the largest units of meaning, whole selections, and only after truly meaningful experiences with whole selections are they asked to respond to smaller pieces such as paragraphs, sentences, words, and letter-sound relationships.

In viewing reading as a process, we know that readers predict that they will read, sample all of the possible cues on the printed page only to the extent necessary to confirm or reject the predictions, and then confirm or reject, predict again, and resample (Goodman, 1967). This view of the reading process causes us to focus on the behaviors of readers as they move from beginning readers to developing readers to mature readers. At each stage we are concerned with observing and recording the behaviors that give evidence of their use of the process rather than their ability to apply a given subskill. Concern for grade scores or instructional reading level is giving way to concern for increased use of semantic cues or the ability to monitor one's own comprehension, for example. This movement is leading to greater reliance on miscue analysis and the development of checklists for processes rather than for skills.

Miscue analysis helps us understand whether a reader is attempting to construct meaning or is simply decoding sound-symbol relationships. For example, if the text word is *house* and the child reads "horse" without noticing the loss of meaning, we can infer that this reader relies much more heavily on graphophonic cues than on semantic cues. If a meaningful word substitution is made, we can infer that the reader relies most heavily on semantic and syntactic cues. By doing a series of miscue analyses across time, we can observe a child's progress toward becoming an increasingly meaning-constructing reader. These observations give us insight into how the reader is using the reading process.

Similarly, we are moving toward process evaluation in writing. We now understand that marking a writing piece with a B+ does not help the student become a better writer. Instead, we examine how the child uses the writing process from prewriting activities to first draft, second draft, editing conferences, rewriting copy, revision conference, self-editing, and publication. By collecting work samples at each of these stages and keeping anecdotal records of our observations of each child in each stage of the process we are able to truly assess and evaluate writing progress.

Here is one of those critical points of peril. Assessment and evaluation must always occur together. Assessment without evaluation is simply nothing more than collecting data on a learner and then doing nothing with it. One of the myths operating in some schools is that portfolio assessment is collecting work samples over time. Teachers simply place samples in folders and nothing more is done with them. Once the samples have been collected, they must be *evaluated*. This evaluation should be done by both the teacher and the learner in light of agreed-upon criteria leading to identification of the child's next learning goals.

Principle Four: Teacher Intuition is a Valuable Assessment and Evaluation Tool

One of the teacher's greatest responsibilities is decision making. Teachers make about ten instructionally significant decisions per hour (Berliner, 1984). One of the most important sources of decision-making data is the teacher's intuition. Yet, in this age of accountability teachers have been encouraged —forced — to discredit their intuition as less valid and reliable than test data. Whole language teachers appreciate the importance of intuition in assessment and evaluation. The things we know intuitively we know without rational, logical explanation of how we know them — we just know them. Our critics insist that we must be accountable for student learning. They insist that we must document student learning gain in a variety of ways — virtually all of them through testing. Certainly teachers must be accountable for student learning. But such accountability does not always have to exist through testing. Teacher intuition that a child knows something is as valid a way of accounting for that knowledge as is testing. This assumes, of course, that teacher intuition is based on careful observation and knowledge of a child's learning.

Principle Five: Teacher Observation is at the Center of Assessment and Evaluation

Yetta Goodman (1978) talks about the importance of the teacher as "kid watcher." It is only through careful watching of children in authentic literacy events that we can bring our intuition as teachers to bear on planning appropriate learning experiences. Informal observations, knowledge about how children become literate, and teacher intuition about why children perform in certain ways form the basis of instructional decisions far more than do test scores (Shavelson and Stern, 1981).

The inexperienced observer (or one with lack of knowledge about literacy development) could look at the scribbles of an emergent writer and see only scribbles. The experienced observer will look at the same piece of writing and see indications of the child's development of hypotheses about the nature of writing, an understanding of the form of a letter, the development of important concepts about print, and a strong literacy set. The experienced observer will not only have spent time watching the writing being created, but probably will have engaged the child in conversation about the writing which will lead to more insightful observation (Johnston, 1987).

In the same way, the untrained observer will listen to a child read and hear only mistakes, whereas the experienced observer who is knowledgeable about the reading process will hear much more. This observer will hear prediction making, prediction confirmation, rereading when meaning is lost, and the growing ability to self-monitor the use of the reading process. Teacher interaction with the student is important here because the teacher can gain insight into the ways in which the reader constructs meaning and can intervene to provide support and suggestions.

Teacher observation of children at work is at the heart of the assessment and evaluation strategies. Central to good observation is a teacher knowledgeable about both child development and literacy processes. At a recent whole language meeting a teacher anonymously wrote the following on the board:

> I used to teach children and evaluate their progress.
> But now I kid watch, facilitate the learning of children,
> And try to discover why learners do what they do.
> I have learned to celebrate children's strengths as language users.

Principle Six: Assessment and Evaluation in Reading Must Reflect What We Know About the Reading Process

We know that reading is an interactive process in which the background experiences, knowledge, and theories (schemata) of the reader interact with the ideas of the author to create meaning. The meaning that is created in this transaction is not exactly the same as that originally intended by the author. In fact, three texts exist in the reading process: the text in the head of the author, the text on the printed page, and the text created in the head of the reader as a result of this interactive process (May, 1990). Assessment and evaluation in reading must acknowledge the interactive nature of the process. This interactive view of the reading process began long ago with Rumelhart's (1977) model of word recognition, and yet assessment and evaluation in reading have not reflected this interactive view.

How can assessment and evaluation in reading reflect this interactive view of reading? The Wisconsin Reading Association has provided some answers to this question in a publication entitled *Toward an Ecological Assessment of Reading Progress* (1990). The Association suggests that assessment and evaluation in reading must consider the factors which influence comprehension. Each of the factors is discussed below.

Prior Knowledge

The knowledge the reader brings to the reading act greatly influences comprehension. Prior knowledge can be assessed in reading tests by giving a multiple choice test that measures prior knowledge, by having children write predictions before they read, or by asking children to write about topics central to comprehension of the passage. When testing individuals, teachers can engage children in conversation about prior knowledge. The assessment of prior knowledge is useful in interpreting performance on a comprehension test.

Text Structure

Narrative selections which conform to a predictable text structure — problem-events-resolution, are more easily remembered than are texts with no discernible structure. Problems in comprehension can be caused by the lack of text structure. Children's knowledge of the various text structures used in expository writing aid in comprehension. Knowledge of text structure should be considered when assessing comprehension. We need to be sure that children understand text structure and we need to determine that texts used in tests have identifiable structures.

Like text structure, it is also important for readers to understand story grammar. Children's understanding of story grammar and the ability to track one's developing understanding of the plot of a story is crucial to comprehension.

Reading Strategies

Metacognition is an awareness and understanding of one's learning process. Applied to reading, this ability is termed metacomprehension. One's ability to monitor comprehension and take corrective actions is crucial in an interactive view of the reading process. Comprehension increases when children are taught what to do when comprehension fails. In individual assessment, students should be asked to demonstrate what strategies they would use in a given reading situation. The degree to which readers ask themselves, "Do I understand? Does this make sense? How can I get help?" and the consequent corrective action is crucial to good comprehension.

Interests and Attitudes

The degree of interest in a topic and the attitude the reader has towards the reading task will influence comprehension. Our understanding of a reader's comprehension ability will be enlightened by knowing the interest and attitude the reader brings to the task.

Others have been working to identify process-oriented ways to handle assessment and evaluation in reading. Valencia and Pearson (1987) reported several formats they are using to "reshape statewide assessment of reading." These innovative formats include the following.

Summary Selection

Students read three or four summaries of a selection written by other students. They select the one they think is best. In an alternative version they are asked to identify the reasons for their selection.

Metacognitive Judgments

Students are asked to think about a way they might have to use a selection after they have read it. An example would be asking readers to think about retelling the selection to a variety of audiences. They rate the helpfulness of several different retellings for each audience.

Question Selection

From a group of 20 questions students select the 10 they think will best help a peer understand important ideas in a selection.

Multiple Acceptable Responses

In recognition of the fact that interpretive and evaluative questions have multiple acceptable responses (despite what norm-referenced test makers would have us believe) students are asked to participate in a group discussion of all responses they find plausible.

Prior Knowledge

Students predict (yes/no/maybe) whether certain ideas are likely to be included in a discussion of a specified topic. In another version students are asked to assess the degree to which they think certain terms would be related to a topic.

Figure 3.1 is a set of contrasts between new views of the reading process and current practices in assessing reading offered by Valencia and Pearson (1987, p. 731).

Figure 3.1   A Set of Contrasts between New Views of Reading
and Current Practices in Assessing Reading

New views of the reading process tell us that...	Yet when we assess reading comprehension, we...
Prior knowledge is an important determinant of reading comprehension.	Mask any relationship between prior knowledge and reading comprehension by using lots of short passages on lots of topics.
A complete story or text has structural and topical integrity.	Use short texts that seldom approximate the structural and topical integrity of an authentic text.
Inference is an essential part of the process of comprehending units as small as sentences.	Rely on literal comprehension test items.
The diversity in prior knowledge across individuals as well as the varied causal relations in human experiences invite many possible inferences to fit a text or question.	Use multiple choice items with only one correct answer, even when many of the responses might, under certain conditions, be plausible.
The ability to vary reading strategies to fit the text and the situation is one hallmark of an expert reader.	Seldom assess how and when students vary the strategies they use during normal reading, studying, or when the going gets tough.
The ability to synthesize information from various parts of the text and different texts is hallmark of an expert reader.	Rarely go beyond finding the main idea of a paragraph or passage.
The ability to ask good questions of text, as well as to answer them, is hallmark of an expert reader.	Seldom ask students to create or select questions about a selection they may have just read.
All aspects of a reader's experience. including habits that arise from school and home, influence reading comprehension.	Rarely view information on reading habits and attitudes as being important information about performance.
Reading involves the orchestration of many skills that complement one another in a variety of ways.	Use tests that fragment reading into isolated skills and report performance on each.
Skilled readers are fluent; their word identification is sufficiently automatic to allow most cognitive resources to be used for comprehension.	Rarely consider fluency as an Index of skilled reading.
Learning from text involves the restructuring, application, and flexible use of knowledge in new situations.	Often ask readers to respond to the text's declarative knowledge rather than to apply it to near and far transfer tasks.

From Valencia, Sheila, and P. David Pearson. "Reading Assessment: Time for a Change." *The Reading Teacher.* vol. 40, no. 8 (April 1987), pp. 726–732.

Another reading assessment strategy that is proving helpful is the process interview (Paratore and Indrisano, 1987). The process is intended to examine how a child views the reading process. The interview includes questions such as:

- How do you choose something to read?
- How do you get ready to read?
- When you come to a word you can't read, what do you do?
- When you have a question you can't answer, what do you do?
- What do you do to help remember what you have read?
- How do you check your reading?
- If a young child asked you how to read, what would you tell him or her to do?

Yet another reading assessment and evaluation strategy that American whole language teachers are finding useful is the Running Record. Running records were introduced to New Zealand teachers by Marie Clay. At the time Ken and Yetta Goodman were doing pioneering work on the reading process in the United States, Clay was making similar inroads to understanding in New Zealand. Running records are a relatively easy way to conduct miscue analysis of a child's oral reading.

Oral reading errors are recorded and analyzed to see which of the cueing systems the reader is using. Miscues are analyzed to see how the reader is responding when meaning is not being constructed. Retellings permit an evaluation of comprehension.

In New Zealand, teachers take a running record on the reading of kindergarten through grade 2 children every three weeks. This frequent and thorough evaluation of a child's reading behavior permits the teacher to accurately track progress in using the reading process. For a very thorough explanation of the form and analysis of running records see Clay's *An Observation Survey of Early Literacy Achievement* (1993).

Principle Seven: Assessment and Evaluation in Writing Must Reflect What We Know About the Writing Process

The first purpose of assessment and evaluation in writing is to inform the child of his or her progress in using the writing process. In traditional classrooms the *product* of writing has been the focal point. Often students are given a piece of their work evaluated by the teacher with only a grade on the paper. Such evaluation does not help children understand how to make the writing better. In whole language classrooms the focal point of assessment and evaluation in writing is the child's growth in using the writing *process*. Consider the differences between a writing program that celebrates the process of writing rather than the product of writing. Figure 3.2 illustrates the differences between writing done as a process and writing done as a product.

Figure 3. 2   Process versus Product Writing

When we write as a Process	When we write for a Product
The writing is student centered.	The writing is teacher centered.
The teacher's role is to model and coach.	The teacher's role is to assign and grade.
We write for many audiences.	The teacher is the primary audience.
The process is evaluated.	The product is graded.
The editing group or editing committee is the primary responder.	The teacher is the primary responder.
We write many, ever-improving drafts.	We write one linear draft.
The entire process of thinking, writing, revising, editing, and publishing is done in class.	A draft is done in class.

If assessment and evaluation are to be consistent with what we know about the writing process, children must be given feedback about their performance and be asked to self-evaluate their performance throughout the process. Thus teachers and students will take critical looks at the child's choice of audience, selection of form, organization of information, rough drafting, getting help, revision, editing, and publication.

Principle Eight: Norm-Referenced Achievement Testing Is of No Help to the Whole Language Teacher

Norm-referenced tests exist to measure virtually every human trait we can imagine. Since World War II we have seen a growing and persistent use of norm-referenced tests in American schools. Whole language teachers recognize the discrepancy between norm-referenced testing and the instructional outcomes we hold important. In fact, norm-referenced test data are essentially useless to us.

Vito Perrone, Director of Teacher Education Programs at Harvard University says of norm-referenced tests,

> While these tests have come to affect Americans of all ages, in all fields, intelligence and achievement tests come down most heavily on the young, those between the ages of 3 and 21. Although problematic for young people of all ages and levels of schooling, they are particularly deleterious for children in preschools and primary grades. For it is in these early years that children's growth is so uneven, so idiosyncratic, that large numbers of skills needed for success in school are in such fluid acquisitional stages. (1990, p. 1)

Perrone goes on to say,

> I cry when I read about young children "held back" on the basis of a test, or placed in one or another of the schooling tracks that support various judgments about children's potential. And I wonder about those who believe that testing young children and then making placement, promotion, or retention decisions on the basis of such testing leads to any constructive end. (1990, p. 1)

The most destructive influence of norm-referenced testing is found in the daily reading activities of children. Reading curriculum has been designed to assure that children do well on the tests. So the activities in which children engage in the name of reading instruction look much more like the tests (fill in the blanks, draw a line from the *d* to the picture of the dog, and so forth), than like authentic reading and authentic writing activities (Edelsky and Smith, 1984). In classrooms where real communicative experiences are of primary importance, teaching to the test is counterproductive. The time spent in test-like activities robs time from the much more important experiences of real reading and real writing.

A vicious circle exists in the production of basal readers. In a test-driven curriculum mentality, the circle begins with norm-referenced tests, the tests influence the design of the basal, workbooks, and accompanying tests, and ends with the norm-referenced tests. (Goodman, Shannon, Freeman & Murphy, 1988). Whole language teachers are committed to breaking this circle with the kinds of assessment and evaluation described in the principles discussed here.

The test items on norm-referenced tests do not look like the real reading experiences children have in whole language classrooms. In Miriam Cohen's book entitled *First Grade Takes A Test* (1980) a child found none of the answers to the questions posed by the test makers acceptable and decided to write in a response "so the test people would know." The test items are at odds with what children have come to expect of authentic texts. Children are accustomed to reading whole texts, not short paragraphs, and to respond to these texts in a variety of ways — positing a variety of possible answers to inferential and evalua-tive questions. A fifth grade teacher recently reported one child's response to a norm-referenced test that she was taking. After reading a selection the child said to the teacher, "Can't we just discuss it?"

Another destructive influence of norm-referenced testing is the appearance of scientific credibility. Teachers have been led to believe that grade scores and percentile rankings are scientific, and therefore more valid than their professional judgment (Harman, 1990). Yet, such standardized tests are designed so that half of the children will score below grade level.

> Therefore, tests cannot simply evaluate what children have learned because then everyone might do well. Some questions must be hard enough — or obscure enough — to guarantee that only a few children will get them right. That is, they must tap what has not been learned. So then schools must begin teaching to those questions, and the vicious spiral of alignment, premature teaching, and drilling whirls on. (pp. 114–115)

Whole language teachers are committed to breaking the vicious spiral Harman describes. This can be done immediately by rejecting standardized tests that are not congruent with classroom practice. In the long run, this can be done by redesigning the tests. Some states are making headway with this effort (Peters and Wixson, 1989).

Arizona, Michigan, and Illinois have all made significant strides in redesigning standardized tests. While it may be impossible to design a standardized test that has the depth and flexibility of running records and retellings, there are some positive changes being made. The new tests use full-length stories and articles rather than the short selections of the past. New tests include questions that invite inference-making and tap into students' knowledge of the reading process. Traditional tests used ranking system scores (grade scores, percentile scores) that only compared one student's performance with that of others. Attempts are being made with new tests to use multidimensional scores that describe the student's depth of understanding, use of the reading process, and use of background knowledge.

Principle Nine: Assessment and Evaluation Instruments Are Varied and Literacy Is Assessed in a Variety of Contexts

Testing is only one form of assessment and evaluation. In addition to appropriate tests, whole language teachers use work samples — recordings of children's readings, samples of children's writing, observations of children in the library corner, and at work in other settings. Teachers watch for indications of growth in the use of the reading process in movement from emergent reading behaviors to developing reading behaviors to maturing reading behaviors. They observe and record ways in which children interact with print, listen to stories, use literacy acts in dramatic play, and make use of environmental print.

Assessment and evaluation are not something teachers do the week before report cards are to be written. Assessment and evaluation are going on in the head of the teacher constantly. They are happening throughout the day as children do the work of being real readers, real writers, and real learners.

Principle Ten: Assessment and Evaluation Are Integral Parts of Instruction

Our traditionally strong reliance on tests as *the* acceptable form of assessment and evaluation has caused us to think of assessing and evaluating as things teachers do before and after teaching rather than as integral parts of the teaching act. Whole language teachers recognize that the best assessment occurs while teaching. Teachers are continually on the look out for indications of children's strengths and signs of what the child needs to learn or be challenged with next. At the same time, teachers realize that evaluation is best done by watching performance on tasks that involve children in literacy acts that have real communicative purpose rather than a test given after the instruction. Because whole language teachers are open to the needs and interests of children, a lesson can take an unpredicted turn, responding to the desires of the students. Just as an instructional objective could not have been written for this new direction in learning, neither could a test have been created in advance. But the lesson most certainly will be evaluated based on the teacher's observations of the processes and products used and created in the act of learning.

It is important to recognize that we cannot test reading comprehension. Comprehension is a process that occurs before, during, and after the reading of a selection. Asking comprehension questions (with someone's answers in the key other than the reader's) is only testing how well the reader's creation of meaning matches that of the teacher or of the author of the test. The real "test" of comprehension is to observe how students engage in the process of reading and how richly they can retell what they read, as they present their creation of meaning. *Comprehension* is a process that must be evaluated *as it is happening,* not a product that can be measured after the fact.

Principle Eleven: Assessment and Evaluation Strategies Are Developmentally and Culturally Appropriate

Whole language teachers believe that children learn to read and write in the same developmental way they learn to speak. Learning activities that honor the developmental nature of literacy focus first on meaning and give children many, many opportunities to practice literacy in ever-increasingly accurate approximations of adult reading and writing. Tests which are designed so that half of the children will be below average are based on the assumption that half of the children will not perform as well as the other half. Yet we know that this is not true in literacy development. Further, when teachers are told to use tests which place one-half of the class below average they are forced to drill children on small bits of information that may be included on the test. This drill is contrary to the ways we know children develop literacy.

Cultural diversity is increasingly a consideration in our classroom. For children whose native language is not American English, five principles should guide our instruction — and therefore our assessment and evaluation. (Ovando, 1989)

1. Language development in the home language as well as in English has positive effects on academic achievement.

2. Language proficiency includes proficiency in academic tasks as well as in basic conversation.

3. A child with limited English proficiency should be able to

perform a certain type of academic task in his or her home language before being expected to perform the task in English.

4. Acquisition of English language skills must be provided in contexts in which the student understands what is being said.

5. The social status implicitly ascribed to students and their languages affects student performance.

It follows from these principles of teaching and learning that assessment and evaluation strategies with culturally diverse students must occur first in their home languages. Such strategies should be sensitive to cultural norms that may differ from those of majority children. For example, in some Native American cultures eye contact and competition are not acceptable. Teachers who do not understand this could form inaccurate conclusions about such students.

Principle Twelve: Assessment and Evaluation Occur Continuously

Collecting work samples and analyzing them periodically for a writing portfolio, recording an oral reading episode for miscue analysis, and making and analyzing entries in anecdotal records are examples of important *periodic* assessment and evaluation activities. These strategies form an important part of the teacher's overall assessment and evaluation plan, but minute-by-minute assessment and evaluation are the heart of the strategy. Teachers are constantly observing children and their work to make mental notes about the latest achievement and the next challenge. The Wisconsin State Reading Association (1990, pp. 54–55) has identified characteristics of expert evaluators that help teachers define what good observation means. The seven characteristics are discussed below.

1. *The expert evaluator recognizes patterns.* When listening to children read, the expert hears patterns, for example, in miscues that lead to an understanding of the cueing systems on which the reader primarily relies.

2. *Expert evaluators have procedural knowledge.* They know how to elicit certain literacy behaviors from children so that they can then be observed, recorded, and filed in some way.

3. *The expert in informal assessment is a listener.* Expert observers hear children's growing abilities in literacy.

4. *Expert evaluators empower learners with responsibility for self-evaluation.* This is a critical aspect of continuous assessment and evaluation.

5. *Expert evaluators are advocates rather than adversaries of students.* The teacher sits beside the child focusing on process, treating the child and the work with the greatest respect.

6. *An expert evaluator's assessment is timely and immediately influences instruction.* The teacher is both teacher and evaluator at once. Evaluation is therefore efficient. This first-hand information is more helpful in planning than second-hand information gained from tests.

7. *Expert evaluators emphasize process and what the child can do.*

Principle Thirteen: Assessment and Evaluation Must Reveal Children's Strengths

Whole language teachers reject the clinical, medical model of educational assessment. In this model one looks for what is wrong with the child, and then writes a prescription to fix it. The child-centered nature of whole language instruction demands that we look first at the strengths of children — what they know, how they can use what they know to learn, and what they can teach us. We also firmly believe that children do not have to be forced or threatened by tests in order to get them to learn. Children are natural learners in environments that seriously invite learning. Their strengths show in such environments. Teachers have found the following strategies helpful in identifying the strengths of children:

1. Make five minutes available to spend with a child. Let the child guide the discussion and discover what you can.

2. Watch the child's social interactions. What communicative strengths does the child have and how are they used?

3. Have children write self-evaluation letters to the teacher or to the parent. Here the child has an opportunity to identify his or her perceived strengths as well as areas for growth.

4. Permit children to identify their next learning step. When

conferring with children, ask first what are the child's goals
for future learning. Then negotiate goals shared by the child
and the teacher and finally indicate goals that the teacher has
for the child. This "Yours, Ours, and Mine" approach to
goal setting permits the child to take the lead and yet
recognizes the teacher's responsibility in instructional planning.

The reader will find Chapter 10, by Jean Church, particularly helpful
in suggesting ways to implement this principle.

Summary

The implementation of these principles of assessment and evaluation
will necessitate a dramatic change from traditional practice. We will have
to come to grips with the fact that current tests do not test what we value
in reading education (Bussis and Chittenden, 1987). Assessment and
evaluation in whole language will move us away from test- and text-
driven measures to student-centered observation.

References

Berglund, R.L. (1988, December/1989, January). Whole language: A
    swing of the pendulum or a whole new pendulum? *Reading Today*,
    p. 18.
Berliner, D.C. (1984). Making the right changes in pre-service teacher
    education. *Phi Delta Kappan, 66*, (2), 94–96.
Bussis, A. & Chittenden, E.C. (1987). Research currents: What the
    reading tests neglect. *Language Arts, 64*, (3), 302–308.
Cambourne, B. (1988). *The whole story: Natural learning and the
    acquisition of literacy in the classroom*. Auckland, NZ: Ashton/
    Scholastic.
Campione, J.C. & Brown A.L. (1985). *Dynamic assessment: One
    approach and some initial data*. (Technical Report No. 361).
    Urbana, IL: Center for the Study of Reading.
Clay, M. (1993). *An observation survey of early literacy achievement*.
    Auckland, NZ: Heinemann Publishing.
Cohen, M. (1980). *First grade takes a test*. New York: Dell Publishing.
Edelsky, C. & Smith, K. (1984). Is that writing — or are those marks
    just a figment of your curriculum? *Language Arts, 61*, 24–32.

Goodman, D. (1989). The whole language umbrella. *Teachers Networking — The Whole Language Newsletter, 9,* 9–11, Katonah, NY: Richard C. Owen Publishers.

Goodman, K. (1967). Reading: A psycholinguistic guessing game. *Journal of the Reading Specialist, 6,* 126–135.

Goodman, K.S., Shannon, P., Freeman, Y., & Murphy S. (1988). *Report card on basal readers.* Katonah, NY: Richard C. Owen Publishers.

Goodman, Y. (1978). Kid watching: An alternative to testing. *National Elementary School Principal, 57,* 41–45.

Harman, S. (1990). Negative effects of achievement testing in literacy development. In Constance Kamii (Ed.), *Achievement testing in the early grades: The games grown-ups play.* Washington, DC: National Association for the Education of Young Children.

Johnston, P. (1987). Teachers as evaluation experts. *The Reading Teacher, 40,* (8), 744 748.

May, F.B. (1986). *Reading as communication: An interactive approach.* (2nd Ed.). Columbus, OH: Merrill Publishing Company.

Ovando, C. (1989). Language diversity and education. In J.A. Banks & C.A. Banks (Eds.), *Multicultural education: Issues and perspectives.* Boston, MA: Allyn and Bacon.

Paratore, J.R. & Indrisano, R. (1987). Intervention assessment of reading comprehension. *The Reading Teacher, 40,* (8), 778–783.

Perrone, V. (1990). How did we get here? In Constance Kamii (Ed.), *Achievement testing in the early grades: The games grown-ups play.* Washington, DC: National Association for the Education of Young Children.

Peters, C.W. & Wixson, K.K. (1989, April). Smart new reading tests are coming. Reading-thinking connection. *Learning 89:* 43–44 and 53–58.

Rumelhart, D. (1977). Toward an interactive model of reading. In S. Dornic (Ed.), *Attention and performance VI.* Hillsdale, NJ: Erlbaum.

Shavelson, R. & Stern, P. (1981). Research on teachers' pedagogical thoughts, judgments, decisions and behavior. *Review of Educational Research, 41,* 455–498.

Valencia, S. & Pearson, P.D. (1987). Reading assessment: Time for a change. *The Reading Teacher, 40,* (8), 726–732.

Wisconsin State Reading Association. (1990). *Toward an ecological assessment of reading progress.* Schofield, Wisconsin: WSRA.

Chapter 4

Reading Evaluation — Miscue Analysis

Dorothy Watson and Janice Henson

Introduction

> I don't know what to do with or for Ted. He is in the fourth grade and
> can't even read the first-grade basal! I've looked at all his test scores —
> the CTBS, and Informal Reading Inventory, the basal end-of-level
> test, and the state achievement test; I still don't know what to do with
> Ted. I'm desperate and ready for suggestions anyone has to offer.

To educators who have voiced similar concerns, the authors suggest
whole language evaluation that includes its most formal technique —
reading miscue analysis.

In this chapter we offer a rationale for the use of miscue analysis, tell
a bit about the background of the instrument, present one form of the
Reading Miscue Inventory (RMI), and perhaps most importantly, show
how miscue analysis can lead to specific strategies within a whole
language curriculum, as well as change how teachers look at students'
reading.

Why Reading Miscue Analysis?

Ted's teacher presents a problem that we feel *only miscue analysis as
part of whole language evaluation can address.* It can help in at least three
ways.

First, miscue analysis provides information about language and about the reading process. Without such information, Ted's teacher is vulnerable: "...I'm desperate and ready for suggestions anyone has to offer." The feeling of desperation may stem from her lack of knowledge about the reading process and about the ways in which language cues support readers in their effort to construct meaning. With information about the natural reading strategies of *sampling* from text and from background experience, *predicting* what is coming up in the text, *confirming* when the reading makes sense and sounds okay, and *integrating* new information with old, the teacher can knowledgeably study Ted's reading. She can also evaluate materials and methods of reading instruction and make decisions consistent with solid information about how language and the reading process work together.

Secondly, miscue analysis provides information about Ted's in-process reading, his beliefs about reading and reading instruction, and about his comprehension. Through *marking and coding* the reading, teachers can judge the proficiency and efficiency with which readers are handling text. The *Burke Reading Interview,* as well as *Reflection on Reading* (self-evaluation) are two parts of the inventory that let the teacher in on what students think about (1) themselves as readers, (2) reading instruction, and (3) their performance on the material they have just read. The student's *retelling* reflects the reader's comprehension of the text.

Finally, miscue analysis enables the teacher to create a curriculum in which students' strengths are valued and used, while their needs are clearly addressed. Miscue analysis points the way to strategies and suggests materials that will help students become more proficient readers.

What Is Miscue Analysis?

The term "miscue" is used in billiards when the cue stick slips off the ball, and in the theater it refers to an actor answering a wrong cue or missing one. Ken Goodman saw some parallels to reading, and made use of the term in his 1964 research, and later in 1973 when he developed the Goodman Taxonomy of Reading Miscues. Goodman rejected the idea that teachers can "get a window on the reading process" by looking at paper-and-pencil test scores, so he proposed an interesting alternative. He asked children to read aloud a story that they had never read before and then to tell what they remembered of it. As students read, they deviated from the text; Goodman called these unexpected responses "miscues." It's important that he didn't call them errors or mistakes; to do so would have meant that the reader was totally responsible (guilty) for the deviation. As Goodman investigated children's miscues, he realized that the miscues were not equal in terms of how they changed the text. In fact, some miscues didn't cause any change in meaning or in syntax, while others destroyed both.

Over the years, many educators helped themselves to Goodman's work, adapting it to their own settings. In 1987, Yetta Goodman, Carolyn Burke and Dorothy Watson built on Goodman and Burke's original *Reading Miscue Inventory* (1972) in order to provide four different miscue analysis procedures. Their work, *Reading Miscue Inventory: Alternative Procedures* (1988), is the basis for the suggestions given in this chapter.

Alternative Procedures of Miscue Analysis

There are four miscue analysis procedures. One (Procedure III) is introduced in this chapter. Procedure I is the most complex and time-consuming option; it offers intensive information about a reader's individual miscues in relationship to all other miscues. Procedure I is recommended for teacher education courses in which there is a focus on miscue analysis and for some research studies. Procedure II assesses miscues within the structure of the sentence. This option is often used by reading teachers or special education teachers who need numbers, profiles, and forms for student records. Procedures II and III provide in-depth information about a student's reading and are similar in their focus. Procedure IV is an informal analysis to be used with students during individual reading conferences.

No matter which procedure is chosen, after doing even one miscue analysis, teachers say they never again listen to students read in the same way. We agree with their assessment, and invite you to investigate this whole language evaluation procedure.

Procedure III is only **introduced** here. An intensive study of miscue analysis requires more information than can be provided in a single chapter; therefore the authors suggest that teachers read *Reading Miscue Analysis: Alternative Procedures,* as well as some of the other works cited at the end of this chapter.

Preparing for Miscue Analysis

Selecting Students

Select a student for miscue analysis who presents a challenge to you — one who is a real puzzle. Ted is a prime candidate. He is not the least-proficient reader in class, but he is the most baffling: "I don't know what to do with or for Ted." Your most troubled reader may produce a discouraging amount of complex miscues and therefore be overwhelming for anyone using the procedure for the first time. Save this reader for a time when you have gained more experience.

Selecting the Story

Although the length of the story used for miscue analysis depends to some extent on the age of the reader, there must be a complete text with a beginning, middle, and end. The story should be new to the reader, but not the major concepts it contains. It must be written in a way that supports readers in their attempt to make meaning. Since a minimum of 25 miscues is needed to give a description of a reader's strategies, the story must be slightly difficult for the student. Teachers usually collect two or three stories that are, in conventional terms, one or two years beyond the grade level indicated by the student's reading test scores. Some teachers use the best stories out of basal readers; this provides a grade level that is understood by skills-oriented educators and parents. Reading time usually takes 15 to 20 minutes, depending on the age and proficiency of the reader.

Preparing the Typescript

The student reads directly from the original source or from a very good black and white copy. If a copy is used, the passage should look as much like the original text as possible. Specifically, the length of lines and pages, the spelling, and any special tables, charts or pictures must be identical to the original text. This gives the teacher information about the influence of the physical text and format on the reader.

The teacher needs a typescript of the text. Three spaces between each line is sufficient room for *recording* miscues on this typescript; a wide right margin allows space for *coding* miscues and jotting brief notations. The last line of each original page is indicated on the typescript by a solid horizontal line. This format helps the teacher determine whether turning the page influences the reader. The line and page number of the original text is typed along the left margin of the typescript; for example, line 4 of page 1 of the original text is typed "0104," line 18 of page 11 is typed " 1118."

Taping the Reading Session

In addition to collecting all the materials and having the tape recorder in good working order, the teacher arranges suitable tables and chairs, proper lighting, and a reasonably quiet location. A neck microphone is preferable, but if one is not available, place a regular mike on a stand or cloth with the mike directed toward the reader and away from any background noises.

The reader and the teacher sit either side by side or across from each other. As the student reads, the teacher marks as many miscues as possible on the typescript. If the student is bothered by the marking, the teacher should discontinue marking until the pupil becomes absorbed in the reading. Since the session is audio- or videotaped, the teacher need not worry about getting all the information on the typescript. Marking the self-analysis of miscues is facilitated by the teacher's familiarity with the story.

Beginning the Reading

Teachers briefly explain to students that they are taping them in order to learn more about their reading. Before a severely nonproficient student sees the story, the teacher might say, "I'd like you to read this story called 'Space Pet,' " or "This story is about something you might be doing this summer — camping."

Students are asked to read the story aloud and to read as if they are by themselves. They are told they won't receive any help and that when they are finished the teacher will take the book and ask them to retell the story in their own words. To assure readers that the procedure won't last all day, teachers let students see exactly how long the story is. Ted's teacher gave the following instructions:

> Ted, thanks for agreeing to read this morning. I think we can find out a lot about your reading. Have you ever read this story or heard it before? (Ted looks at the story and shakes his head no.) It's six pages long. (Ted checks the number of pages.) Please read aloud; I'm going to record your reading. When you come to something you don't know, do whatever you would do if you were reading all by yourself. I won't interrupt you. (This lets Ted know that he isn't going to receive help.) When you're finished, I'll take the book and then ask you to tell me the story in your own words. Any questions?

Reading Miscue Inventory: Procedure III

The components of the RMI should not be viewed as parts of a formula. Teachers and researchers must decide the focus of their evaluation and use the components accordingly. We believe, however, that the following will provide abundant information for the teacher who is faced with a problem reader:

1. Initial interview
2. Oral reading
3. Retelling: unaided, aided, cued
4. Reflection on reading
5. Analysis of miscues: marking, coding, profile
6. Curriculum planning

Initial Interview

The instrument most often used to initiate the RMI is the Burke Reading Interview, but teachers may want to devise their own set of interview questions. Examples from the Burke Interview are provided below and the entire interview follows this chapter. No matter what form it takes, the purpose of the interview is to find out how students feel about themselves as readers and about the reading process. Question one of the interview helps teachers learn how students handle difficult text. This example from Karen, a third grader, illustrates the kind of information obtainable (T = Teacher, K = Karen).

T: When you're reading and you come to something you don't know, what do you do? (Burke Q1)

K: ...it's pretty fun to me when you read and you say blank or something and you go back and you try to figure out what the word is. It's like a mystery to me.

No interview should be seen as a script to be followed slavishly. Many times, follow-up questions need to be asked: (C = Connie)

T: When you're reading and you have some trouble, or you come to something that gives you a problem, what do you do? (Burke Q1)

C: Tell the teacher.

T: What do you tell her?

C: I tell her I have a problem with my reading.

T: Let's say the teacher wasn't there and you had a problem with reading. What would you do?

C: I'd go find her and tell her what I need.

T: Do you ever do anything else when you have a problem?

C: When I'm at home I tell my parents. And when my dad and mom's...my sister...I ask her about it.

These answers to follow-up questions suggest that Connie has one major strategy to fall back on when she has trouble reading: She usually relies on help from others. It is important to find out if Connie expects the teacher to give her similar help in this situation.

Questions may be added to any interview. This question about family literacy provided information about Mike, a fifth-grade boy in a remedial reading class.

T: Who reads at your house, Mike?

M: No one, hardly.

T: Nobody.

M: Just my uncle.

T: Does he live with you?

M: Yeah.

T: What does he read?

M: Car books or something, you know, how to fix your engine or something...and like getting parts for his motorcycle or something, just reading.

The influence of reading in this family became evident when Mike was asked about the kind of things he liked to read:

M: Like, I don't like stories that much, but I like, like how to build things or something, or 'struction, how to take things apart or something.

Carol's views of reading practices are revealed in these interview questions.

T: Would you like it if your mom (still) read to you?

C: Yeah, to bring good memories back.

T: What kind of good memories?

C: How fun it was when she read to me...

T: What do you like about how reading is taught?

C: Teacher reading to you.

T: How do you feel about that?

C: It reminds me of when my mom read to me, when I was a kid.

Carol has a less positive response to another instructional method:

T: Which do you like best, silent reading or oral reading?

C: Silent reading.

T: Why is that?

C: Because I like reading to myself…because…I'm embarrassed to read books.

T: You're embarrassed to read books out loud?

C: Most of the time.

T: Why is that?

C: 'Cause I miss words and the class laughs at me.

Oral Reading

Unaided oral reading provides a "window on the reading process." The reader is allowed to work through the text without help or interference. This not only reveals in-process comprehending (see below), but it provides information about the student's view of instruction. When third grader Sarah read "Zoo Doctor," she kept hesitating, waiting for her teacher to supply unknown words. When she wasn't given the expected help, she said, "My teacher last year said to skip it. Do you want me to skip it?" Sarah didn't trust the strategies she had been taught and needed confirmation that they were okay. When she found out that she could rely on strategies that moved her along in the text, she began to read the story with relative ease and with comprehension. If the teacher had supplied unknown words or corrected Sarah's miscues, none of this information would have come to light.

Checking oral reading against the retelling of the story helps teachers check alternative approaches to instruction. Mitch, a fifth grader, remembered very little of the story, "First Kill." Without the oral reading, his teacher might conclude that Mitch had problems reading the words in the text. This wasn't the case. Listening to Mitch read orally revealed that he was excellent at "recoding," going from print to sound. What he didn't do well was invest himself in the reading, which became evident when he was unable to retell the story. Without that commitment to the text, Mitch was unable to monitor his meaning construction process. Mitch actually skipped entire paragraphs without changing his speed or without correcting himself.

Retelling

Comprehension or lack of it can never be based on reading performance alone; therefore, retelling is a vital part of miscue analysis.

Unaided retelling consists of readers retelling the story in whatever way they prefer. Unaided retelling is introduced simply with, "Tell me all you remember about the story." With this prompt, some students willingly recreate the story, often including plot, characters, and underlying theme. If encouragement is needed, the teacher can provide non-content related prompts such as, "Tell me more" or "What else do you remember?"

In *aided retelling,* the teacher picks up on anything the reader has mentioned during the unaided retelling. Here the teacher must be careful not to put words in the student's mouth. Sam, a third grader, said during the unaided retelling, "And he saw something bad. And he, he saw something coming out of Mrs. Miller's window, and the fire truck came, and it took the house somewhere...that's all I know of." The teacher aided the retelling with, "...you say the fire truck came and took the house. Tell me more about that."

Misconceptions can be cleared up during aided retelling, as when Sherry, a fifth grader, read "Zoo Doctor" and substituted the word *indigestion* for *injection.* On the second encounter with the word she substituted a non-word. She never said *injection.* During the retelling, however, she discussed the elephant getting a shot and the danger of the needle breaking off if the elephant moved. Sherry obviously understood the author's intended meaning.

Cued retelling is a way of telling readers that there is more in the story to be told; for example, in one story, five animals helped the princess escape the evil knight. Sally tells in great detail what three of the animals did. When it was obvious that she was not going to tell more, the teacher said, "Sally, you mentioned how the dog, the kangaroo, and the cat helped the princess. Were there any other animals that helped her?" Such a question obviously cues the reader that there were other animals and that it is important to report that information.

Reflection on Reading

This procedure involves self-evaluation and self-reporting. Students often have reading problems that are difficult to pinpoint and to understand. When teachers need more information or need to confirm information they have gained from the miscue analysis and retelling, it makes sense that the students themselves should be consulted. After the cued retelling, the teacher asks the student to reflect on the reading by posing questions such as:

How do you think you did with your reading?
How do you think you did on your retelling of the story?
When did the reading go well? (Return the book to the student.)
Where did you have trouble? (Student may point to a specific word or mention a confusing concept.)

Why did you leave out this word?
Do you remember what you said for this word? What do you think it means?
Did the pictures help or bother you?

To help reflect on her reading, Kate's teacher asked her about specific miscues. Kate, a third grader, liked to read, but her oral reading was particularly dysfluent. She often made miscues that seriously affected the meaning of the story. Kate's teacher expected her to have just as much trouble with the retelling, but such was not the case. In her retelling, Kate included most of the major elements of the story, and was correct on many of the details. To help understand this apparent discrepancy, Kate was asked to comment on some of her miscues. Here a more complete picture emerged. Below we see how Kate attempted to bring her knowledge of language into the meaning making process in order to work through an unfamilar concept. She actively tried to construct meaning even though she didn't know the word. Kate read a sentence about filling a water *trough,* for which she substitutes the word *through.* She was asked to respond to her miscue (Italics ours):

T: What does that mean, "I filled the water *through* twice?"

K: That, well, I don't know if that's the true word, but like, "*through* twice," I thought that was because he poured it in, but now I just noticed that, 'cause when it [goes] *through* when you, like, when you go *through* a hoop it just goin' straight *through,* but I know you don't pour water *through* it.

T: So what do you think about that?

K: That *maybe that it could be a different word,* or that maybe there's a word like it, like homophones, or there's another one, but it's the opposite of homophones, maybe it's one of those, like the word's the same, if they're spelled the same but they mean different.

At other times, Kate was able to come up with the author's intended meaning, even though it wasn't apparent from her oral reading.

T: Would you read this paragraph?

K: While they *whipped* the medicine and water from their faces, the (inaudible) were figured out what to do next. (Text word is *wiped.*)

T: What does it mean, "They *whipped* the medicine"?

K: Like they, I was thinking that maybe they shoved it in, or they gave it to her really fast and then, she… threw it out, the water really fast, too. And then she *wipe,* they *wiped* their faces from it. They *wiped* their faces from the, see, from their face, they *wiped* the medicine and water from their faces, well…

T: Oh, so *whipped* means what?

K: That maybe they *wiped* their face, they *wipe* all their clothes off.

When information from the student's reflection on reading is added to the other RMI information, a more complete picture of the reader is constructed. In Kate's case, she did far better on retelling than anyone expected considering the large number of miscues she made. This would indicate that her active approach to constructing meaning was paying off.

Analysis of Miscues

Understanding any cognitive process is difficult. We can't see into the mind, and so must rely on the very best observable information available. Reliable evidence for understanding and reading process comes from an analysis of a readers' miscues. In this analysis the teacher looks for patterns that tell something about reader's use of the cues of language and the strategies they use to process written material.

The first step in analysis is to mark the typescript. Some marking can be done as the reading takes place, but even so it is necessary to listen to the recording to confirm exactly what the student did. Tapes of readings can also be used to show the longitudinal development of students.

Most of the RMI marking is very straightforward. Substitutions are written above the word in the text.

fresh   bones

Something was wrong inside those four tons of flesh and bone.

Read: Something was wrong inside those four tons of fresh and bones.

Omissions are circled:

He reached through the bars to lay a hand on (the) elephant's trunk.

Read: He reached through the bars to lay a hand on elephant's trunk.

Repetitions of a word are marked with an "R" and a line under the repeated text:

(R)

As ⌊Jim left the hospital with a box...

Read: As Jim Jim left the hospital with a box of cones...

The same notation is used when a miscue is repeated:

⑧ *six*
About | sixteen million units of penicillin…

Read: About six six million units of penicillin…

Multiple repetitions are indicated with lines below the repeated text. Each line represents a repetition: ⑧

When there was no more smoke the firemen…

Read: When there was no more smoke the the the firemen…

Insertions are marked with a caret:

said
What's the matter, old girl? ⋀ the zoo doctor asked.

Read: What's the matter old girl? said the zoo doctor asked.

Corrections are marked with a "C" and a line under the text that is read. The line should stop at the end of the last word spoken before the correction.

ⓒ *those*
He reached | through the bars to lay…

Read: He reached those the bars, through the bars to lay…

ⓒ *said*
…and | she ⋀ isn't going to like it.

Read: …and she said isn't going to like, she isn't going to like it.

ⓒ
Don't talk to her, Doc, | the keeper / said)

Read: Don't talk to her, Doc, said the keeper, the keeper said.

Unsuccessful attempts to correct are marked with "UC." (Non-words are marked with a $.)

⑯ $*scissee*
$*sooks*
The zoo has no | scale big enough to weigh Sudana.

Read: The zoo had no $sooks $scisee big enough to weigh Sudana.

I filled her through twice.

Read: I filled her water twice, through twice.

...down the length of her rough leg...

Read: ...down the length of through her though her leg...

Occasionally a reader will say the correct word and then replace it with a miscue. This is called abandoning the correct response and is labeled "AC."

...they figured out what to do next.

Read: ...they figured out what to, what do, we do next.

Some miscues are complex and difficult to mark. If you are unsure of a marking, it is best to write out in the margin what the reader said and number each attempt. In all cases, the criteria to use when marking are: accuracy, clarity, and efficiency. In other words, your marking must accurately reflect what the reader did, should be possible for others to interpret, and should be relatively easy to record.

Coding

The purpose of coding is to facilitate the analysis of miscues. An important assumption of miscue analysis, based on extensive research, is that all miscues are not equal. A simple counting of errors does not provide usable information, but through an analysis of miscues teachers can learn how the student handled the cues of language and what strategies were used.

At the most basic level, miscues are analyzed in terms of their syntactic and semantic acceptability. In other words, if a miscue is made, does the sentence result in something that sounds like English (syntax check), does it make sense (semantics check), and does the miscue change the meaning of the story? An additional question gives information about the graphic (letter) similarity between any substitution and the text item for which the word is substituted. Four questions are asked in this RMI procedure:

Is the sentence, as finally read by the student, syntactically acceptable in the reader's dialect and within the context of the story?

Is the sentence, as finally read by the student, semantically acceptable in the reader's dialect and within the context of the entire story?

Does the sentence, as finally read by the student, change the meaning of the story? (Question 3 is coded only if Questions 1 and 2 are coded yes [Y]).

How much does the miscue look like the text item?

The questions are answered by reading the sentence as the reader left it. Consider Kate's sentence:

ſ Suffle   *weight*   *where of very*
The sulfa would have to be weighed out; sixty grams (of sulfa) were used for every thousand pounds of elephant.

Read: Her suffle would have to be weight out; sixty grams where used of very thousand pounds of elephant.

The answers to the RMI questions:

1. Is the sentence syntactically acceptable?   No

2. Is the sentence semantically acceptable?   No

3. Is there a meaning change?   Yes

Not all miscues result in such a dramatic change in syntax and semantics. The highest level miscue is one that does not substantially change either syntax or semantics:

Susan
Sudana was sick.

The sentence is coded as both syntactically and semantically acceptable. The substitution of "Susan" for "Sudana" does not change either the grammar or the meaning of the sentence. This sentence would be coded: "Y" (syntax), "Y" (semantics). In this case, the reader read "Susan" for "Sudana" throughout the story; therefore there was no change of meaning either at the sentence or story level and the miscue is marked "N" (no meaning change).

The following sentence is very different.

fresh
Something was wrong inside those four tons of flesh and bones.

Read: Something was wrong inside those four tons of fresh and bones.

This sentence is coded "N" (syntax) and "N" (semantics) because it is not grammatically acceptable to say, "Something was wrong inside those four tons of fresh and bones," and the resulting sentence does not make sense. There is a change of meaning at both the sentence and story level and the sentence is therefore marked "Y" (meaning change).

A sentence can be syntactically acceptable, but not be a meaningful sentence. This most often happens when there is a substitution of a non-word (marked with a $):

ears *her $thrit and through*

He slipped his hand under her ear, down the length of her rough leg and back along her body.

Read: He slipped his hand under her ears, down her $thrit and through her leg and back along her body.

The non-word "thrit" has the characteristics of an English noun, making it an acceptable placeholder in the sentence. Despite the many miscues, Kate followed the rules of English syntax.

Occasionally miscues will partially change the meaning, either of the sentence or of the story, as in this example:

said *came*

He saw Mrs. Miller come home from the store.

Read: He said Mrs. Miller came home from the store.

To code graphic similarity, the marking of "H" (for a great deal of similarity), "S" (for some similarity), and "N" (for no letter similarity) is placed on the typescript in a circle directly above the word-level substitutions.

The right margin of the typescript serves as a coding form for the first three questions. The summary of the RMI can be presented as follows:

Syntactic Acceptability	__Y __%	__N __%		
Semantic Acceptability	__Y __%	__N __%		
Meaning Change	__Y __%	__ P (Partial Change)__%	__N __%	
Graphic Similarity	__H __%	__S __%	__N __%	

To compute the first three questions, count the number of sentences coded and divide that number into each raw score. To determine percentages of the graphic similarity, divide each "H," "S," and "N" count by the number of coded word-level substitutions.

Management Issues

Although miscue analysis is time consuming, it can be incorporated into the whole language classroom. It is interesting, but unnecessary to analyze the reading of students who are progressing and enjoying their literacy. Select the students for miscue analysis whose strengths and weakness are a puzzlement to you and possibly to themselves, students such as Ted.

Scheduling the data collection must not require a major revamping of the class schedule. One 30-minute block for the reading and retelling, 15 minutes for the Burke Reading Interview and possibly a 15-minute follow-up interview will be needed. Teachers might ask a student teacher or aide to take on class responsibilities while they work with a reader. If no such help is available, call in a trusted parent volunteer, or make arrangements with another teacher to schedule an activity that involves both classes (of course, reciprocate with a later, multiclass activity). Perhaps older students can read, tell stories or sing with your class; they might present a project they have been working on, or work individually with students on a math or science concept, or on your students' research projects. That should take care of the 30-minute block of time needed.

The reading interview and any follow-up needed to clarify a student's answer might be worked in during regular conferencing time. If conference time isn't available, search your schedule for those times when students can do just fine without your supervision. The rule of thumb might be, "What am I doing for students that they could do for themselves?"

The analysis of the data must be done when the teacher has time to study the reading phenomena. It isn't possible to say how long it will take to mark and code the miscues, and analyze the retelling and reflection-on-reading; it depends largely on the reader's responses. Normally the process can be done in an evening.

Application to Curriculum Planning

The major purpose of reading evaluation is curriculum planning. Miscue analysis is especially suited for classroom application because it provides a great deal of indepth information; this information must be analyzed before it can shape the curriculum for Ted or any other reader. One method of analysis is to look for trends or patterns that present the complete reader. These patterns often emerge as questions, like the following. Answer these questions in light of all available data.

1. How do the readers feel about themselves as readers? How do they feel about reading?

2. What strategies do they see as legitimate? Do they know when a strategy is not working? Do they have alternatives?

3. How well do their strategies work? How compatible is their meaning construction with the original text? What conditions facilitate meaning construction? Which ones hinder it?

4. How do the readers define literacy? What do they see as the main purposes of reading and writing?

5. What is the role of literacy in the family?

6. What instructional procedures do the readers perceive as facilitating learning? Which ones have an adverse effect?

Answer these questions in light of all analysis of miscues:

1. What percentage of sentences make sense within the context of the story?

2. Do the readers correct miscues? What type of miscues are usually corrected? What type of miscues are usually left uncorrected?

3. Do the readers substitute words that look or sound like the words in the text?

4. If the readers substitute blank or non-words, how are they used?

5. What kinds of words are most often miscued on? Are they usually function words or content words?

6. Do the readers have many regressions? Do the regressions result in corrections?

7. Do the readers attempt to "sound-out" words? Are there multiple attempts at a word? Are the readers usually able to produce the intended word?

8. Do the readers omit sections of the text? Are these omissions noted by the readers?

9. Do the readers change the punctuation? Do these changes result in meaningful sentences or non-sense?

10. For all of the above, were there trends? Did the trends change as the reading progressed?

A case study is presented here to illustrate the kind of information obtainable from a Miscue Analysis and to illustrate how that information can inform the curriculum.

Case Study

Sue is a fourth-grader in a class that uses basal readers exclusively. She is in the low reading group, and is reluctant to read, resisting the teacher's every attempt to get her to do so. With the exception of workbook assignments, Sue often doesn't complete her homework. She does not volunteer answers to questions, and when asked for answers, she is often incorrect. Her oral reading is not fluent. She makes many miscues, and usually waits for the teacher to supply the correct word. She frequently causes behavior problems and spends much of her time sitting in the hall.

Her teacher sees Sue's behavior as incomprehensible. End of level reading tests suggest remedial activities, but none of them appear to work. In fact, Sue's attitude and reading performance get steadily worse. Miscue Analysis provides Sue's teacher with information that suggests a reading program to capitalize on her strengths and to meet her needs.

Interview

From the interview, several important concepts emerge. As can be seen from this dialogue, Sue's early training with reading stressed perfection.

T: How did you learn to read? (Burke Q8)

S: By my mom setting me on the couch and telling me to read this book.

T: What did your mom do...?

S: She...would read a page and then...I would have to listen so I would know the words when I came to them, so when she was done reading, I had to read the page and then if I messed up I would have to read it over until I got it right.

Almost all of Sue's reading instruction in school supports the idea that reading should be flawless. Despite the fact that she lists several strategies for dealing with unknown text (sounding out, using context, skipping words, saying "blank"), she doesn't truly think good readers ever use such strategies. Sue believes good readers can always effortlessly say the correct word.

T: What would you like to do better as a reader? (Burke Q9)

S: Know the word and you wouldn't have to stop all the time.

T: You say you wouldn't have to stop. What do you have to stop for?

S: Words that I don't know.

T: But why do you have to stop?

S: Well, sometimes I'll stop to try to sound it out, and I can't sound it out...

Because of her belief that reading must be perfect, Sue feels she must stop to sound out any unknown word. She knows this breaks up the flow of her reading, but she doesn't think she has a choice. Her stress on letter-perfect reading interferes with her ability to concentrate on meaning.

T: What is your biggest problem with reading?

S: I don't understand the books mostly.

T: Why do you think that is?

S: Well, I don't read. I try the words so hard that I just don't get them out right, and they come up wrong.

By asking her questions about instruction, the teacher gains information about successful and unsuccessful teaching strategies. For example, when Sue's teacher introduces new words before a lesson, it establishes a mind set that is restricting and deepens her fear of the unknown.

T: What are the hardest things for you to read?

S: Books like we have in the fourth grade ...like *Weavers*... and sometimes we have to read *Gateways*.

T: Why are your reading books hard to read?

S: Because they have new words that, that you don't know.

T: How do you know they have new words?

S: Well, sometimes she tells us to go ahead and look through the book, and the story that we're gonna read next, go ahead and just skim through it. And you see all these words in there that you don't know.

Basal reading assignments given as homework are also counterproductive. Rather than reading the stories, Sue asks someone at home to read them to her. Also according to Sue, the homework assignment doesn't leave any time to read for pleasure and only increases her aversion to reading. Sue sums up her feelings in this way: "I have a lot of trouble reading and...usually I let my mom or dad read the story to me and...when they read it to me, I'll just listen and I won't look at the words to see what they are."

There are instructional activities that work well with Sue. She likes to write because "People say I have a good imagination." She also likes to use her imagination in other ways.

T: What do you like best about reading class?

S: When you can visualize pictures and draw them.

T: What does that have to do with reading?

S: We'll read the stories and the pictures that they don't have in there, we get to visualize them and draw them.

T: Why is this your favorite thing?

S: Well, because I like drawing, and then I can see the picture, and then I can read the part over...

There are times when Sue does enjoy reading and is able to respond to the reading, as is shown in this dialogue:

T: Why don't you read much?

S: I don't like to read.

T: Have you ever liked to read?

S: Well, sometimes I'll get a spooky book, and I like to, I like to get (unintelligible) books: ...I have it here right now. There's a whole bunch of books. I had one...for the summer, and his little sister said that she had a doll, and she said that the doll said that there was a ghost in the window... (She continues telling the story.)

Sue also recognizes the importance of motivation in reading:

T: Is there anything you like reading about?

S: Well... it's like you like that book and then...you're interested in it, so you want to read it, so you try the best you can to...get the... words right so you can understand what it's about.

From the interview the teacher can get a great deal of information on how to help Sue, but in order to gear instruction to her needs, she must know how Sue handles unknown written material without assistance. In other words, what strategies does she actually use?

Oral Reading

Sue's reading is somewhat hesitant, but not dysfluent. There are no pauses longer than two seconds, and she only occasionally repeats the first letter of a word. She does not skip any portion of the story longer than a word, and her phrasing matches the punctuation of the story.

Retelling

From the retelling we learn that Sue is a better reader than she thinks she is. She understands most of the major points of the story. She has one misconception at the end that may be related to a lack of prior knowledge.

Reflection on Reading

One of Sue's most telling comments comes when she is asked how she feels about her reading. She answers that she hasn't done well because of the number of times she stopped. This statement is significant because there were no noticeable pauses. What she interprets as stopping was not perceived as such by her teacher. When asked why she stopped, she said it was to sound out words quickly. This is another indication that she expects reading to be flawless.

Analysis of Miscues

Trends in the miscue data provide more information about Sue's reading. Sue often corrects her miscues. This indicates that she is monitoring the reading based on her knowledge of syntax and semantics, as in these two examples:

We had a little|trouble hiding her...

Sue recognizes that *table* does not make sense in the entire sentence, and she corrects the miscue to make the sentence meaningful.

But|we liked her too much to take a chance...

Read: But we knew, we, but we liked her too much to take a chance...

The commoness of the phrase "we knew" compels Sue to substitute the word "knew" for "liked." These two words have no resemblance phonetically and, except for the letters "k" and "e," have no resemblance orthographically. The substitution of "knew" for "liked" in the sentence does not change the meaning substantially. Nevertheless, Sue notices the difference and corrects her miscue.

A second trend is revealed by Sue's treatment of unknown multisyllabic words. Usually she substitutes the word "blank" for the text word. There is only one instance in which she supplies the correct word; the remainder of the "blanks" are left uncorrected.

This tendency to use "blank" as an uninflected placeholder, rather than substituting a word that makes sense, is another indication of Sue's reluctance to take risks. In this example she substitutes "blank" for "divided."

blank

But we found it easier to think of time as being divided into day and night.

She does not add a past tense inflection ("ed") to the placeholder ("blank"). She also doesn't substitute a reasonable word, such as "broken." She doesn't go back after finishing the sentence in an attempt to substitute a meaningful word for "blank." For all intents and purposes, the placeholder "blank" is simply a way to skip the word.

Applications

Only by looking at the whole picture can we get an idea of how to help Sue. We know that she feels reading must be perfect and flawless. She doesn't meet her own expectations. She doesn't have confidence in her own abilities, and so she avoids reading. Requiring skill sheets, comprehension drills, and multiple readings does nothing but encourage these negative feelings.

Despite this, Sue is able to read for meaning. She even enjoys reading and responds with a "lived through experience" if the book is one she chooses. She likes to write and visualize scenes that are evoked by the stories she reads and writes. These are encouraging signs and things to capitalize on.

There are many strategies for Sue's teacher to consider. Her major goal should be the creation of a classroom where risk-taking is maximized, risk is minimized, and literacy learning is meaningful. Such a classroom has several characteristics.

Students are encouraged to take linguistic risks. When this happens, miscues occur. When Sue's miscues do not change the meaning of the text, they should be ignored. All deviations from the text are seen as opportunities for students to learn new reading strategies and to use the appropriate strategies they already know. Strategy teaching, however, should only be done after the reader has worked through the text without assistance.

Students have many opportunities to experience reading and writing as ways of communicating. Sue needs to see herself as an author. In order to do this, she must write every day, but the writing must be authentic. Grammar drills or writing in response to story-starters will not make students feel like authors. Authentic writing satisfies some felt need: To tell a story or to communicate an idea. This can only happen if students have control of topic and genre and if there are opportunities for students to share their work.

The writing must be risk free. Risk is diminished when students are allowed to concentrate on ideas and intentions rather than perfection in their first drafts. Later in the writing process, students work on conventions such as spelling, grammar, and handwriting.

The classroom should be organized in a way that invites self-initiated learning and promotes a community of learners. This can only happen if students are allowed to interact with each other. Interactive, student-centered learning can take place without sacrificing classroom order if the classroom is thought of as a teaching/learning strategy. Materials need to be easily available and as varied as possible. Students must understand the guidelines for class organization and be involved in establishing rules within their classroom community. Above all, the classroom must be built on mutual trust among all learners, including the teacher.

Students need choice not only in what they read, but in the total curriculum. A reading strategy that allows students a certain measure of choice is literature study in literature discussion groups. This strategy, with its emphasis on cooperation and meaning making rather than "one right answer," could be especially helpful with Sue because of her lack of confidence in her own abilities as a reader.

Literature discussion groups are formed based on a common interest in a book, thereby tapping into Sue's increased motivation to read books she likes. Several times a week the groups meet for discussion. Topics of discussion are free ranging, but certain themes usually emerge. As the students and teacher discuss these themes, they learn how to work through reading problems. They find out that good reading is not necessarily flawless reading, and that there can be many different interpretations of a text. The groups may plan projects in order to re-experience their literature. Participation in projects offers Sue an excellent opportunity to use her imagination and artistic abilities. Through these groups and other student-centered activities, the classroom becomes a community in which students learn from each other and discover their own strengths. Sue needs such a classroom to help her feel the joy of literacy.

If we had infrared vision, the world would appear to be a very different place. We would see colors, ranging from dark blue in hot spots to dark pink in cold spots. The world wouldn't change, but our perceptions of it would. Learning miscue analysis is something like putting on infrared goggles. Every literacy encounter becomes an opportunity to learn more about readers and about the process of reading. There are many ways that miscue analysis changes the way teachers view reading. We discuss a few of those ways here.

Discovering the Giftedness in Each Student

The best reason for learning miscue analysis is to discover students' hidden abilities. Miscue analysis can reveal remarkable abilities in students who, according to test results and performance with basal readers, have serious reading problems. That's because tests are designed to reveal weaknesses. Miscue analysis, in contrast, enables teachers to see past weakness to discover strengths.

For example, speaking a non-standard dialect is often seen as an academic weakness. A dialect that includes sentences such as, "Wait 'till he baby be born" may cause problems on typical reading tests. However, by not correcting miscues, and listening for consistencies (or inconsistencies) in them, it is often possible to distinguish between reading problems and dialect differences.

Tim

For instance, a seven-year-old rural Missouri boy named Tim, while reading a story about secrets being whispered into animals' ears, substituted a word that sounded like "our" every time he came to "ear." He never changed or corrected this substitution or hesitated before the word. During the retelling, he retold the story, using "our" as if it were the word "ear." This is evidence of a phonological dialect difference, rather than a reading problem. As far as Tim knew, "ear" was pronounced "our."

Jimmy

One of the main reasons why typical assessment procedures don't reveal student strengths is because they do not capitalize on student interests. With miscue analysis, student interests can become part of the assessment. Taking student interests into account can sometimes result in dramatic revelations, as happened with Jimmy, a student I was tutoring. He was nine when we first met.

I was told that he could not read a word and didn't even know the alphabet. I saw him for about six hours, scattered over the span of a semester. Throughout that first year, it appeared that the only words he could read were his name and the names of some family members. I saw Jimmy a few more times during the second year. During Black History Month, I wore a button bearing a picture of Martin Luther King, Jr., along with a quote by him. Jimmy was interested in the button so I gave it to him.

He wanted to know what the quote said. I read it to him and then wrote the words on a piece of paper. I read the quote again, pointing to each word as I read. I then asked Jimmy to read it to me. He gave his customary "I can't read" response. I asked him to point to any words he knew and read them. The quote and Jimmy's response follow:

We   to   together as brothers or we are go
We must learn to live together as brothers or we are going

to   together as fools.
to perish together as fools.

After the first attempt, I asked him to try again and he read every word except "must" and "perish."

Jimmy's teachers at school didn't know that he had learned to read because he had never gotten the chance to initiate reading based on his own interests. As a result, at school during reading group, he did as he had always done: When he came to a word he made a feeble attempt at sounding it out and then waited for the teacher or another student to tell him the word. By having him attempt to read something of his own choosing, without assistance, I discovered that he was on his way to becoming an independent reader.

Henry

Henry, a fifth grader, lives on a Navaho reservation and is in the Chapter One program in his school. He has little confidence in his abilities and seems more interested in joking than in learning.

One morning, I read the book *Buffalo Woman* by Paul Goble to a group of four boys, including Henry. When I had finished reading, Henry asked me a question about something in the book, so I told him to read the page to find out. He immediately started reading out loud until he came to the sentence: "My Grandfather is chief of the Buffalo Nation." At the word "chief" he stopped and looked up at me. When I didn't tell him the word, he asked me what it was. I told him that I wasn't going to tell him the word, so he would have to skip it or put in something that made sense.

He skipped the word and finished the sentence and then asked me again what the word was. I told him, "Put in a word that makes sense."

He substituted the word "chicken." I said, "Does that make sense?" He laughed and said "No." "So why did you say 'chicken,' " I asked. He said it was because they both started with a "c." I said, "Forget about the 'c,' " and I took the book away from him. "Now," I said, "tell me a word that makes sense." " ' Leader,' " he said.

Henry and I learned a lot from this encounter. He learned that "making sense" is what is most important. I learned that he tended to rely too much on sound/symbol cues, but that he was capable of using meaning to help him figure out words. I would never have discovered this if I had told him the word or if I was not aware of the different cuing systems of language that are part of miscue analysis.

Bryan

Bryan, a fourteen-year-old boy who says he isn't a good reader because he reads slowly and stumbles over words, reads a newspaper article about a local basketball star. Just as he said he would, he reads slowly and stumbles over words. He has many miscues. Then he is asked to retell what he has read. He asks, "Do you want it told back in the order it happened or the order it was in the newspaper?"

He then proceeds to retell every detail of the story, including addresses, times and dates, and number of points scored. During the reading he omits the word "heckle," but during the retelling, he explains that the crowd at the game was making "nasty" remarks about a player. Bryan does indeed "sound like" a poor reader, but through miscue analysis, it is possible to discover his remarkable abilities to comprehend detailed information.

Carol

Carol, a fourth grader who likes to read and says she is a good reader, has few miscues as she reads a difficult story, but she substitutes the word "shouldered" for "shuddered" and does not correct it or use the word "shuddered" in the retelling. She is asked how she figures out the meaning of an unknown word. She says that she uses the meaning of the sentence to figure out the word and explains the process in this way:

> Well, if the sentence read "There is poverty on Main Street"... I would know that...means the people were poor because Main Street might be a trashy street and then it might say there is poverty on Main Street. [It's] like Hide and Go Seek!

From her description of the reading process, coupled with her success as a reader, it is possible to conclude that Carol's miscue was not significant enough to be considered a problem.

Tim, the seven-year-old with the rural Missouri dialect, sometimes skips "little" words and sometimes transposes letters in words, as he did in this example.

First I have ~~tell~~ my ~~trigger~~ said Oliver. Oliver
First I have to bell my tiger, said Oliver. Oliver

        (d)   (d)
whispered ~~the~~ seket into his tiger's our.
whispered the secret into his tiger's ear.

A teacher trained in miscue analysis would not consider any of Tim's problems significant because the omissions didn't cause a loss of meaning during the retelling and because he corrected "trigger" to "tiger" in the second sentence.

Roger, aged nine, read the following sentence,

I waited and waited and waited at the cellar door

in this way:

I waited and wished and waited at the cellar door.

It appears, to miscue-trained ears, that Roger was using his knowledge of story and of syntax to jazz up an otherwise boring sentence.

Potential Problems

Once teachers are trained in miscue analysis, they can also spot potential reading problems. For example, when first grader Susan tries over and over again to sound out every single word she sees without making any attempt to make meaningful substitutions, then it could be a sign that she is relying too much on a single cuing system. Or the same could be true when Sean correctly sounds out the word "mischief" as "mis-chief" without ever trying to combine the two syllables into a recognizable word.

The Burke Interview (1988) can be a source of information about many potential problems. Finding out that students do not like to read, or that they think they are bad readers can help teachers to adjust curriculum to their needs. It is also important to find out what student interests are. John, a fifth grader, said he didn't like to read in school because the emphasis was so much on fiction. John wanted to read about things like "'struction" (construction) instead of having to read stories.

Another example took place in a secondary reading class. According to tests, Alan was classified as borderline mentally retarded and was reading on a second grade level. He expressed interest in books about horses and dogs and asked if he could read *The Red Pony,* by John Steinbeck. I told him he could, but the book might cause him some trouble. I went about my teaching duties and occasionally glanced at Alan.

He sat for almost an hour, slowly turning pages, all the time paying rapt attention to the book. Finally, he came to me and said he was confused about the Pony, it seemed to disappear after the first chapter. I had many other things to do at that moment, so I told him to reread the last two pages of the first chapter. In a few minutes he came up to me with a look of complete satisfaction. He said, "Now it makes sense. The Pony died." I confirmed that revelation and told him to reread chapter two with that information in mind. I spent, at the most, five minutes with Alan, but in that five minutes I learned more about his reading ability than I could from any test.

By viewing Alan as someone who could use all of the cuing systems of language to make meaning from print, I allowed him to attempt reading that should have been far too difficult for him. By regarding reading as a process of making meaning, I was able to get a great deal of information about Alan's abilities to get meaning from print as he reads.

I saw the attention of a normally restless boy held by the act of reading; I saw him struggle to make meaning from the text, without asking for assistance until he was unable to make sense of the story; I saw him reread the text and correct his misinterpretations. I saw all of this as I went about the business of teaching. At the time, I jotted a few words down in my ever-present notebook (I call mine "What I Noticed"). At the end of the day, I took a minute or two to transfer the information to his folder.

Once teachers learn to view reading through the lens of miscue analysis, it becomes the basis of all their reading assessment. This doesn't mean that these teachers are doing miscue analysis on all of their students all of the time. That would be far too time consuming. Instead, as they go about their teaching duties, they keep their eyes and ears open for examples of students using language. The earlier example, where Henry substituted "leader" for "chief," occurred as part of a reading lesson. When it happened, I made a note of it and later transferred that information to Henry's folder. The whole procedure took about 60 seconds.

Conclusion

This chapter is an introduction to a Reading Miscue Analysis procedure that provides teachers with immediate and accessible information about the reading abilities and needs of students. The authors encourage teachers to pursue the study of this whole language evaluation instrument by delving into the references and resources listed below. We hope, too, that teachers will investigate the informative qualities of the Reading Miscue Inventory — by using the inventory, along with the reading interview and other suggestions given above, to gather information about a student who poses curricular questions and uncertainties. We feel such a comprehensive study will provide an abundance of data on which a strong and appropriate reading program can be built.

Note: Excerpts are from interviews that were done as part of a Weldon Spring Grant, University of Missouri, 1987–88.

Bibliography and References

Theory and Research

Gollasch, F.W. (Ed.). (1982). *Language and literacy: The selected writings of Kenneth S. Goodman* (Vols. 1 and 2). Boston: Routledge and Kegan Paul.

Goodman, K. (1969). Analysis of reading miscues: Applied psycholinguistics. *Reading Research Quarterly, 5*(1), 652–658.

Goodman, K. (1984). Unity in reading. In A.C. Purvis and O. Niles (Eds.), *Becoming readers in a complex society.* Chicago: University of Chicago Press.

Goodman, K. (1985). *What's whole in whole language?* Toronto: Scholastic.

Goodman, Y. Kidwatching: An alternative to testing. *Journal of National Elementary Principals, 57*(4), 41–45.

Goodman, Y. & Burke, C. (1972). *Reading miscue inventory manual: Procedures for diagnosis and evaluation.* New York: Richard C. Owen.

Marek, A., Goodman, K., & Babcock, P. (1985). *Annotated miscue analysis bibliography* (Occasional paper No. 16). Tucson: University of Arizona.

Whole Language Curriculum and Instruction

Buchanan, E. (Ed.). (1980). *For the love of reading.* Winnipeg: CEL Group.

Cochrane, O., *et al.* (1984). *Reading, writing, and caring.* Winnipeg: CEL Group.

Edelsky, C., & Smith, K. (1984). Is that writing—or are those marks just a figment of your curriculum? *Language Arts, 61*(1), 24–32.

Gilles, C. (1990). Collaborative literacy strategies: "We don't need a circle to have a group." In K. Short & K. Mitchell-Pierce (Eds.), *Talking about books: Creating literature communities.* Portsmouth, NH: Heinemann.

Gilles, C. (1989). Reading, writing, thinking and learning: Using literature discussion groups. *English Journal, 78*(1), 38–41.

Gilles, C., & VanDover, M. (1988). The power of collaboration. In J. Golub (Ed.), *Classroom practices in teaching English 1988: Focus on collaborative learning.* Urbana, IL: National Council of Teachers of English.

Gilles, C., Bixby, M., Crowley, P., Crenshaw, S., Henrichs, M., Pyle, D., & Waters, F. (1987). *Strategies that make sense for secondary students.* New York: Richard C. Owen.

Goodman, Y., & Burke, C. (1980). *Reading strategies: Focus on comprehension.* New York: Richard C. Owen.

Goodman, Y., & Watson, D. (1977). A reading program to live with: Focus on comprehension. *Language Arts, 54*(8), 868–879.

Harste, J., Woodward, V., & Burke, C. (1984). *Language stories and literacy lessons.* Exeter, NH: Heinemann Educational Books.

Newman, J. (1986). *Whole language: Translating theory into practice.* Exeter, NH: Heinemann Educational Books.

Rhodes, L. (1981). I can read! Predictable books as resources for reading and writing instruction. *Reading Teacher, 34*(5), 511–518.

Watson, D. (Ed.). (1987). *Ideas and insights: Language arts for elementary children.* Urbana, IL: National Council of Teachers of English.

Watson, D., Burke, C., & Harste, J. (1988). *Whole language: Inquiring voices.* Toronto: Scholastic.

Chapter 5

Whole Language Assessment and Evaluation Strategies

Ward A. Cockrum and Maggie Castillo

This chapter covers whole language assessment and evaluation strategies of developmental checklists, interview sheets, journals and logs, portfolios, and holistic scoring. We describe format, purpose, and use of each of the strategies and provide sources of published examples of instruments and suggestions for the development of your own instruments. We begin the chapter by discussing the power of observation because these whole language assessment and evaluation strategies are based on observation. The chapter concludes with a rationale for marking report cards based on the data gathered using whole language assessment and evaluation strategies.

Power of Observation

Observation is the primary method of gathering data for evaluation in a whole language classroom. Goodman stated that "whole language teachers are constant kid watchers" (1986, p. 41). This observation or kid watching can take many forms. It can be as informal as watching the child play games on the playground to using a checklist while conducting an interview with the child. Regardless of the structure of the observation, using observations for assessment and evaluation should not be undervalued. Observation can be very powerful in developing a complete picture of a child's literacy development.

Observation as the basis of evaluation requires active participation on the part of the teacher in the child's language acts. Standardized tests or even teacher-made tests place the responsibility for evaluation in the instrument. This can result in a teacher being upset with a child's score on an exam because the teacher "knows" the child performs at a much higher level in class. A whole language kid watcher trusts his or her evaluation of a child because he or she is a part of the child's language use. Whole language teachers are as involved in the child's language development as parents are with a child learning to talk.

Observation as the basis of evaluation requires ongoing kid watching. The evaluation of the child's literacy development needs to be based on many observations in many contexts at many different times. The power of using observations to evaluate a child is directly related to the amount of observation used to form the evaluation. Too few observations are just as dangerous as one-time testing to evaluate a child's language development.

A good kid watcher is always looking for what the child can do. The total language development picture the teacher is attempting to build is based on what he or she has observed the child do, not on what he or she has not seen. It is assumed that any abilities the child has not demonstrated are ones which will develop in the future. For instance, inaccuracy in language use is a sign that the child is in the process of developing that ability. Those abilities not visible may require a change in the instructional approach so that the child has an opportunity to develop them. But, never should a child be made to feel that he or she is lacking or deficient; instead he or she should always feel that he or she is a capable learner.

Observation makes the evaluation process less stressful for the child and the teacher. The focus on what the child can do and the continuous nature of observation helps to limit stress in the evaluation. Observation does not generate negative behavior because the child is not placed in a powerless situation. When observation is used as a basis for evaluation, the learner's view is important to the observer and the observer needs to communicate on a one-to-one basis with the child to be sure the observations are accurate reflections of the child's ability.

When observations are used in evaluation of a child's literacy development, self-evaluation is possible. The child can look at his or her own work and tell the teacher what he or she is attempting to do. The child can see from models provided in the classroom what is needed to reach the standard of the model. The child can keep examples of and notes about his or her own work in portfolios, which then become part of the observation-evaluation process.

Observation also is a powerful method of evaluation because the teacher is in the role of a learner. As a teacher uses observation strategies to determine the child's literacy development, he or she becomes more knowledgeable about literacy development. The teacher becomes an expert in the way literacy develops in the classroom. He or she doesn't wait for the results of a test to report whether achievement in literacy has occurred. He or she knows, because he or she is a part of the literacy community in that classroom.

The most powerful aspect of using observation as the basis of evaluation is that it can reflect the "real world." Society has expectations as to the literacy abilities of people graduating from the 12th grade. They are frequently disappointed. Business people complain about recent graduates' lack of ability to do as simple a task as correctly filling out a job application. Parents decry the lack of interest in reading in their children. College professors tell us students come to them ill prepared in the area of written communication. Some of these problems may be attributed to the method used to determine a student's literacy development. When only multiple-choice questions or fragments of language are used to determine success in language development, educators and students can be misled. Job applications don't have multiple-choice responses, nor can high school English teachers follow students to college to find their spelling errors for them. A more valid view of a 12th grader's literacy development can be obtained by observing his or her actual reading and writing. What children do in their own reading and writing in school is a more accurate reflection of what they will do in their own reading and writing out of school. This issue is essential to the value of whole language assessment and evaluation. Many times whole language instruction is attacked on the basis of standardized test results. Such results are, however, "inappropriate for judging whole language programs" (Goodman, 1986, p. 42). The true test of the success of whole language programs will be in the total literacy development of students as they enter the world after formal education.

Strategies for Observing Literacy Development

Several strategies have been developed to provide structure to the observation done for evaluation and assessment purposes. Two strategies, developmental checklists and interviews, are in the form of instruments; two others, portfolios and journals and logs, are a way of organizing student-produced work. Each of these strategies can be used for both instruction and evaluation and can be modified to use for self-evaluation.

Developmental Checklists

The developmental checklist is the most frequently used method of guiding observations for whole language assessment and evaluation. The term "developmental" has two meanings, both of which can be applied to these checklists. One refers to the maturation of the child and implies that certain stages of language development occur as the child grows older. This type of development can be seen in very young children and some checklists in the kindergarten and first grade are based on stages of maturation.

However, most checklists used in whole language assessment and evaluation are based on the view that development in language ability occurs because the child has been provided the opportunity to use language. The checklists based on this view of development help the teacher see how effective the classroom environment has been in allowing the children to develop their language ability.

Format of Developmental Checklists

Developmental checklists usually contain a list of the language traits for which the teacher is watching and some system to mark the occurrence or quality of the traits when they are observed. An example of a checklist to evaluate a kindergartener's awareness of environmental print, titled "What Can I Read," is shown in Figure 5.1.

Purpose of Developmental Checklists

Checklists are used in whole language assessment and evaluation to keep the observer focused, to provide a method of recording observations that requires a minimum of writing and to provide consistency from one observation to the next. In addition they can be customized to match the instructional focus of a given teacher.

Uses of Developmental Checklists

The number of specific uses for developmental checklists may be unlimited, since any literacy event can have a checklist designed to facilitate the observation and evaluation of that event.

Figure 5.1 Sample Developmental Checklist

What Can I Read?

Name _____

Date _____

Level of Attainment

	NR	NC	C	NL	DC
I. **Most Common**					
Butterfinger	☐	☐	☐	☐	☐
Cheerios	☐	☐	☐	☐	☐
Corn Flakes	☐	☐	☐	☐	☐
Lunchables	☐	☐	☐	☐	☐
Mayonnaise	☐	☐	☐	☐	☐
Pizza	☐	☐	☐	☐	☐
Salt	☐	☐	☐	☐	☐
Spaghetti	☐	☐	☐	☐	☐
II. **Next Most Common**					
Burger King	☐	☐	☐	☐	☐
Kmart	☐	☐	☐	☐	☐
McDonald's	☐	☐	☐	☐	☐
Pizza Hut	☐	☐	☐	☐	☐
Jack in the Box	☐	☐	☐	☐	☐
Safeway	☐	☐	☐	☐	☐
Taco Bell	☐	☐	☐	☐	☐
III. **Least Common**					
TV Guide	☐	☐	☐	☐	☐
IGA	☐	☐	☐	☐	☐
Ranger Rick	☐	☐	☐	☐	☐
Daily Sun	☐	☐	☐	☐	☐
Newsweek	☐	☐	☐	☐	☐
Time	☐	☐	☐	☐	☐

NR = No Response

NC = No Contextualization, response does not fit context, e.g., says Jello when shown candy bar wrapper

C = Contextualization, response does fit context, e.g., says candy bar when shown candy bar wrapper

NL = Names Letters, response fits context and indicates some sound symbol recognition

DC = Decontextualization, able to read product name when written on index card

(The three categories of product names were established by asking children to bring in things they could read at home. Category one contains those products that 10 or more students brought, category two—5 to 10, category three—less than 5.)

The editing stage of the writing process provides a nice example of the use of developmental checklists. The mechanical aspects of writing (use of capitals, use of punctuation, and so forth) are put on a checklist. Levels of attainment of the use of those mechanics (present, absent, or not observed) are also put on the checklist. The teacher can then look at a sample of the child's writing while using the checklist to record observations. The teacher can document changes in the student's use of writing mechanics by repeating the use of the checklist at a later date. The teacher can also evaluate the effect of the learning environment on the student's use of the mechanics of writing.

The same checklist can be part of classroom instruction. The student can fill out the checklist prior to an editing conference with the teacher. The teacher and the student can then determine those concepts related to writing mechanics which the student has not yet attained. Letting students self-evaluate their writing allows them to develop independence. Students become responsible for finding and fixing their own errors.

Several authors have included examples of developmental checklists that could be used for evaluating writing. One appropriate for the early elementary grades can be found in Marie Clay's book, *What Did I Write?* (1975). Two that seem to be useful in the upper elementary grades appear in *Now We Want to Write* by Jan Turbill (1984) and *Spell by Writing* by Wendy Bean and Chrystine Bouffler (1987). And Evelyn Lerman (1984) designed a writing checklist for grades seven and eight.

Checklists for the assessment and evaluation of other language uses are also available. A selected listing is included here:

The Concepts About Print Test in *The Early Detection of Reading Difficulties* by Marie M . Clay (1979) has been used in the United States as a screening device for reading readiness (Stallman & Pearson, 1990). The checklist helps determine the knowledge a child has about how books work and how print works in books.

The Whole Language Evaluation Book by Kenneth Goodman, Yetta Goodman, and Wendy Hood (1989) has samples of kindergarten checklists, a writing checklist, and a thinking and language checklist.

An excellent "Response to Literature Checklist" can be found in *Grand Conversations* by Ralph Peterson and Maryann Eeds (1990). They have also included checklists for recording students' participation in literature studies.

Two more global checklists are currently available. The Whole Language Behavior Inventory in *The Administrator's Guide to Whole Language* by Gail Heald-Taylor (1989) is a very complete checklist which covers speaking, listening, writing, and reading. This checklist is also designed to cover kindergarten through sixth grade. A complete evaluation package that includes observation forms developed in England is the *Primary Language Record Handbook for Teachers* (ILEA/ Center for Language in Primary Education, 1989). The Primary Language Record is designed to be used for a child's entire elementary school years.

Deciding which checklist to use requires a knowledge of the behaviors that can be observed as a child's experience with language increases. It is helpful to become familiar with the literature on literacy development before using any developmental checklist.

Teachers should freely modify existing checklists or develop their own. One of the most powerful characteristics of developmental checklists is their adaptability. As a teacher gains experience using the checklists and his or her knowledge of literacy development grows he or she will want to revise the checklists he or she is using.

Interviews

The second most common observation instrument used in whole language evaluation and assessment is the interview sheet. Interview sheets are also known as conference recording forms.

Format of Interview Sheets

In its general form, an interview sheet has a set of questions that the teacher will ask the student and blank space to record the child's response. However, there are many variations of the interview sheet. One type used with older students suspends the interview and has students fill out the sheet independently. Another variation uses a forced-choice response format whereby the student selects from a given set of responses the one that best matches how he or she feels or thinks. An example of an interview sheet titled "Literature Interview Form" can be seen in Figure 5.2.

Purpose of Interview Sheets

The purpose of most interviews is to gain insight into how the student views his or her own literacy ability or feelings toward some literacy event.

Figure 5.2   Sample of an Interview Sheet

Literature Interview Form

Reader's Name _____ Date____/____/____

Interviewer's Name* _____

       Book Title _____

       Author _____

1. Whom did you like the most in the story?
2. Whom did you least like?
3. Where does the story take place?
4. When does the story take place?
5. Why did the story keep your interest?
6. Did the author do anything that surprised you?
7. What was the saddest part of the story?
8. What was the happiest part of the story?
9. Did any part of the story make you laugh or cry?
10. What do you wish you could ask the author?
11. What do you think you will always remember about this book?
12. What type of person do you think would most enjoy reading this book?

---

*Interview may be done with the teacher, another student, or independently.

Uses of Interview Sheets

Interview sheets can also take many forms and have many uses. The Reading Interview in the *Reading Miscue Inventory* (Goodman, Watson, & Burke, 1987) is an interview sheet in which the interviewer asks the child questions such as: "How did you learn to read?" and "What do you do when you come to a word you don't know?" The child's response is evaluated to gain insight into how the child views the act of reading and how he or she processes print.

Regie Routman, in *Transitions From Literature to Literacy* (1988), describes a simple two-question interview used with her first graders. She wanted to determine the impact her classroom had on her students' views of reading and writing. On the last day of school she asks the students in her class "What is writing?" and "What is reading?" The responses were very enlightening.

Interview sheets can be used to conference with individual students about how their writing is progressing or how they respond to a piece of literature they have read. Examples of interview sheets used for writing conferences can be found in *Understanding Writing: Ways of Observing, Learning, and Teaching,* edited by Thomas Newkirk and Nancie Atwell (1988) and in *A Researcher Learns to Write,* by Donald Graves (1984).

The interview is used by the teacher to confirm other observations or to gather new information about the child. Self-evaluation occurs for the student when they answer the interviewer's questions.

Journals and Logs

In whole language classrooms journals and logs are primarily used for instruction. But, journals and logs are excellent records of a student's language development and can be used in assessment and evaluation, as well.

Format of Journals and Logs

Journals and logs generally take the form of a booklet. Several blank pages are stapled together and placed between a front and back cover. The pages can include dates for entries that will be made in the journal or log and designated spaces for the entries.

Purpose of Journals and Logs

Students may write anything they wish in their journals, while logs provide a place for learners to respond to some agreed-upon topic. The evaluation uses of journals and logs change with the age of the student. Teachers, however, should make clear to students at all levels exactly how their journals and logs will be used for evaluation.

Uses of Journals and Logs

The use of journals with beginning writers lends itself to both instruction and evaluation. The first journal entries of the writers in a kindergarten provide the teacher with an initial opportunity to determine the children's level of development in writing.

Students' journal entries may be pictures (picture stage), some may have scribbles like writing with their pictures (scribble stage), others may have random letters along with their pictures (alphabet stage), while still others may have written stories in invented spelling to accompany their pictures (invented spelling stage). A knowledgeable teacher can recognize that each of these groups of students is at a different level of development in writing.

By responding to each child in writing, using the child's words in the response, a teacher can provide a model for the kindergarten writer. The journal becomes a dialogue between the teacher and student and provides a constant source for evaluation of the students' writing development.

The journal becomes a record of the child's development from a picture stage, to the level of invented spelling. It also shows when the child abandons a particular invented spelling and moves to the arbitrary standard spelling.

The journal is also a method of self-evaluation for the kindergarten writer. The teacher's response gives the child feedback about the meaning he or she was able to put into his or her writing. The words and sentence structure used by the teacher provides a model for the child to compare with his or her own writing.

The more capable a writer becomes the less journal entries should be evaluated by the teacher. The self-evaluation role of journals will be viable with writers at all levels of sophistication. But, the day may come when the journal writer does not want the teacher to write in his or her journal or to even read it.

A child can use literature logs to give a response to books he or she has read. He or she can make entries while the book is being read or after it is finished. The teacher can respond in writing to the child's entries and establish a dialogue about the book. Literature logs can also be established for specific books. Each child who reads the book can write an entry and can compare his or her reaction to the book with those of his or her peers.

Children can also start logs to enter their views of their own writing. They write about how they feel their current writing project is progressing or what they hope to express in their stories, and the teacher can respond. In this way, a dialogue starts that focuses on the children's writing.

Portfolios

Portfolios have become one of the primary assessment tools in whole language classrooms. In the most rudimentary form, portfolios are simply collections of students' work. In advanced forms developed by many whole language teachers, portfolios have become dynamic vehicles for combining assessment and instruction. Portfolios have also been used to cross over content boundaries to integrate growth of content knowledge with the development of language communication skills.

Format of Portfolios

In general form, a writing portfolio is a folder that contains a selection of an individual student's writing. The physical appearance of the folder varies from teacher to teacher, but it seems that the more professional-looking the folder, the more pride the child takes in owning it. A recent technological adaptation used in some classrooms is to have the portfolio on a computer disc.

The internal format of the portfolio follows no established rules, but usually has the student's work arranged in chronological order. Additional sections may be present for organizing the work on the basis of genre, favorite and least favorite selections, reflection sheets, or checklists and interview forms.

Purpose of Portfolios

The portfolio is a place to save examples of a student's work. The number of pieces in the portfolio should grow as the school year progresses. Permanent portfolios containing samples of the student's best work can move with the student from grade to grade or school to school and become their property upon completion of high school.

Uses of Portfolios

A major use of portfolios has been in the development and assessment of writing ability. The writing portfolio documents the child's development in writing ability. By comparing earlier pieces with his or her current work, the degree of progress becomes clear to both the teacher and the student.

The two major users of the writing portfolio are the teacher and the student. The student needs to have ownership and control of the portfolio. The student's reflection upon and self-evaluation of his or her own work makes the portfolio a powerful step in moving the child to a position of independence in learning. The child should make the final decision about including a piece in the portfolio.

The teacher, in the role of a consultant, can use the material not only to guide the student's development of the mechanics of writing but also to develop his or her own voice. The teacher can use the writing portfolios to examine the student's work for consistent errors for which he or she may need to have a model. The teacher can focus the student's attention on the model and then see if the child transfers that model to his or her own writing. The teacher can also see what impact the instruction in the classroom has had on the student's writing.

The examination of the writing samples can reveal changes in the child's writing style. The teacher can examine growth in the child's ability to write interesting stories and can evaluate the use of specific story elements.

The student can use the material in the portfolio for reflection on his or her development of writing ability. The student can take control of his or her writing and use the teacher as a consultant to help answer questions he or she has about writing.

In addition to reading and writing, portfolios have been used in the content areas of math, science, and social studies. Students can reflect on both the development of the written work in the content folders and the knowledge gained about that content area.

The construction and use of portfolios have been widely documented. Sheila Valencia (1990) describes the use of portfolios for reading assessment. *Portfolio Assessment: Getting Started* by Allan A. De Fina (1992) provides an excellent source for beginning users of portfolios, and Regie Routman (1991), in *Invitations,* describes the struggle of moving toward the use of portfolios. And a very complete resource for literacy portfolios is *Portfolio Assessment in the Reading-Writing Classroom* (Tierney, Carter, & Desai, 1991).

Holistic Scoring

One of the few whole language evaluation and assessment procedures that results in a number is the holistic scoring system. The system usually has a rubric to limit inconsistency in scoring.

Format for Holistic Scoring

Holistic scoring is usually done with a piece of written work. The child is aware that he or she will be scored and should have the opportunity to produce an example of his or her best work. A rubric is used to guide the evaluation of the written work. The rubric may include information about the prompts made to the students when the work is collected and have established characteristics that need to be in evidence for each level of the scoring scale. The teacher or scorer reads the piece and awards a score based on his or her impression of how well it meets the characteristics on the scoring rubric. It is assumed that this impression is influenced by the writer's ability to use the mechanics of language as well as the quality of the content.

Purpose of Holistic Scoring

Holistic scoring provides a system to evaluate a large number of pieces of writing. Holistic scoring results in a comparative ranking of the pieces of writing that were evaluated.

Uses of Holistic Scoring

Holistic scoring is used to evaluate the writing programs of whole schools or school districts. It is also used as a method of determining how well an individual's writing skills are developed in comparison to others at the same age or level of education. All students being evaluated need to write on the same topic and their work needs to be evaluated by "equivalent" scorers.

A second use of holistic scoring is to evaluate students' responses on an essay test. After the test is returned, a sample of answers that were evaluated at each level, from 1 to 5, can be put on an overhead sheet and students as a group can then determine why each response received the score that it did. In this way students can determine how to improve their own responses.

Julia Jasmine has developed examples of holistic scoring rubrics for grades one through six. The rubrics are available in her book *Portfolios and Other Assessments* (1993).

Making Your Own Instruments for Whole Language Assessment and Evaluation

While you can adopt published instruments for use in your own classroom, it will probably become necessary at some stage to make your own instruments using published ones as your models.

There are several stages in designing your own instruments. First, list those literacy traits you hope students will develop while in your classroom. (You may also need to include those traits that the school district expects to see developed.)

Next, cluster those traits logically into the categories of reading, writing, speaking, and listening. Then subcategorize the traits by the context in which they can be observed. For example, group together all traits which can be seen in a child's formal writing, or all traits which can be observed during a literature study.

Finally, sort the subcategories by method of observation. The method of observation most appropriate for gathering evidence of the development of any given group of traits will provide the format of the checklist or interview sheet.

An instrument which was developed for use in a first through third grade multi-age classroom can be seen in Figure 5.3. Because it was intended for use in a multi-age classroom, three levels of development of reading ability — emergent level, early level, and fluent level — were identified and reading behaviors grouped into each level.

The process used to develop this instrument included determining the items which would be evaluated. The local district and the state curriculum guides suggested specific skills which should be acquired by the first, second, or third grade students. This instrument was designed to go beyond those specific skills and give a comprehensive view of the students in the class. It was believed that the reading behaviors listed subsume the specific skills listed in the district and state curriculum guides. This instrument was a listing of the goals that each student could demonstrate in his or her reading.

The goals are intentionally stated in the first person so that each student is part of the evaluation process. As a teacher or the student recognize that one of the listed behaviors is being demonstrated, the date is entered into the blank preceding the stated goal. The student is made aware of his or her progress as it is observed, and he or she is part of the evaluation process in the classroom.

A sample portion of a specific-skills instrument can be seen in Figure 5.4. In this instrument the teacher decided that keeping skills came from the teacher's knowledge of those sub-skills and state and district curriculum guides.

The teacher has frequent conferences with each student and evaluates the student's reading by listening to him or her read a short selection aloud from his or her current self-selected trade book. Levels of attainment for each skill are listed across the top and the teacher simply places a check mark in the appropriate spot.

One advantage of having teachers develop their own instruments is that the resulting instrument can more closely reflect the philosophy they subscribe to. As a teacher grows in his or her knowledge and ability to operating in a classroom, she or he can revise the instruments used in the class.

Figure 5.3   Example of a Teacher-Made Evaluation Instrument

Reading Goals for the Integrated First, Second, and Third Grade

Emergent Level

Date Demonstrated

_____I am able to locate the front, back, and spine of a book.

_____I am able to follow print from left to right.

_____I have one-to-one correspondence.

_____I can tell the beginning, middle, and end of a story.

_____I am able to recognize upper and lower case letters.

_____I am able to show one letter in a word.

_____I am able to show a capital letter in a book.

_____I can recognize the difference between a letter and a word.

_____I am able to recognize some high-frequency words.

_____I am able to recognize similarities in words.

_____I am able to listen to stories.

Early Level

_____I can sit for short periods of time and read.

_____I am able to use meaning as a cue.

_____I am able to take risks in reading.

_____I am able to read beyond a word I don't know.

_____I am able to use text and pictures to sample, predict, and
confirm.

_____I am able to self-correct.

_____I am able to integrate strategies and cross check cue sources.

_____I am able to retell stories.

Fluent Level

_____I am an independent reader.

_____I am able to read silently.

_____I am able to read with expression.

_____I have had an emotional response to something I have read.

_____I am able to differentiate between fiction and nonfiction.

_____I am able to choose suitable reading material.

Figure 5.4   Example of a Sub-Skills Evaluation Instrument

	Not Developed	Developing	Fully Developed
Word Recognition Recognizes Initial:			
b			
c			
d			
f			
etc.			
Comprehension Answers:			
main idea questions			
detail questions			
sequence questions			
etc.			

A Comprehensive Language Evaluation Strategy

The goal of the Comprehensive Language Evaluation Strategy is to develop a complete literacy picture of a child. A convenient way to organize the system is to break literacy into the four language functions of reading, writing, speaking, and listening. The strategy should include instruments to collect data in each of these language areas.

The teacher should evaluate each language area with at least two instruments. Each of those instruments should be used in a different context and should gather data in a different way. By gathering data in different ways at different times and in different contexts the validity of the child's literacy picture is much greater.

The teacher then enters a synopsis of each of the instruments onto the Comprehensive Language Evaluation Chart and a summary statement made for each category on the chart. A copy of the Comprehensive Language Evaluation Chart is shown in Figure 5.5.

The teacher can use the chart when conferencing with parents and/ or the child, or when evaluating the effectiveness of the classroom environment for that child's literacy development.

Whole Language Assessment and Evaluation and Report Cards

One very pragmatic concern of classroom teachers is how to determine a grade for a student's report card. Many teachers feel that whole language evaluation and their current report cards are not compatible. We agree with their view and would hope that districts will either modify their current report cards so they can be used with whole language assessment strategies or that individual teachers be allowed to produce their own versions of report cards.

Figure 5.5   Comprehensive Language Evaluation Chart

Instruments Used/Analysis

L a n g u a g e A r e a	Speaking	Instrument 1- Instrument 2- Summary-	_____ _____ _____
	Listening	Instrument 1- Instrument 2- Summary-	_____ _____ _____
	Writing	Instrument 1- Instrument 2- Summary-	_____ _____ _____
	Reading	Instrument 1- Instrument 2- Summary-	_____ _____ _____

Unfortunately school districts seem slow to change their practices and many whole language teachers may still be required to give letter grades on mandated report cards. We offer the following information for those teachers.

Grades on report cards are usually based on one of two criteria. The first criterion compares an individual student's performance with that of the other students in the class. Points are totalled in some manner and each child's total ranked in terms of the rest of the class. Arbitrary levels are then established for each letter grade. In this system most students would receive an average or middle grade. While comparisons with other students is not part of whole language evaluation, it is still possible to use the data collected to form a rough class ranking and then award grades based on that ranking.

The second criterion in traditional grading schemes gives some predetermined numeric level for each letter grade. Every child reaching that predetermined level receives the same grade. Data gathered in whole language assessment can be used in the same way. Each child demonstrating the development of a specific set of literacy traits or a specific number of literacy traits receives the same grade.

Both of these methods are completely incompatible with whole language instruction. However, the second scheme is preferable, especially when the predetermined criteria is such that all children in the class have a chance to attain it. Also, the teacher must be sufficiently knowledgeable to set appropriate criteria. In either case, the grades awarded from whole language assessment data can be as valid as those determined by a traditional point system.

References

Atwell, N. (1988). Making the grade: Evaluating writing in conference. In T. Newkirk & N. Atwell (Eds.), *Understanding writing* (pp. 236–244). Portsmouth, NH: Heinemann.

Bean, W. & Bouffler, C. (1987). *Spell by writing*. Rozelle, NSW, Australia: Primary English Teaching Association.

Clay, M.M. (1989). *The early detection of reading difficulties* (3rd ed.). Portsmouth, NH: Heinemann.

Clay, M.M. (1982). *What did I write?* Portsmouth, NH: Heinemann.

De Fina, A.A. (1992). *Portfolio assessment: Getting started*. New York: Scholastic.

Goodman, K. (1986). *What's whole in whole language?* Portsmouth, NH: Heinemann.

Goodman, K.S., Goodman, Y.M., & Hood, W.J. (1989). *The whole language evaluation book*. Portsmouth, NH: Heinemann.

Goodman, Y.M., Watson, D.J., & Burke, L.B. (1987). *Reading miscue inventory alternative procedures*. New York: Richard C. Owen.

Graves, D.H. (1984). *A researcher learns to write: Selected articles and monographs*. Portsmouth, NH: Heinemann.

Heald-Taylor, G. (1989). *The administrator's guide to whole language.* Katonah, NY: Richard C. Owen.

Jasmine, J. (1993). *Portfolios and other assessments.* Hunting Beach, CA: Teacher Created Materials.

Lerman, E. (1984). In N.M. Gordon (Ed.), *Classroom experiences.* Exeter, NH: Heinemann.

Peterson, R. & Eeds, M. (1990). *Grand conversations.* New York: Scholastic.

The primary language record handbook for teachers. (1989). Portsmouth, NH: Heinemann.

Routman, R. (1991). *Invitations.* Portsmouth, NH: Heinemann.

Routman, R. (1988). *Transitions: From literature to literacy.* Portsmouth, NH: Heinemann.

Stallman, A.C. & Pearson, P.D. (1990). In L.M. Morrow & J.K. Smith (Eds.), *Assessment for instruction in early literacy.* Englewood Cliffs, NJ: Prentice-Hall.

Tierney, R.J., Carter, M.A., & Desai, L.E. (1991). *Portfolio assessment in the reading-writing classroom.* Norwood, MA: Christopher-Gordon Publishers, Inc.

Turbill, J. (1984). *Now, we want to write!* Rozelle, NSW, Australia: Primary English Teaching Association.

Valencia, S. (1990). A portfolio approach to classroom reading assessment: The whys, whats, and hows. *The Reading Teacher, 43,* 338–340.

Chapter 6

A Collage of Assessment and Evaluation from Primary Classrooms

S. Jeanne Reardon

I notice that the subjects and verbs consistently disagree in Trang's writing. She writes "the bird fly," "kids runs," and so forth. As I sit down beside Trang I ask her how she decides to put "s" on some words. She smiles and explains to me, "Easy. 's' here (kids) I put 's' here (runs). No 's' here (bird) and no 's' here (fly)." Now that I understand Trang's reason I can help her. I explain that, "It doesn't work that way in English. In English…"

This chapter brings the reader into a primary grade classroom where the children and I work to understand the written and spoken language we use together to learn and live. The classroom I refer to in this chapter is a composite of many kindergarten through third grade classrooms in which I have taught. All of these classrooms are part of a large suburban public school system (over 100,000 students). Most of the classrooms are in schools identified as Chapter I, having a significant number of children from low-income households, many of whom speak English as a second language. Readers who are part of large school systems are familiar with the nature of the school bureaucracy and the routine use of tests to measure student and teacher performance. I have not found that the data generated by national, state, and school system tests help the students or me to understand what it is that students know and do as they use written and spoken language.

The discussion in this chapter is limited to examples of assessment and evaluation which have been useful to us in our classroom community.[1] My assessment is not a response to outside forces. I am compelled to assess because that is how I teach. There is information I need and questions that the children and I must consider in order for us to learn.

What's going on?
When does Shirley revise her speech, reading, writing — and how?
How do we know if someone understands what we're saying or writing — and what do we do when they don't understand?
What makes us keep reading a book — or stop reading?
What does Jenny do in her writing to make us laugh?
What do you do when you can't read the word?
How do you know your story is finished?

I am constantly searching and re-searching to understand — to understand language, and the child as a language learner and one who uses language to learn. Put simply, what I assess is what I teach and value — understanding, revising, and wondering. This is how I teach.

Before I give specific examples of how I assess children's language use and language learning, it is important that we begin together, by recognizing the assumptions upon which my teaching and assessing are based: I always assume that children's language activity is purposeful — that children have reasons for what they are doing. Assessment enables me to see language from the perspective of the child, to begin with the child's reasoning and to extend the child's understanding.

I accept the complexity of the literacy behavior of young children. I agree with Taylor (1990) that children's literacy does not develop in an orderly, sequential, predictable manner.

Finally, I believe that evaluation demands simultaneous understanding and wondering. I don't think we can understand without wondering first, and wondering comes from noticing, and noticing comes from wondering, and our understanding may be limited to the specific situation and time. The ambiguity, complexity, and confusion of the previous statement will not surprise you if you live with children in a primary grade whole language classroom. You recognize that assessment will be ambiguous, complex, and sometimes confusing. That is what makes it so fascinating and exciting.

Imagine that you are in an art gallery studying a collage. At first you are attracted by the colors, shapes, and materials, but confused by the seemingly unrelated juxtaposition of the elements. You do not follow the interaction, or feel the relationships between the distinct forms. Then, after studying the collage, the artistic design emerges. This chapter presents an assessment collage. There are distinct elements: the teacher assessing, the child independently evaluating, the data collected by both teacher and child. There are intersections and overlappings as children and teacher collaborate and share in the evaluation process. Since I view assessment as a collage, the design of this chapter may at first appear confusing. Keep in mind, children have reasons for their literacy behaviors. Our job as assessors of language is to discover and understand their reasons so that we may teach from their perspective.

The Data Collection

Assessment for understanding literacy requires data, and in a whole language classroom there is an abundance of data! The teacher's biggest problem is *what* to collect. Then come the questions of *how* to collect and organize all of this information so that teachers and children can use it. I find observations, conferences, collections of student writing, and reading records are my most useful sources of information.

Teacher's Observations

Most of the data that I use for assessment is gathered through observation. I observe children as they read and write, I note the reading and writing processes of individual children, and the resulting products. (The product of reading is understanding, or comprehension; the product of writing is the text.) I have purposefully chosen the word "processes" and not "strategies." It has become popular to speak of "strategies" children use as they read and write. There are checklists of thinking strategies, decoding strategies, and writing strategies. I agree that all of us use strategies while thinking, reading, writing, computing, observing... In our room we work to become aware of the strategies we use; we talk about them to understand how they work for us and to make them available to others. I do note the strategies a child uses, but my greater interest is how these strategies work for the child within the child's larger reading or writing process. An emphasis on identification of discrete strategies or dependence upon strategy checklists often replaces the more fruitful understanding of process.

Process Observations

To assist in understanding process within the context of the classroom environment I record as much as possible of what I see and hear. This means that I make wide-ranging, open observations of process and product. I also make focused observations to answer specific questions. Again I make focused observations of both process and products. Remember the collage? All of these observations are not going to be distinct and separate; some are going to overlap.

Our classroom is active most of the day, an ideal setting to observe language learning. It is easy to say one should observe all of the time, but in practice some times work better than others. Within our day's structure there are times that especially lend themselves to both wide and focused observation. One such regular observation time is the first 45 minutes of the day.

When children come into the room each morning they sign in and return books checked out overnight from our room. They order lunch, look over the Message Board, put up their own messages, and read. Some read alone, others read in twos or threes. Most read on the floor and out loud. (By third grade those who read alone usually read silently.) This is an informal, social reading time for the children. I tend to the beginning-of-the-day routines and talk with the children about the books that went home overnight. Then I walk around and observe and listen to children reading. Some children select books immediately, others select children and read whatever their friends are reading. There are those who come in already knowing what they will read this morning, those who always go to the "New Books" display, and others who read the familiar "old friends" first. The children record their reading in their Reading Record and bring their books to the rug for Reading Talk.

I have an opportunity to observe natural reading, writing, and conversation during this 45-minute block of time. My book check-in conversations focus on the home audience and response to reading. I find that children sometimes select different genres or "levels of difficulty" for their at-home reading. Since our goal is to have children become lifelong readers, this out-of-school reading is of great interest to me. We keep a record of at-home reading as well as at-school reading.

At Home Reading

When Amy checks in *Strega Nona* (dePaola, 1975), I find that Amy's grandma only reads and understands Russian, but she

> ...likes to listen to me read and she looks at the pictures. I can't talk to her much... I can tell when she figures out the story... She started talking a lot in Russian when the pasta was coming out of the pot and

all over the floor, and she laughed when Big Anthony came slidin' out of Strega Nona's house on top of all that pasta. When Papa came home he told me about a Russian story like that. That's what Grandma was talking to me about. It's just like all the different Red Riding Hood stories.

Six-year-old Amy understands personal response to literature and uses her understanding to select the books she reads to her grandma. She knows that there are many versions of folk tales and that frequently her grandma knows these tales. Amy has begun using a storyteller's voice when she retells stories. ("Big Anthony came slidin' out of Strega Nona's house on top of all that pasta.") I make a note on my self-stick pad. (See Figure 6.1.)

Knowing the out-of-school reader and writer is important to understanding the in-school learner. As much as I would like to, I do not find time to visit homes and chat with families about reading. My glimpse into home literacy comes from in-school conversations such as Amy's and from parents at conference time. In my weekly, or bi-weekly, letters to parents I describe our program, snatches of classroom conversation, and share literacy events and ideas for home. I invite parents to share literacy happenings and pass these on in my letters. These chatty letters also give me the opportunity to explain the connections children are making in their reading and writing. It is my assessment of children and their learning that enables me to describe these connections.

Classroom Reading and Writing

The book check-in is at a large rectangular table adjacent to the Message Board. Many children sit there while composing their messages. I watch and listen as children write notes.

Often they begin talking with a friend about something that has happened, then decide to write a message about the event. "Tell 'em where you found it," Mike says as Carl writes about his silver rock. Mike's sense of audience is just beginning; only two weeks ago he was writing, KM C ME (Come see me) and pinning it unsigned on the board with little thought to the needs of the reader. I make a note of this comment before I leave the table. (See Figure 6.1.)

I move around the room to watch and listen as the children read. There is much to be learned without even hearing the words read. It is the watching that enables me to move outside my adult perspective of language and to understand the child's purpose. Some of my most useful insights into children's reading behaviors have begun by watching

Figure 6.1   Examples of Observational Notes Taken
from Student Pages in the Red Notebook

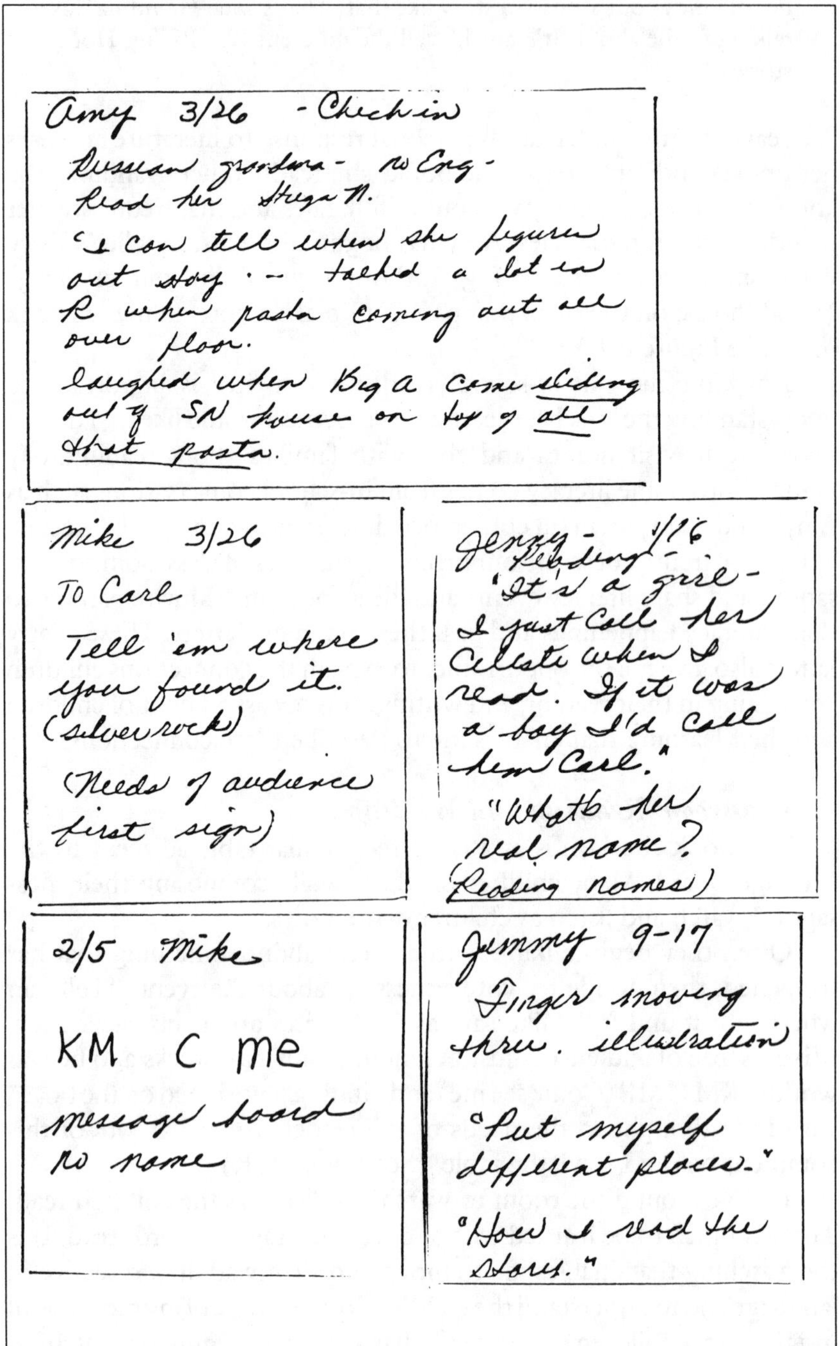

without listening. Certainly my most productive questions come after a few minutes of watching. I had noticed Jimmy moving his fingers through illustrations, often pausing and talking to himself. After observing Jimmy do this with many books I asked him, "How do you read the illustrations?" He explained that he put himself "different places to see how things look from there. It's how I read the story." This was September of third grade and Jimmy read very few words, but he gave the most thoughtful response to the books I read aloud to the class and asked the most provocative questions in writing response groups. Other insights have come through listening while children read or write without looking at their words. Perhaps it is easier for me to see from the child's point of view if I, like Jimmy, limit my observations.[2]

Conversations and Conferences

Most of my reading (and writing) conferences are quick and informal. Every day I try to have three- to four-minute informal conferences with five children, and once each quarter I have a formal reading and writing conference with each child. Most of the reading conferences take place during the social reading time, the first 45 minutes of the day. There is no particular order to my conferences. I see or overhear something of interest and confer with these children, then on Friday I pick up any children I may have missed during the week.

It is a Wednesday morning in January in first grade; I am thinking about children's book-selecting behavior, and wondering how it has changed now that the children are reading more words. First I watch and make some observational notes. Three six-year-olds, Milagro, David, and Sean are standing next to the counter where a collection of winter books is displayed. Milagro looks across the counter, picks up *Brave Irene* (Steig, 1986), studies the cover, turns each page slowly, pauses, and goes back to a previous page before continuing through the book. She takes the book over to where her best friend Kehinde is reading. She repeats the process with Kehinde, the two talk, then sit down to read on the rug. David picks up book after book, looking only at the cover. If the book is nonfiction he turns to the contents page, scans it and holds onto the book. After he has collected three books he takes all of them back to his table and begins reading. Sean picks up the first book he touches and walks around the room with it, never opening it or even glancing at it. He returns it and picks up another book. After three trips to the display he leaves and goes over to sit with two boys who are reading to each other. He listens to them read for the next 15 minutes.

On that Wednesday morning I spent a few minutes observing, then I had short conferences with David, Milagro and Kehinde, Sean, and another reader, Jennifer. My notes show that David came to the winter display with several questions and was looking for books that would answer them. When I talked with him he pointed to the table of contents in one of the books. He was trying to decide which of the chapters would answer his questions about snow and ice crystals. I showed him the index in the back of the book. David located "crystals" and began telling me what he already knew about crystals. I left him looking for answers to his crystal questions. Milagro said her older sister had been reading fairy tales to her and she thought that the "pictures in *Brave Irene* look like fairy tale pictures." The two girls read a couple of pages to me. Both substituted words freely and the story came out fairly close to Steig's — not his text, but his story. Sean and I talked about the stories he had listened to his friends read. We discussed what he liked about those stories, and about listening to them. My next conference was with Jennifer who was using her modification of a reading strategy she had overheard me discussing with another child. I had been explaining that sometimes when I read I don't know how to pronounce the name in a book, but this does not keep me from understanding and enjoying the book. When that happens to me, I said, I just make up the name the best I can, or if it is a very long, complicated name I just keep track of the character by the first letter of the name. Jennifer explained to me that she was substituting the name of someone she knew whose name began with the letter of the unknown name. (See Figure 6.1.)

All of my notes go in a loose-leaf notebook. It doesn't have a name — the children call it The Red Notebook. There are pages of unlined paper for each child in the class, and I stick my notes on the child's page. I have found it much easier to keep pads of self-stick notes in my pocket, than to carry around a big notebook. The sticky notes are wonderful. I can take notes in any order, there is nothing to copy and I can rearrange my notes as I read them over and begin to see patterns. (I also write analytical notes in the notebook.) One year, at a friend's suggestion, I decided to use pads of three different colors. Blue was for reading, yellow for writing, and green for speaking. The idea was that it would help me see threads that crossed expressive and receptive modes. That's not how it worked. I would pull out the wrong color pad from my pocket and write on it. Then I'd have to copy my notes onto the correct color. I quickly abandoned the idea. Record keeping is a very individual matter; each teacher must experiment and find a system that will work for her.

Figure 6.2   Reading and Writing Conference (Writing)

READING AND WRITING CONFERENCE- (writing)

Name: Conference on *11/16*

* Writes during journal writing time and writing workshop.

(usually)   sometimes   once in awhile
i write a lot in my journal

* Knows and uses several ways to get started. *Draw the pictures*

* Knows what s/he likes--and when writing works.
When say the word over — like far, far away.

* Enjoys playing with words. *faster and faster + faster*

(quite a bit)   some   not really

lots of * Has tried out different kinds of writing: (letters), stories,
(about self writing) explaining, poetry, how-to writing,
informing, lists, thinking/figuring out writing, riddles,
plays, . . . *phone numbers, messages*

* Helps classmates by listening to and talking about their
writing.

(pretty often)   sometimes   hardly ever
my friends

* Thinks about other kids' suggestions.

usually   sometimes   (not really)

* Uses supports in the room: other children, charts, books,
adults . . . *first made to still in books*

pretty often   (sometimes)   once in awhile

* Changes writing to make it better.

pretty often   (once in awhile)   not yet
when I leave out some of it

* Participates in sharing time as a listener and reader.

(almost always)   once in awhile   hardly ever

Plans:
*Finish my soccer book and write another
one.*

Figure 6.3   Reading and Writing Conference (Reading)

```
              READING AND WRITING CONFERENCE--(reading)

 Name:                              Conference on  11/9

  * Reads during Everybody Reads time.

 usually            sometimes            not very much
                  a little and  a lot

  * Can explain how s/he chooses books.
 favorite books - you read.  What I like   I ask somebody
                                       that can read it.
  * Talks about what s/he reads.  Know what s/he likes.
                                       yes
 a lot to say       some             not much to say


  * Likes to read to self--and others.
                  sometimes to friends if they ask me


  * Reads different kinds of materials: stories, information,
 how-to, messages signs, poetry, pictures, books, magazines,
 letters plays, jokes, riddles, experiments, records, cards . .
 phone numbers, menu.  Happy Birthday Moon
                       I, Egg and Ham    Didn't Frighten me
                       Oh Brother
  * Uses illustrations to figure out words and to check meaning.

 a lot              sometimes            not much


  * Use the rest of the writing to figure out words and check
 for meaning.

 quite often        sometimes        hardly ever beginning
 I read it all over from the very beginning
       and when I come to it I have the word
  * Uses letters and sounds to figure out words and check for
 meaning.

 quite often        sometimes            hardly ever

  * Can read words as soon as s/he sees them.

 quite a few words   some words        just a few words

  * Plans:
 just do what I'm doing -maybe read
 slower so I can talk more about it.
```

named
books!

For the formal Reading and Writing Conference I use forms to focus our discussion and provide a basis for comparing responses over the year. (See Figures 6.2 and 6.3.) Before the first quarterly conference we talk about what interests us, is important to us, and what we know about ourselves as writers and readers. I also share the questions I am interested in talking about. (By November the children are quite accustomed to my note taking, and my "I noticed... I wonder...; I heard... I wonder..." musings. They come to assume that is the way we learn in this room.) I type a form that will be the basis for our conference discussion and share it with the class so everyone will have a chance to think about his/her response. Nancie Atwell (Atwell, 1987) works differently with her middle school students. She has quarterly evaluation conferences that begin with an interview response to questions. Three of her four or five questions remain the same through the school year.

The children and I look forward to these conferences. It takes one week for us to complete the writing part of the conference and one week for the reading part (five to ten minutes per conference). I have tried doing both parts at the same time since I think of reading and writing as intertwined, but have found that with young children the conference works better if we talk about writing while children are writing — and reading while they are reading. And so we do them separately. We do think of them as a Reading and Writing Conference even though it comes in two parts. When we have the second half of the conference we take some time to talk about writing and reading and how they fit together. As the year goes on we compare our current response to earlier responses and talk about how we have changed as writers and readers. You have noticed that assessment is a part of my teaching.

Collections of Student Writing

Children's writing is an important source of information. In our room each student keeps a Writing Folder, a Thinking/Learning Log, a Writer's Notebook, a Science Journal, and a portfolio. The Writing Folder is a comprehensive collection of the child's writing for the current quarter of the school year. The Thinking/Learning Log contains quick writes and responses to prompts across the curriculum. ("What science did the author/illustrator need to know to write/ illustrate your book? What questions did the author answer in the book you read? Do you think those are the important questions? Were they your questions? What do you need to know to teach someone to tell time? etc.") The Writer's Notebook contains the child's collection of words and phrases she or he has selected to save, and ideas for future writing. The children keep a separate science journal that holds their observations, comments, questions, explanations, and data collection from investigations. Mathematics thinking goes in our Thinking/ Learning Log, but science seems to need its own book.

There are student writing samples that do not fit any of these categories. There are signs, notes, lists, phone numbers; there are cards, letters and gifts of writing that go directly to the recipient. There are games, messages, how-tos, sign up sheets, casual scribblings... How can a teacher, let alone a child keep track of all this writing? We don't keep track of it all, but we save enough to construct an understanding of the child as a writer.

My writing observation and conference notes, made on self-stick pads join other notes in The Red Notebook. These notes are about all kinds of writing — single draft and multiple, finished and incomplete — across all content areas. At the end of the day I look over the room for environmental writing that I may have missed during the day.[3]

My writing observations are about the children's composing processes, the forms, functions, and purposes for their writing, structure, and use of conventions. Each week I try to review writing folders, notebooks, and my observational notes of three or four children and then make entries in the Red Notebook. (See Figure 6.4.) This means that I look closely at the child as a writer every two months. Often I copy a selection if I have made reference to it in my notes. Figure 6.5 is a selection written by the child referred to in my notes of Figure 6.4.

Our county writing curriculum requires that over the year each primary grade student will write, and take through the writing process at least one piece of expressive, literary, informative, and persuasive writing. My comments in the Red Notebook include the intent or purpose of the writing, the audience, theme, or topic. Beyond that I comment on prominent features of the piece rather than covering items on a check list. My comments lead me to questions and further conversations with the child writer (see Figure 6.4.)

Children's writing has been an interest of mine for years. I have studied thousands of pieces of children's writing, and have read widely from books and articles about writing and writing research. For those who have had little practice looking at the composing processes and writings of young children I would suggest meeting with teacher consultants from state branches of the National Writing Project and reading books and articles about writing. I would particularly suggest

Figure 6.4   Notes About Writing Samples of First Grade
Boy Taken from the Red Notebook

2/1   Poetry, continuing seasonal / weather theme
new idea - put 4 short poems into long
poem with refrain. Repetition of
-ing words. Lines getting shorter,
feeling stronger, rhythm
stronger.
First evidence of large scale revision in
poetry - Change in form.
Had not worked on poems since Winter
Break - Distance ?? ask
Wants to publish or add to Poetry Collection

2/5 - 2/12   Chicken pox

2/12 - 2/20 · Wandering, watching others (Believe
writing behavior as failure)

2/26   Drawing, underwater ships, sea creatures,
labels, cartoon bubbles, lots of action
in drawings. Audience off. ← Note -
Gave 2 drawings away.

3/3   Working w. yy · Nate on filmstrip adventure
Sharks, Subs, People   Conflict: Can you
add to somebody's illust? Who gets to
decide story line

3/19   Ninja Turtles. (see sample pg 1.) completed
6 pages Pages end w. dramatic tension.
"Almost like how Chptrs. end." Illust.
are moving off or coming into page - each pg.
Literary language.
Standard end punct.   " "around
speaker rather than
Signs of revision   dialogue
adding on

Figure 6.5   Writing Sample of Child in Figure 6.4

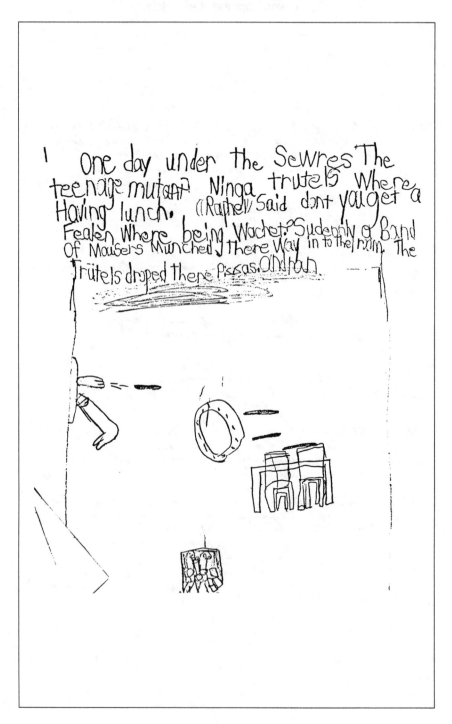

reports from the Center for the Study of Writing and books and articles by Dyson, Hansen, Atwell, and Bissex (see References).

At the end of each quarter children select one piece of writing to keep in their portfolio and the rest of the writing goes home. Nine weeks is a long time to wait to take home something as valuable as writing and so we have established a policy of checking out pieces of writing overnight — just as we check out books from our room. We try to wait until the end of the quarter to take home all of the writing, but it doesn't belong to me. We also have a box for writing to be photocopied so that originals can go home. Letters and notes need to go home the day they are written.

Using the Data Collection

All of these writing samples and observations are not worth much unless they are used by the teacher and the children.

My observations of children, their writing samples and follow-up questions have confirmed my belief that there are many roads to literacy. Some are more heavily traveled, but there is not one correct, best, or normal route. Assessment enables me to understand the various routes taken.

One alternate route which my assessment has shown me is the "copy" road. For many years I noticed one or two children in the class who would copy from books rather than compose their own writing. I would be disturbed by this, and say something like this to the child: "Oh, that book has already been written. Do you want to take it home to read?" or, "I can make a copy of that page for you on the copy machine. Right now we are writing for ourselves." Or I might ask, "What are you doing?" And the response would come back, "Writing." Then I would go on with my "You don't need to write it again. It's already been written."

Many of these copiers had begun school in other countries or inner-city schools and I attributed their behavior to previous experience and teacher expectations. But it continued to bother me, and I worked hard to stamp it out. Eventually, I decided to watch a little more closely. In the past four years I have concluded that this is just another way into writing for some children. What begins as the copying of a page, gradually shrinks until only the lead sentence is copied and the rest is composed by the child. After several months the child has mastered that genre, form, or theme and writes on his or her own. But when attempting a new kind of writing the child will again begin by copying.

If I had not observed closely over a long period of time I would not have respected or accepted this as a legitimate way of learning.

Using Portfolios

Many school systems are now requiring teachers to maintain portfolios of student work. Portfolios must be more than archives. (For a discussion of portfolios by classroom teachers see Graves and Sunstein, and Smith and Ylvisaker in References.) They do provide documentation of change, but they must also assist children and teachers in assessing, analyzing, and understanding reading and writing. This means that I must reflect upon my own reading and writing process and analyze my products. I must ask questions which help my students reflect and recognize what it is they do as they read and write. Rhodes and Shanklin's work (see References) is an excellent resource. It is not enough for children to select pieces of writing and samples of reading to include in portfolios, they must explain and give reasons for their choice. (See Figure 6.6.)

Figure 6.6   Examples of Evaluative Questions to Help
Children Become Aware of How They Know,
What They Think About Writing

How do you decide if writing is good writing? What makes one piece of writing better than another piece of writing? How do you decide if your writing is good writing?

If someone asked you to help them write a (story, poem, report, description...) what would you do for them?

Does it make a difference whom you are writing for when you write? Whom you are writing to?

Who helps you write? How do they help you? What do they do when they help you? If you could get someone to help you write a _____ what would you have them do to help you?

How do you go about writing? What do you do when you write? Do you ever get stuck? What do you do then?

What part of writing do you like the most? the least? How do you explain that?

What are some of the things that writers do?

Reading Records

Records are another source of data. In our room the children keep records of their in-class and at-home reading; my book sign-out and media center circulation records also keep track of books. I look for patterns in these records. I notice that in each class reading session Kehinde begins by reading "an old friend" — something familiar, and then moves to something new. Other patterns relate to length, difficulty of reading material, or genre. For example, there are patterns of long and short, short, short; patterns of difficult and easy, easy, easy; of one genre or one author for months and then a switch. (Because of my observational notes I know that some children choose children to read with, rather than books to read, and so the titles of books read by these children do not tell me about their personal reading preferences so much as their reading habits.) Book sign-outs may indicate the influence of audience on book selection; only my conversations with children and conference notes can tell me.

The Red Notebook contains literacy data and analysis for our classroom. It is a broad collection of observation notes about the children's literacy development, writing samples, and the children's reading records. But it is more than just a collection of data. It also contains my reflections, generalizations, and analytical comments. It functions for me in the same way that the Descriptive Biographic Literacy Profiles do for the New Hampshire teachers who work with Denny Taylor (Taylor, 1990). It enables me to know the children and talk, teach, and learn with them in a different way. Certainly my teaching is more child specific, but there is something else. The more I know and am able to see through the children's eyes the more I share their goals. Perhaps because I understand more I am better able to adjust to fit the children's goals. Such assessment keeps my teaching honest.

Student's Self-Evaluation

The Red Notebook and my increasing understanding of how children learn and use language is part of the assessment collage; another part is the children's evaluation of themselves as language learners and language users. Just as assessment is an integral part of my learning and teaching, self-evaluation is a natural part of the students' own learning. Children engage in evaluation without our help, and we need to understand their personal forms of evaluation. This section explores the self-evaluation of speaking, reading, and writing that goes on in our classroom.

When children revise as they are reading or talking, they are demonstrating a form of self-evaluation. Reading teachers use the term "self-corrects" when a child goes back and gives an accurate word reading of the text. I find it more helpful to think of the behavior as evaluation and revision. It occurs quite early and naturally in speech, and continues through adulthood. (Only a few minutes of observation of yourself or other adults speaking will provide numerous examples of revised speaking. I assume that is the result of evaluation based on knowledge of audience and the intent or purpose of the talk.)

I have found that self-evaluation also occurs naturally in reading. While reading, young children frequently revise the printed text to fit or make their own meaning. If we think only of correctness and errors in the match between print and spoken text then we miss understanding how the child is reading. The realization that children purposefully revise the printed text to fit or make their own meaning came after many years of teaching and I believe it is very important. Recognizing how a child is reading is critical to a teacher's planning. When I listen to a child's thoughtful and meaningful, but inaccurate, reading I note revisions that fit logically into the whole. I am not listening at the word level, as in miscue analysis. I am speaking of meaning analysis. I listen for revisions that produce coherence in the whole piece, that fit the literary structure of the piece, that are consistent with the child's experiences and knowledge. This revision of the text to fit the child's construction of meaning is one form of self-evaluation.

Another form of reading self-evaluation is revision of one's meaning to fit the printed text. This is the type of evaluation teachers have typically valued. It is not helpful to the child to judge one type as better than the other. Both are evidence of evaluation and understanding of language — just different understandings.

Young children whose primary speech is not standard English automatically revise the text as they read, substituting their own speech for the author's. Randal was a child who would match his reading to the printed text ("accurate reading") then stop and go back to translate it into his own English. When he was in my third grade classroom he had perfected this to simultaneous translation. I may not have understood what he was doing if he had not been in if my first grade classroom. In first grade I noticed that when he read a book with a predictable pattern he would begin with accurate word reading and as soon as he recognized the pattern he would shift to translation, inaccurate word reading. In a few pages when the pattern changed he would catch himself — revise his language to match the new printed pattern, then once it was established begin translating into his own English again.

When we teachers make open observations and follow them with focussed conversations about how children are reading or using language, then we see from the child's perspective and are open to understanding. If we observe only from our own, limited sense of correctness, we are often closed to understanding and unable to help the child learn.

When thinking about revision we more typically think of writing revision than of speaking and reading revision. In whole language classrooms where writing emerges as a natural form of interaction and expression, children seem to engage in writing evaluation and revision on their own. Kindergarten children often tell stories from their written text. I do not think of this storytelling as writing evaluation, but when children add thoughts and words in the oral rendition of the written text then they begin to evaluate their writing. My experience with third grade children who have not had opportunities to write for themselves, but have only experienced taught writing, is that they do very little self-evaluation and revision of their writing. On the other hand, when I have had the same children in first grade and again in third I frequently see evaluative comments written in the margins of writing in progress. My favorite example is Maggie, who would write such comments to herself as, "Starts here — the good part," or "Think about this." She would also make little caricatures of faces in the margin, which she explained to me were her readers. (Her audience was on the paper as well as in her head!)

I don't want to leave the impression that all I and other teachers need to do is provide the environment and evaluation will take care of itself. Our job with naturally occurring evaluation is to recognize it, make the child aware of what and how he or she is evaluating, and make the many forms of evaluation apparent and available to other members of the classroom community. I point out how and what we are evaluating by having the children talk and write about their own evaluation, and I expect it. My frequent invitations to evaluate begin, "I noticed..." and continue, "Can you explain what you do — or how you...?"

And there are the "almost by yourself evaluation" times when I push or nudge. There are times when I pause to recognize or listen for effective language while reading aloud to the class, and ask the inevitable questions, "How do you think (Robert McCloskey — or an author in our room) wanted you to feel?" "Why do you think...?" There are times when I direct the children to evaluate their own or other printed text. Remember the collage? I am moving into the area of greatest overlap — collaborative evaluation.

Collaborative Evaluation

In collaborative evaluation I assist the children by focusing attention on a particular facet of language or language learning. The evaluation may begin with reflective questions posed to a single child during a conference, a small group of children, or the whole class. Later such questions become part of the children's own inner evaluative conversations — part of the repertoire of self-evaluation.

As I sit down at a table where children are writing I am asked, "Want to hear my story?" Andrew begins to read, hesitates, and stops. "I can't read what I wrote." "You were writing about when the monsters chased you and locked you in the closet. Just make it up," helps Philip. Andrew continues reading his story. We talk about the story, and I say to the children at the table, "I've noticed that sometimes it's easy to read what you write and sometimes it's hard. What do you think makes it hard or easy?" (My question is an invitation to analyze, and a model question for the self-evaluation process.) The children think about themselves as readers and writers. Andrew doesn't have any ideas yet. "I can just read it or I can't," he reports. Katie is very clear and says, "I know a lot of letters and I talk and write it at the same time. Only the spaces are hard. You know, the spaces aren't the same when you talk and when you write." She shows us her writing. "You have to put in lots more writing spaces than you do talking spaces, an' sometimes I can't remember where they go." She pauses. "You say it, 'Onceupona time,' " (two words, one space) but you write it like this." (1 Z AP N A TM, five words, four spaces.) "There's lots more spaces in writing." Philip explains, "I draw lots of pictures, and write, and draw some more, so I can read the pictures and the letters at the same time."

In our room, assessment requires collaborative data gathering to help us think about and understand our literacy questions. One morning I overheard six-year-old Laura ask Ferhad, "Will you help me read *The Snowy Day* (Keats, 1962)? During Reading Talk I comment on what I had heard, and Laura explains what it was that she wanted when she asked for help. Then we all think, write, and discuss our response to the questions, "What helps you read?" "What kind of help do you want when you want someone to help you read?" For days we ponder these questions as we read and ask for and receive help from each other.

Together we assess help and how it works for each of us as we write, talk, read, and listen. (This is an example of self-evaluation of a process.) The children share their understanding of help. During the discussion I also share what I know about myself as a writer, what I have figured out about the help I need, how I get it, and how I use it. We evaluate, we share, and we enlarge and modify our personal understanding. That is how collaboration works. If the assessing we do and the data we collect does not lead us to an understanding of what we are doing, then the assessment has no value for us.

When having a whole-class discussion, we take time to write before we talk. This gives us all time to think and reflect, and it commits us to our own ideas. Every child tends to contribute to discussions if given an opportunity to write first. Examples of evaluative questions we have discussed are listed in Figure 6.6.

Often the collaborative evaluation discussion springs from one of my observational notes. We are all meeting together just before we have Writing Workshop. I begin, "Yesterday I heard Jimmy asking Guillermo about the end of his story. Can you two describe the problem for us?" Jimmy explains that he can't tell when his story is finished. Guillermo's solution is to write THE END; that's what he does. I ask the class to think about how they know when a story is finished — to think about their own writing and about stories and books they have read. All of us write in our Thinking/Learning Logs and then the discussion begins. Some may call this problem solving; others call it reflection. I call it self-assessment. In this case each one of us is assessing what she or he knows about story structure and how it works. (This is a self-assessment of knowledge.) During the discussion that follows our Quick Write we have a chance to rethink our understanding, and maybe modify or add to it, as we listen to our friends' ideas.

Other times the evaluation topic comes directly from a class member to the group. Marla, a third grader, says, "In our response group we never raise our hands and we do just fine. How come we have to raise our hands during Reading Talk?" We have a discussion (mostly raising our hands) about talking, listening, and how it works. "How do you get into a small conversation?" "Who stops when two begin talking at once?" "Can you talk to someone if they're not looking at you?"

A large group of children decides to investigate our questions. Splinter groups form around different issues. Teams of investigators observe in our classroom, the lunchroom, on the playground, and at home. Reports come back over the next month. The class decides that six is the magic number — "Sometimes six can really talk and listen, but any more and you have to have some way to take turns." Is this research? Yes. Is it evaluation? I think so. Certainly these children now know more about how spoken language works and how they and others use it in a variety of situations, for a variety of purposes. They have assessed and evaluated the data. They have revised (modified and extended) their understanding — they have learned.

These accounts are examples of individual evaluation in a whole-class setting. Evaluation does not need to be solitary and silent to be effective evaluation (Eidman-Aadahl, 1988). How one reaches an understanding, or if one is the first to understand, is not important. What is important is that one becomes a literacy insider, a person who understands how written and spoken language works for oneself and for others. Part of my job is to provide the time, the space, the atmosphere, and questions so that this "becoming a literacy insider" will happen. I am not the only one who assists in self-evaluation. The children continually assist each other through their responses and questions. Evaluation and learning are social activities. Social interactions provide peer feedback that almost demands self-evaluation.

There is another, more formal way in which I assist the children with evaluation. Just as I use a formal Reading and Writing Conference sheet (Figures 6.2 and 6.3) to assist me in assessing the current state of a child's language understanding, the children use formal evaluation sheets to assist themselves in self-evaluation. Each year the children develop new response sheets for a variety of purposes. The sample in Figure 6.7 was developed to help third grade students look at their persuasive writing. We have developed other sheets to evaluate our understanding of literary forms, reader's theatre presentations, handwriting that is to be read by the public... The evaluation sheets are always developed by the class after analyzing the important features of the particular genre, form, intent...

The Evaluation Sheet for Writing to Convince came in response to a flurry of persuasive writing. Young children engage in persuasive speech as a part of normal interactions with their peers and adults. Some children are experts at verbally convincing others of the importance of an idea or action; others have a very limited repertoire of techniques to persuade. One year in third grade there were many children with a limited understanding of how verbal persuasion worked. They tried other avenues of persuasion. Increased volume or higher pitch accompanied by hitting, grabbing, and shoving were favorites. Through

Figure 6.7   Evaluation Sheet

EVALUATION SHEET FOR WRITING TO CONVINCE *Mom and Dad*
(person)

Chris
(author)

Meg
(partner)

	author	partner	Mrs R.
PERSUASION			
What I want the reader to do or think is clear. *Not walk my sister to school*	✓	✓	✓
There are logical reasons given. *Yes!*	✓	✓	✓
There is evidence that I know the reader and have anticipated and answered problems or arguments the reader may have.	✓	✓	✓
CONVENTIONS			
Paragraphs are used for separate ideas.	✓	✓	✓
Punctuation follows our rules sheet. (Ending punctuation, commas, apostrophes) *-fw*	✓		✓
Capital letters are used where needed.	✓	✓	✓
Words are circled that may be misspelled. (draft) Words are spelled correctly. (final copy)	✓	✓	✓
Handwriting meets our standards for writing that will be read by others.	✓	✓	✓
WRITING PROCESS			
I told my partner all about the person who had to be convinced.	✓	✓	
I tried out my persuasion with my partner.	✓	✓	
I told my response group what to listen for.	✓	✓	
I considered the comments and questions of my response group.	✓		
I listened and reacted as the person to be convinced when other kids read their letters.	✓		
REVISION HELP			
The purpose sentence is underlined in red. The reason sentences are underlined in blue. The anticipation of problem sentences in green.	✓	✓	✓

drama, discussion, reading, more discussion, and practice the class became more adept at verbal persuasion. Then letter writing took hold. These children were very serious about their ideas, and the importance of convincing others to change or act. This response sheet reflects the class's analysis of persuasion, understanding of audience, conventions of written language, and a writing process. The entire class helped in its development, I typed it, and it was available for those who were doing persuasive writing. Those students mailing their letters had conferences that utilized the draft letters and this evaluation sheet.

It is not this particular evaluation sheet or any of the others we develop that is important. What is important is the process used to develop the sheet, the student analysis of language, and the function analysis plays in revision. Self-evaluation leads to revision, and revision, the modification and extension of understanding, is learning.

Before I conclude I must acknowledge my familiarity with a more common form of evaluation which is called grading. I do not put grades on papers or on students. Grades and grading are a concern of children, teachers, and parents which needs to be addressed. This chapter is limited to a discussion of assessment which is useful to the children and to me. I am a teacher of children, and comparative or numerical evaluation does not meet my needs. It does not assist me in my assessment and understanding of children as language users and language learners. Grades given by me, even if based on my assessment and understanding of a child's emerging literacy, cannot substitute for a child's self-evaluation. Grades given by me will not lead children to become literacy insiders engaging in self-evaluation, but my careful assessment and collaborative evaluation will. I leave comparative and mathematical evaluation to those who have a use for it.

Summary

Back to the collage — I had planned to summarize with a collage — a visual representation of assessment and evaluation which would show all of the component parts and their relationships. The teacher would be there noticing, wondering, questioning, analyzing, revising, understanding, questioning again, sharing, collaborating. There would be children who, in the midst of written and spoken language are also noticing, wondering, questioning, evaluating, and revising. There would be conversations and conferences, observations, reading records, writing samples... and the relationships would now be clear. I tried to construct the collage, but found I needed three dimensions, not two. Perhaps it should be an evaluation and assessment mobile.

What is clear to me is my goal: that the children become literacy insiders who routinely engage in self-evaluation. It is self-evaluation that leads children to revision. And revision, the modification and expansion of understanding, is learning — that is what teaching is about. While I believe children engage in self-evaluation on their own, I also believe they are assisted by collaborative evaluation with teachers who use assessment as the foundation for their teaching.

Endnotes

1. For a discussion of a teacher's handling of mandated reading assessment, see Reardon (1990).

2. The collection of articles in *Observing the Language Learner* (Jaggar & Smith-Burke, 1985) is useful to the teacher who is interested in learning more about observation.

3. See Loughlin & Martin (1987), especially Appendix B, "Environmental Evidence for Literacy Growth."

References

Atwell, N. (1987). *In the middle. Writing, reading, and learning with adolescents.* Portsmouth, NH: Heinemann Educational Books.

Bissex, G. (1980). *GYNS AT WRK: A child learns to write and read.* Cambridge, MA: Harvard University Press.

DePaola, T. (1975). *Strega Nona.* Englewood Cliffs, NJ: Prentice-Hall, Inc.

Dyson, A. (1988). *Drawing, talking and writing: Rethinking writing development.* Occasional paper No. 3. Berkeley, CA: Center for the Study of Writing, University of California, Berkeley.

Dyson, A. (1988). *Negotiating among multiple worlds. The space/time dimensions of young children's composing.* Technical Report No. 15. Berkeley, CA: Center for the Study of Writing, University of California, Berkeley.

Eidman-Aadahl, E. (1988). The solitary reader: Exploring how lonely reading has to be. *The New Advocate, 1,* (3), 165–176.

Graves, D. & Sunstein, B. (Eds.). (1992). *Portfolio portraits.* Portsmouth, NH: Heinemann Educational Books.

Hansen, J. (1987). *When writers read.* Portsmouth, NH: Heinemann Educational Books.

Jaggar, H. & Smith-Burke, T. (Eds.). (1985). *Observing the language learner.* Urbana, IL: IRA/NCTE.

Keats, E. (1962). *The snowy day.* Bergenfield, NJ: Viking Press.

Loughlin, C. & Martin, M. (1987). *Supporting literacy: Developing effective learning environments.* New York: Teachers College Press.

Newkirk, T. & McClure, P. (Eds.). (1992). *Listening in: Children talk about books (and other things).* Portsmouth, NH: Heinemann Educational Books.

Reardon, S. (1990). Putting reading tests in their place. *The New Advocate, 3,* (1), 29–37.

Rhodes, L. & Shanklin, N. (Eds.). (1993). *Windows into literacy: Assessing learners K-8.* Portsmouth, NH: Heinemann Educational Books.

Smith, M. & Ylvisaker, M. (Eds.). (1993). *Teacher's voices: Portfolios in the classroom.* Berkeley, National Writing Project.

Steig, W. (1986). *Brave Irene.* Scranton, PA: Farrar, Straus & Giroux.

Taylor, D. (1993). *From the child's point of view.* Portsmouth, NH: Heinemann Educational Books.

Chapter 7

Holistic Assessment in Intermediate Classes: Techniques for Informing Our Teaching

Yvonne Siu-Runyan

Good teaching...is created and crafted through a continual process of revision. (Bird, 1989, p. 15)

Assessment and instruction go hand in hand. Assessment enhances teachers' powers of observation and understanding of learning. (Teale, Hiebert, & Chittenden, 1987, p. 773)

To use assessment information for revising one's teaching, as these experts suggest, requires a different kind of data collection. It requires going beyond relying on numerical results from the commonly used standardized and criterion-referenced tests packaged by publishers or developed by school districts.

While numerical scores from standardized and criterion-referenced tests can yield useful information about how well students, schools, and districts do in comparison to others, they do not provide information useful for daily instruction. A numerical test score cannot tell us:

- What our students think about reading and writing.

- What strategies they use when reading and writing various texts.

- How they use reading and writing to make meaning, to evaluate the relevance of knowledge, to verify and revise their own thinking, and ultimately to direct their own learning.

Further, scores from tests are not helpful for teachers who want to involve their students and themselves in the process of continual self-evaluation for reflective teaching and learning. They cannot help both teachers and students seriously examine questions such as: "How am I doing? Are things going as I planned? What can I do to see that things go better next time?" (Goodman, 1989, p. 13).

Because of the limited information test scores can offer teachers, and because teachers want assessment data that can empower them to revise their teaching, many teachers are asking, "What else can I use that's more helpful than test scores to inform myself about what my students know, what they are struggling with, and what do I need to help them become more strategic readers and writers?"

Assessment Techniques for Intermediate Classrooms

When discussing assessment, several experts point out the need for overcoming our habit of using once-yearly, product-oriented assessment techniques. They suggest putting more emphasis on using:

- Assessment data which reflect ongoing student learning over long periods of time (Jaggar, 1985).

- Assessment data that reflect the active nature of learning and can be used as feedback for reflective practice and as the basis for cooperative decisions about curriculum and instruction (Browne, 1989; Costa, 1989).

- A broader range and variety of assessment techniques (Valencia & Pearson, 1987; Pikulski, 1989), which include teachers' assessments (Hiebert & Calfee, 1989).

- Authentic assessments such as direct observation of behavior, portfolios of student work, long-term projects, logs and journals, student interviews, video- and audiotapes of student performance, and writing samples (Costa, 1989; Shepard, 1989).

- Assessment instruments which are directly linked to a teacher's instruction, instructional goals, and assessment questions (Rhodes, 1993).

From my past experiences as a classroom teacher working with children in grades 3–6 in a mountain schoolhouse that has approximately 40 children (K–6), I have learned that there are several sources of information that yield information valuable for assessing student understanding and ability, and directing instruction. These techniques involve talking with students, using anecdotal records, involving students in long-term projects, learning from student portfolios, observing how students use reading and writing in their everyday lives, how they talk about their own literacy and the literacy of others, and how they use literature to inform their writing.

In addition teachers may want to use other assessment techniques such as audiotapes and videotapes, and logs and journals, neither of which are addressed in this chapter. Those interested in information about these assessment tools may want to read page 121 in *Portfolio Assessment in the Reading-Writing Classroom* by Tierney, Carter, and Desai (1991) and Norma Mickelson's chapter which answers the questions: Can we measure whole language? How do we handle evaluation in a whole language classroom? in *Questions and Answers About Whole Language,* edited by Orin Cochrane (1992).

Regardless of what assessment procedures teachers decide to use, we need to keep in mind that these procedures need to reflect the dynamic, constructionist nature of language learning and not the mastery of discrete skills. Further, I encourage teachers eager to move toward holistic assessment techniques to jump right in and do it. Don't feel as though you need to know everything there is about these techniques before you try them. There is no rigid formula for their use. As you use the various assessment procedures, you will learn what works best for you and your students. You will learn from your mistakes and refine your own techniques.

Talking with Students

Some of the most useful sources of information we teachers can use for assessment are the conversations we have with students about their reading and writing. These conversations can inform us about:

- Student understanding of reading and writing.
- How reading and writing affect students' thinking and learning.
- The things teachers do that are helpful and not helpful to students.

- Student interests — the things about which students like to read and write.

- The areas where students want help.

To learn about one's teaching and how students view reading and writing.

Two questions that lead to interesting conversations with students and that I have found to be extremely useful for assessment and teaching are:

1. What kinds of things do I do that help you as a writer?
2. What kinds of things do I do that help you as a reader?

When I first asked my students these questions, I received either no response, very little response, or general statements that had little value for instruction. Besides having limited or no experience responding to questions like these, I think the students were unsure of my sincerity. They didn't want to be penalized for being honest with me. Initially, students typically offered comments like these:

> You help us. (Zephyr, 3rd grade)
> You like us. (Travis, 4th grade)
> You help me with spelling. (Geoff, 5th grade)
> I don't know. (Ashleigh, 4th grade)
> You don't yell at us. (John, 6th grade)

However, because I was interested in finding out what my students thought about my teaching, I kept asking them these two questions. To assure the students that I was sincerely interested in finding out about the things I did that they perceived as helpful, as I received useful information about my instruction from the students, I began sharing it with the entire class during mini-lessons in reading and writing. For example, one day Lucas, a fourth grader, shared, "I like when you share your writing with us." The next day, I informed the class about Lucas's comments and proceeded to show them how I go about revising a piece. Eventually, the students realized that I was interest in them giving me honest feedback, and to my delight they actually started to do so.

What did I learn from asking these two questions?

From Zephyr (3rd grade), I learned how important the language I use with children is. He said, "I like when you (long pause), I mean some teachers I've met are really serious and if I get something wrong they'll yell at me. I like that you don't do that. You offer suggestions, but not meanly. And then I choose if I want to follow your suggestions. I don't feel stupid."

Zephyr was the first to point out that how I spoke with the students was important. As a result of Zephyr's response, I became much more aware of how I spoke with the students. I noticed that when I was dictatorial and directive, the students tuned me out. And that when I offered suggestions and spoke with them as reader to reader and writer to writer, they were much more invested in their own learning.

With practice and close attention to the kind of teacher talk I used, I became more of a facilitator of children's learning, rather than the director of their learning. Zephyr taught me that helping children learn is more a matter of what we do than of what we ask our students to do.

As I became more skillful at using language that empowers them as learners, appreciation for the way I talked with them was later expressed by other students.

> I like the way you talk to me about the stories I read. You're really interested in what I like...and by getting to know us and the kind of stories we like to write. (Stephanie, 5th grade)
>
> I like the way you talk to me about the stories I write, and how you help me put conversation in my stories. (Cara, 4th grade)
>
> I like the way you talk to me to help me when I get stuck. (Travis, 4th grade)
>
> I feel good after I talk to you about my story. You tell me what you like and you help me think about what I want to say. (Geoff, 5th grade)
>
> I like it when you read stories to us and we discuss them. It gives me ideas for my own stories. Learning how to write from a web was also helpful. (D.J., 6th grade)
>
> I like it when you read to us. It makes me want to read the book too. (Ben, 5th grade)
>
> When you show us what you do when you read and write. (Mike, 6th grade)

From the comments like the ones above, I learned several things:

- To stop and think before I speak.
- The students understood that writing is using written language to communicate. They are first concerned about their message instead of the mechanics. This indicated to me that they have a good grasp of the writing process.
- The books we read and discussed helped my students generate ideas for their own pieces.

- It was important for the students to share their pieces with others.

- Teaching them how to brainstorm and web ideas provided them with helpful strategies to use as writers.

- That students liked it when I read, wrote, and shared with them.

Two other questions that were much more difficult for students to answer were:

1. What kinds of things do I do that are *not* helpful to you as a writer?

2. What kinds of things do I do that are *not* helpful to you as a reader?

I found that when I asked students these two questions, they had, at first, an incredibly difficult time formulating their responses. I believe two things caused them concern: (1) they had not had previous experience answering questions like these and didn't want to be put on the line, and (2) they were unsure of how I would respond.

To assure the students that I was sincere and wouldn't punish them for their responses, as I received useful information about my instruction from the students, I began sharing it with the entire class during mini-lessons in reading and writing. For example, one day John, a 6th grader, told me, "I don't like it when you tell me to read a book during silent reading time, when I'd rather read a magazine. I like magazines. I learn interesting things in them." The next day I informed the class about what John had told me. The students were amazed that I took John's comments to heart. I openly discussed with my students how I made this grave mistake because I wanted all of them to read great literature, and had forgotten how important reading other kinds of materials is. Then I thanked John for his bravery and honesty.

After this discussion, other students began responding to these questions honestly and sincerely, and as a result I was able to break new ground for my thinking. From Silas (4th grade), I learned that just telling kids to get busy and write isn't always helpful. In response to these two questions, Silas said, "I like that we can read what we want. But, I don't like it when you tell me to just get busy and write. I have a hard time getting busy when I don't know what to write about."

Stephanie (5th grade) taught me that when a student is sitting and daydreaming, it doesn't mean he or she isn't writing. Stephanie related, "I don't like it when you tell me to get busy. Lots of time I'm thinking about my story. And when you tell me to get busy, it makes me nervous."

Missy (5th grade) taught me that it was important for them to share their reading and writing with one another. She offered, "I don't like it when we are right in the middle of a discussion about a book or a story we are writing, and you tell us to stop."

As a result of the information gleaned from asking students to tell me the ways in which I was helpful and not helpful to them as readers and writers, I became a much more reflective and responsive teacher, and in the process I improved my teaching. For the first time in my life, I was not afraid to ask these hard questions. In fact, I learned that in order to be an effective teacher, I had to seek answers to these difficult questions.

To find out what students want to learn next.

The way curriculum guides and published materials are developed and packaged leads many teachers to rely on them to direct their teaching. We rarely, if at all, ask students what they want to learn next in order to become a better reader and writer. And yet, this may be one of the most important questions we can ask our students. Jane Hansen (1989, p. 21) offers, "Asking kids these kinds of questions is really important to teaching. I'm wondering how in the world I ever taught before because I didn't ask students what they wanted to learn, nor did I ask how I could help them. So I was putting things together in my head very differently from the way children saw things. No wonder school didn't seem to be all that meaningful."

What did I learn from my students when I asked this question? I learned that students can articulate what they want to learn. From this information, I could better assess their understanding of reading and writing, and this influenced how and what I taught next. I learned that teaching became a lot easier, more dynamic, and fun for all of us. I learned that I was a more effective teacher when I took my lead from the students. I learned that the students were more invested in learning when they focused on things important to them.

When I first asked the question: "What would you like to learn next in order to become a better reader or writer?" I received very little response from the students. When they did offer comments, they were vague ones like:

> Learn how to read better. (Ben, 5th grade)
> Write better. (Geoff, 5th grade)
> Who knows? You're the teacher. (Travis, 4th grade)

Once again, I needed to demonstrate my sincerity and interest in learning from them what they wanted to learn next. After about a month of my asking this question over and over again, students slowly began telling me what they wanted to learn next. As I garnered this much-needed information, I began presenting mini-lessons based on what the students told me they wanted to learn. As a result, my lessons became much more useful to the students. They even began to take more responsibility for their own learning, and became more aware of their own strengths and weaknesses as readers and writers.

Here is a sampling of the things they wanted to learn:

> I want to learn how to read inside my head, instead of out loud. (Ben, 5th grade)
> I want to learn how to put conversation in my stories. (Ashleigh, 4th grade)
> I want to learn about other words to use in place of said. (Mike, 5th grade)
> I want to learn how to punctuate the conversations in my stories. (Lucas, 4th grade)
> I want to learn how to find topics to write about. (Silas, 4th grade)
> I want to learn how to type on the computer. Finding the keys is hard. (Cara, 4th grade)
> I want to learn how to develop my characters. (D.J., 6th grade)
> I want to learn how to spell the word "probably." (Thomas, 5th grade)

From the children's comments, I learned that they knew a lot about reading and writing. They knew that reading is not sounding out words, and that writing is not primarily spelling words and forming the letters of the alphabet correctly. They knew that one reads for understanding, and one writes to communicate. And, most importantly, their suggestions showed me that students can tell us what they want to learn if we just ask them.

Using Anecdotal Records

Anecdotal records include teachers' observations about any of the following:

- What students are reading and writing.
- Student comments about reading and writing.
- How students approach reading and writing.
- How students respond to instruction.
- How students use reading and writing to learn.
- Teacher questions and comments.

While it is helpful for teachers to record their observations daily, it isn't always feasible. Nevertheless, if teachers can write a minimum of only one sentence every day about their observations, they will learn a lot. This information is vital if teachers are to move from being mangers of materials to being reflective decision makers in charge of their own teaching. Sometimes teachers feel as though they must make insightful comments or evaluative comments about their observations. But I have learned that just recording one's observations is often enough. Insightful or evaluative comments are drawn from the many observations recorded over time.

To illustrate what I mean let's examine some excerpts from my anecdotal records.

8/31/87—Most of the children are struggling with their pieces. They want to write grand stories, but don't know enough about their topics to write well. They want to write fiction, and not personal narratives, which is what I think would make a difference for them.

9/2/87—The students are abandoning pieces like mad. Even though I did a lesson on brainstorming ideas for writing topics, most are still struggling with topic choice.

9/8/87—Thomas is writing a piece about war. It's really a replay of the war stories on television.

9/14/87—I wish the kids were more invested in writing. They are wasting a lot of time, because many don't know what to write about. I am getting worried.

10/7/90—Kids of concern: Zephyr, Tom, Travis, Geoff, Cara, Ashleigh, Lucas, John, Ben, Missy, Mel, Rojana, and Mike. These kids are still not invested in their writing. I'm beginning to feel like a failure.

When I reviewed the observations recorded on the dates listed above, I knew I had to do something to help these children and soon. I then realized that I hadn't written with them, nor had I modeled how literature inspired me to write. "Perhaps, if I model this technique, the students will take their lead from me," I thought. "It's worth a try."

So, the next day (10/8/87), I read *The Important Book* (1949), written by Margaret Wise Brown. After reading the book, I said, "You know, reading this book has given me an idea for writing." Then during writing time, I wrote my own important story, which included every student in my class. I shared my emerging drafts and read the final story to the students.

Entries in my anecdotal record notebook dated after the 10th of October reveal what happened when I used this approach.

10/14/87—Lucas and Melissa are writing their own important stories. I am so pleased that they are trying their hand at this. Perhaps now others will use literature to help them learn about writing. Now to keep the momentum going. I must be careful about what books I choose to share. I must remember to select personal narratives with an obvious design. I think this will help the kids a lot.

10/20/87—Read *My Mom Travels A Lot* (1981) by Caroline Feller Bauer. Discussed the design of the book. Created several stories verbally following the opposite design pattern of this book. Today Cara developed her own story from the model presented. Great!

10/26/87—Read *Fortunately* (1954) by Remy Charlip. The design of this book is very similar to *My Mom Travels A Lot*, except that the events are connected. Guess who decided to write a similar story? Cara. She's really taken off on using the opposite design pattern for her stories.

11/2/87—Read *If You Give A Mouse A Cookie* (1985) by Laura Joffe Numeroff. Discussed circle plot structure with the class. Made up two stories verbally. Thomas is starting his own story modeled after this book. Wonderful. Thomas has a hard time organizing his thoughts. I wonder how he'll do.

12/7/87—Since the beginning of November, Thomas has written several stories modeled after *If You Give A Mouse A Cookie*. He's written "If You Give A Chipmunk A Peanut Butter Bread," "If You Give A Bear Some Crumbs," and "If You Give A Goat Some Grass." Tom is obsessing on this pattern. I'm wondering if I should be concerned. But he is writing. And his stories are more organized than they have ever been before. He had definitely learned how to spell the word, "probably." Rhoda, the special education teacher, told me that he has never written anything before as organized as these three stories. We think the structure of the design helped him to organize his thoughts. Rhoda also said that Tom loves the word, "probably." He refused to take it out of his story. Now that's investment.

From my anecdotal records, I discovered the importance of discussing the design of stories with my students. I also found out that if I wanted to encourage my students to take risks in writing, that I must write with them, model how I use the writing process and literature to help me write, and become one of the participants in our reading/writing workshop.

Further, to help my students understand that effective authors write from a position of knowledge and experience, I started asking, "What do you think the author had to know or experience in order to write this piece?" Once we started discussing their responses to this question along with the design of various pieces, I noticed the empty war stories and TV violence replayed on paper slowly vanished.

In addition, anecdotal records have also been useful in helping me determine the areas in which my students need help in order to improve their writing style, and how they use reading to help their writing.

11/23/87—Students are writing, writing, writing. They love writing and share it easily with others. I have noticed however that there are a lot of wents, gots, and saids in their stories. Perhaps now would be a good time to discuss strong verbs.

11/30/87—D.J. is noticing character development in the story he's reading. In fact, it is not uncommon for him to follow me around the class reading excerpts from his book to me.

12/2/87—Steph's piece has the words *treeCAP* in it. She said she learned that from the book, *Tuck Everlasting* (1975) by Natalie Babbitt.

12/7/87—Kids still think that revision is editing. They do not really understand **RE-VISITING** a piece.

12/11/87—I need to get the kids to become more independent. They need to learn how to rely on each other more, instead of always coming to me. Help!!

They need to learn how to ask each other questions so that revision can occur.

12/14/87—D.J. said that he wants to write descriptive leads instead of leads which put the reader right into the action.

The kids are moving along very well. They are learning about writing from stories they read. Pointing out things that authors do when they write the books we are reading and discussing is proving to be useful for me personally and for the students, too.

When reviewing the previous anecdotal records, I learned that I needed to now focus attention on:

- Making public how and what the students were learning about writing from their reading.

- Helping the students learn how to ask questions that help the writer with revision.

- Helping students understand how important it is for them to write about something they know.

- Using strong verbs.

It is interesting to note that these four very important aspects of reading and writing are not part of the district's language arts/reading curriculum guide. Had I taken my direction for developing lessons from the curriculum guide only, I would not have seen the opportunity to teach my students how to learn about writing from the literature they read, how to ask each other questions which help with revision, and how to use strong verbs rather than weak ones.

Involving Students in Long-Term Projects

Assessment should determine whether students are able to monitor their own understanding, use strategies to make questions comprehensible, evaluate the relevance of accessible knowledge and verify their own solution. The best way to check for these indicators is to make assessment measures resemble learning tasks (Shepard, 1989, p. 7).

In the school district where I last taught, a task force was organized to develop a plan for assessing students' writing ability. The plan that the committee finally approved was suggested by Miles Olson from the University of Colorado. Because we wanted this activity to be an authentic task for students, Dr. Olson suggested having the school librarians write a letter to the students in their respective buildings asking for input about the authors, topics, and books they would like in their school libraries. A sample letter was developed for teachers to follow. In this letter, the students were asked to help select books by telling who their favorite authors were and what topics they were interested in. The students were also told that it would be helpful if they included in their letters titles of books by their favorite authors and titles of books on their favorite topics. And finally, students were informed that decisions about which books to purchase would be based on how well the students were able to convince the school librarian that their choices were the best ones, and on how well their letters were presented. The students were given two weeks to finish this project, and all writing had to be done in school.

In order to complete this assignment, the students decided they needed to have a discussion about how to proceed. (I merely acted as facilitator. I did not direct them or give suggestions about what to do.) Their discussion surprised me. I discovered that the students knew a lot more about the writing process and books than I had originally thought, and that they had definite opinions about the authors, titles, and topics they wanted to read. These were the activities in which the students engaged to complete this project:

Rehearsal:

1. They brainstormed favorite authors and topics.
2. They talked with one another about favorite authors and topics.
3. They did research to find titles of books written by favorite authors.
4. They did research to find out titles of books on favorite topics.
5. They went to the card catalogue to find out what books and how many copies of certain titles were already in the school library.
6. They developed and conducted surveys to find out if other students wanted the same authors, titles, or topics they had chosen.

Drafting:

1. They wrote and shared their emerging persuasive letters with one another to check for clarity.
2. They used each other as well as the resources in the

classroom to find spelling and punctuation errors and correct them.

3. They used the language arts textbooks to clarify the correct form for writing letters.

Final Copy:

1. They wrote final copies in long hand or on the computer using correct letter format.

2. They had concrete reasons for their choices.

3. They had suggestions for titles, authors, and topics.

4. Their letters were organized.

5. They understood a lot about punctuation. A few of the 3rd graders, most of the 4th graders and all of the 5th and 6th graders underlined the titles of books and used the colon appropriately. Most of the 3rd and 4th graders and all of the 5th and 6th graders used ending punctuation and commas in a series correctly.

6. They all demonstrated their knowledge of writing and literature, their love of books, and their ability to research, collect, and analyze data.

Here is Silas's (4th grade) letter at rehearsal and in final copy. Notice that his preparation for writing his draft is thorough. He first brainstormed all his favorite authors and topics (Figure 7.1). Then he selected his most favorite topics and authors and did research to determine how many books, if any, were included in the collection (Figure 7.2). After that Silas interviewed the other children to find out if they were interested in reading books on topics and by authors he had selected.

Once he had collected all the data needed for writing his letter, he proceeded to write his draft (Figure 7.3). After the draft was written, Silas shared his emerging letter with other students, received feedback from them, and wrote the final copy (Figure 7.4).

Notice how much Silas understands about the writing process and the skills he knows. Silas knows how to brainstorm ideas, gather data using the card catalogue and *Children's Books in Print*, conduct a survey, organize the information, and write a persuasive letter from draft to final copy. Silas also knows how to use ending punctuation, the colon, commas in a series, parentheses, and capitalization. In addition, he also knows correct letter format and that book titles need to be underlined.

Figure 7.1

Silas 2-22-89

FEB 24

Brainstorming Sheet

Author _____   TOPICS

Author	Topics
1. Franklin W. Dixon *	1. Mystery *
2. Wilson Rawls	2. Adventures *
3. Richard Adams *	3. Survival *
4. Wintharp	4. Fiction *
5. Jack Pearl *	5. Wild Life X
6. Beverly Cleary	6 Mamels
7. Chris VanAllburg X	7. Drama X
8. E.B. White	8. Dogs
9. Shel Silverstein*	9. Cats
10. Gary Paulsen X	10. Rodents X
11. Sheila Burnford *	11. Secpene
12. James Hewe	12. Reptiles X
13. Audrey + Don Wood	13. Poems X
14. Jack London *	14. Forest X
15. Brock Cole X	15. lizard
16. Robert N. Pech X	16. fishing X

Figure 7.2

Library Research

Silas 2-27-89

Authors	Topics
FranBlin Dixon	Mysterys
	We have: 63
We have: 7	
	Adventures
Rickard Adams	We have: 1
We have: 0	
	Survival
James Howe	We have: 10
We have: 5	
	Sports
Jack Pearl	We have: 0
We have: 0	
Jack London	
We have: 2	
Shel Silvestein	
We have: 1	

Figure 7.3

Silas 1989   X

RESONS

1. I like Franklin W. Dixon. Other kids like him to. These are some people: Lucas, Ben.B, Adam, and Sean and other people do to.

2. I like Franklin W. Dixon because he writes exsideng Mystery/Adventures. He writes Hardy Boys. Here are a few of his casefile book: "Border line," "Perfect Get Away," "Cult of Crime," "Edge of Destruction," and "Lazus Plot." Another Author that I like is Richard Adams. He writes books about Ficional anamals. They would bring enjoment to the class (Espercaly D.J.). These are a few books I would like you to order: "Shardik," "Watership down," and "Pleoge Dog."

Figure 7.4

March 8, 1989

Dear Gail,

I like Franklin W. Dixon. Other kids in our class like him, too. These are a few people that like Dixon: Lucas Ben. B, Adam, Sean, and other people in our class.

I like Franklin W. Dixon because he writes exciting mystery/adventure stories. He writes the Hardy Boys Here are a few of his casefile books: Bordrer Line, Perfect Get Away, Cult of Crime, Edge of Destruction, and See No Evil

Another author is Richard Adams. He writes fictional novels. They would bring enjoment to the class. (Especialy D.J.) These are a few books I would like you to order. Shardik, Watership Down, and Plage Dog.

Sincely,

Silas

The results of this project showed me my students' knowledge of writing and literature. It also provided me with insights about instruction. When I reviewed the rehearsal activities, drafts, and final copies of the letters, a glaring hole in my instruction surfaced. I noticed that not one student developed a graphic organizer of the information they wanted to include in their letters. Consequently, that was one of the strategies I immediately taught my students how to use when writing. We had used graphic organizers (webs) when studying content areas and for reading comprehension, but I had neglected to teach them how to use graphic organizers for writing.

This long-term, persuasive letter project gave the students the opportunity to write a real piece for a real reason. It was developed so that the writing situation would be a natural one, and revealed not only what the children knew about writing, but also about books and authors. The students were give sufficient time and a supportive environment where they could actually demonstrate their ability to use the writing process and the resources needed to complete this project. In long-term projects like these, students are better able to demonstrate their knowledge in authentic, meaningful ways.

Learning from Student Portfolios

> Portfolios allow teachers to get to know their students — as readers, writers, thinkers, and as human beings (Reif, 1990, p. 24).

Using portfolios for assessment is valuable for teachers, students, and parents. Since "...portfolios should be viewed as a growing, evolving description of students' reading and writing experiences" (Farr, 1989, p. 264), they show growth over time and provide useful information about the unique literacy development of each student in the class in the following ways:

1. Portfolios can help parents understand the ongoing development of their children as readers and writers. With this kind of frame, parents are less likely to put undue value on the results of test scores. They come to realize that numerical scores provide only limited information about their children's abilities.

2. By putting together a portfolio students can examine concretely for themselves how they have grown as readers and writers.

3. Portfolios can help teachers discover the strengths and weaknesses of their students and thus better develop lessons and literacy experiences for them.

When putting together literacy portfolios, I ask students to do the following:

1. Select samples of your best writing and arrange them in some way.

2. In preparation for our conference about your portfolio, think about why you selected the pieces you did, and what you want to say about them. Think about:

    a. What parts of your piece do you really like and why?

    b. What you were trying to accomplish in this piece and do you think you were successful?

3. Look at all the pieces you selected for your portfolio and think about what you learned about yourself as a reader and writer by putting together your portfolio.

4. Now that you've thought about your development as a reader and writer, what goals do you have for yourself as a reader and a writer?

To illustrate the value of portfolios and their "...potential for placing teachers and students — not tests and test scores — at the very center of the assessment process" (Pikulski, 1989, p. 81), I have chosen to share D.J.'s portfolio. I chose D.J. because of his ability to reflect on and talk about his reading and writing, and to use what he had learned to self-evaluate his reading and writing development and to set goals for himself in these areas.

According to his 5th and 6th grade results on the California Achievement Tests (Forms E&F), D.J. scored:

	5th Grade Results	**6th Grade Results**
Vocabulary:	NP=75%; Range=67-82	NP=89%; Range=84-93
Comprehension:	NP=62%; Range=56-69	NP=79%; Range=70-85
Total Reading:	NP=70%; Range=63-75	NP=87%; Range=82-89
Language Mechanics:	NP=39%; Range=28-54	NP=62%; Range=49-74
Language Expression:	NP=30%; Range=23-38	NP=65%; Range=54-75
Language Total:	NP=33%; Range=27-40	NP=63%; Range=54-71

While D.J.'s scores on the CAT tests indicate that he scored above the national average (50th percentile) for reading while in 5th and 6th grades, below the national average for language while in 5th grade, and above the national average for language while in 6th grade, these scores do not provide me with information that I can use to guide my instruction. In fact, these scores did little in terms of informing me about D.J. as a reader and a writer. The scores also didn't tell me anything about how D.J. uses reading to inform his writing, or what he thinks about himself as a reader and a writer. Compare the usefulness of the scores from the CAT tests with the information gathered from D.J.'s portfolio.

D.J. selected nine pieces (three realistic fiction, a biography, an essay, two adventure stories, a science fiction, and a folktale that used a story within a story plot structure with a surprise ending) to include in his portfolio. When I asked him why he selected these pieces, he responded with, "I picked these because they show more of my strong points."

D.J. ranked his piece entitled, "The Season" (realistic fiction written in grade 6), as his best. Here is a portion of the conversation I had with D.J. about it.

Yvonne: Why did you choose this piece as your best?

D.J.:   This is the fourth piece I was really pleased with and I took it around and showed it to people. I am really proud of this piece.

Yvonne: What was good about it?

D.J.:   I like the descriptive words I used to show what my character is like. I also like how my story flowed.

Yvonne: Was this hard for you to write? Did it take a lot of effort?

D.J.:   The part that took a lot of effort was trying to describe the character's feelings and show what this character is like.

Yvonne: Look through this piece and pick out some of the parts where you feel you did a good job of accomplishing your objective of showing what the character is like.

D.J.:   In this part, Jim had just gotten through with practice in the story.

At the end of practice I was exhausted. I slid into my 1970 V-8 orange jeep and sped out of the parking lot.

"I don't know how I could hit so many red lights."

The light turned green.

VROOM! SCREECH.

"I hate coaches!" I sighed. "Why do I have to play their way?"

I looked back only to see lights flashing. I slowed down and turned to the side of the road.

A wirey haired man came up beside me and looked at me. His square jaw moved mechanically as he said, "Do you know how fast you were going?"

"Ya! Thirty-five like the sign said!"

"Try sixty-five," the officer said curtly. "Will you step out of your jeep please? Now, can you walk a straight line?"

Jim walked a straight line.

"Can I smell your breath, please?"

"Sure."

"Just in a hurry, huh?" the officer sighed.

"Yeah."

Yvonne:	Why did you like this part?
D.J.:	It showed how he was aggravated because he had not done well at practice and he was angry at the coach, and it showed how he took out his frustrations. It shows what kind of person he was.
Yvonne:	What were you trying to do in this particular piece?
D.J.:	In the whole piece I was trying to bring his attitude from a pretty bad attitude to a good attitude where he would be always trying and listening. I wanted to show that he was basically a good player with a good attitude, but at first he was too cocky to play with the majors.
Yvonne:	And do you think you successfully did that?
D.J.:	Yes, I think I successfully brought the story around to where Jim learned he had to change his attitude if he wanted to play in the majors.
Yvonne:	Was this hard for you to write?
D.J.:	It was kind of hard. It was a fun piece, but it was hard to get everything just the way I wanted it.

Yvonne: Did you learn anything about writing from writing this piece?

D.J.:   I learned how to use experiences from my life and put it into a story. I learned I could describe things better if I knew something about it.

When discussing the other eight pieces D.J. chose to include in his portfolio, it was interesting for me to learn that he selected them because in each one there were three common threads. In each, D.J.:

- had tried something that was new for him.
- had learned something about writing.
- felt he had accomplished what he had set out to do in the piece.

What follows is a listing of the other eight pieces D.J. chose to include in his portfolio, and unfortunately, because of limited space, only a sample of what he said about each one can be shown here.

2nd Best — "Alexi Grewal," biography written in grade 6.

This was the first time I had actually done a web to help me with my writing. I made up questions to ask him. Then I interviewed Alexi on the tape recorder. I thought this was very good, because as I listened to the interview on tape, I webbed the information. As my questioning went to different things I just brought out different circles, and as I went to write the piece I looked at my whole web and decided what I wanted to say first, second, third and on down. This was a lot easier than working from notecards.

I learned how to take notes and ask questions and how to use the answers to write a biography. I also learned how to web the information and write from a web. I thought it was a good piece for a short biography. If I had to do this again, I would ask more questions, and I would look to see what areas I didn't have as much information on and I would ask him about those things so that there is more complete information about him in the piece. But this was only my first biography.

3rd Best — "The Wrong Game," realistic fiction written at the end of grade 5.

I chose this piece, because in this piece, it was the first time I thought about developing my characters. I got the idea of developing characters from a book I read by Clive Cussler. Cussler really does a good job of developing his characters and I like that in his books. I wanted to show how sometimes good kids get caught doing bad things because of peer pressure. And I wanted to show that because he was basically good, he had trouble with his conscience. Here is one part I like:

> Tony thought to himself that it sure was lucky they were all spending the night together, but something kept bugging him. Who else were they going to meet at midnight? Tony had a hard time sleeping that night. But finally he dozed off. Suddenly Tony felt a nudge on his ribs.
> "Come on, come on," whispered B.J.
> Tony had butterflies in his stomach as they jumped out of his bedroom window. He sure hoped his parents slept real sound tonight.

I like it here, because I think I did a pretty good job of showing what kind of person Tony really was. Tony just got in with the wrong gang, but basically he was a good kid. He knew the difference between doing good and bad.

4th Best—"Mesa Verde," folktale with a story within a story design and a surprise ending written in grade 5. (This piece won third place in a young writers' competition sponsored by the Colorado Council of the International Reading Association.)

I got the idea for Mesa Verde after you read us a book about an Indian grandmother. We talked about the plot structure of the book and how the author used the story within a story design for the story. After we talked about this, I was getting ready to write a piece and I thought why not try it out. And I had just gotten back from taking a trip to Mesa Verde this summer so I thought why not put the setting there. I liked writing this piece. I had a good time writing it.

5th Best — "Why I Love Reading and Books," essay written in grade 6.

This was just a little thing I had written telling what I thought about reading and books for an essay. I thought I had written it well. I liked it when I wrote this part: "Books are like friends. You start to read one and you want to read more, just like you want to see your friends more." I like it because it tells what I think about books. When I find a book I really like I want to find out how the story ends, but when it ends, I wish it was still going on. And it's kind of like losing a friend.

The piece tells you that I categorize books as friends and that I like to read. And when I start liking something, I just don't want to stop reading. Like the essay says, I also read books to learn how to write. And I read to learn about cultures and things like that too. When I read a book I can go into another world and just have fun reading. From reading books, I learn more about words and ideas and things like that.

As a writer, I use books to help me learn different words and get ideas for my stories. And if you have ever seen me reading a book, then you probably have seen me using ideas I learned from the books in my writing.

6th Best — Adventure story with no title written in grade 6.

Even though I really like this piece, I put it towards the back because I didn't really write this piece. Gary Paulsen really did. I liked the book *Hatchet* (1987) so much that I wanted to rewrite the story. And I liked the way Paulsen repeated his words in the story. So, I thought of writing an adventure story following Paulsen's style. I think I did a pretty good job of following his style, but I also rewrote his story. So that's why I put this towards the back. I like this part:

> I realize the worst thing that could've happened had happened. The pilot was dead. I screamed three times and thought, "Get a hold of yourself. You are Corry Williams. You are in a plane, and the pilot I think had a heart attack. What should I do? I might be able to fly the plane, but after the pilot had jerked the plane, I don't know which way to go. I am like a bat without sonar, helpless."
> I realize I would have to go down, but trees meant certain death. I had no parachute. I would wait till the plane ran out of gas. I began to cry.
> "Death, death, I was going to die."
> Suddenly, the plane roar stopped. I had to glide to a lake and skid along the edges. "Lake, lake," I thought. Then I saw the lake.

This part shows how I used Paulsen's style of repeating certain words to make it sound almost like a poem.

7th Best — "Futuristic Fiddle Faddle," science fiction written in grade 5.

This was just a fun piece to write. I like it because it was a different kind of writing I don't usually do. I just wanted to have some fun. I really got into conversation in this story, and used different words for said. Like here when I wrote.

"That's it!" Frank and Joe yelled spontaneously.

"Give us a hundred."

Joe and the guy got in a big fight. While they were fighting, Frank picked up fifty Pepsi's and started shoving them down his pants and anywhere else he could find. He did the same with Joe. Then he saw an EXIT sign. They ran out clanging all the way. Finally they reached the ship. They jumped in.

"I am driving," yelled Frank. He took off full bore. Joe fell to the floor.

"You!"

"I'm just going to your motto!" Frank laughed.

"Let's start hyper-warp drive," Joe said.

"Warp 1, 2, 3. . .9.9, BOOM!"

They went full bore so they could coast in with no power. They lined up with the runway and flew in. Boom! The lights were out.

"EMERGENCY POWER!" Frank bellowed. Then the lights were on.

8th Best — "Pool," realistic fiction written at the beginning of grade 5.

Even though this piece is short, I think it shows what I was trying to do. In this piece, I was trying to write about something that I wish would happen to me. I was playing a lot of pool with my friends and I always wanted to get all the balls in at once. And so that's what I decided to write about. I like my beginning when I introduce Don. It sort of sets up the situation. "Don Majestic woke up in a cold sweat after dreaming Allan Wiggins, the worst pool player in the world, beat him in a game of pool. Don was the fifth best player in America." I think it shows the tense situation he was in.

9th Best — "World War VIII," adventure story written at the beginning of grade 5.

I didn't use any conversation in this piece. I just told what happened. When I wrote this piece, I never used to think much about conversation. In this one, I like all the action. I like some of the words I use like "counter-attacked," "kicked-rear," and "got nailed in the knuckle." I like how I used these words to show action. I can't believe I used to write stories like this.

I learned a lot about D.J. as a reader, writer, and learner from having him put together a portfolio and talking with him about the pieces he chose to include in it. I learned that D.J.:

1. Loves to read, and that he uses reading not only for personal enjoyment and pleasure, but he uses reading to learn about life and other cultures, and to inform his writing. D.J. reads deeply, critically, and in a most sophisticated way. He reads with the eye of a writer.

2. Enjoys writing. He likes to try out different things that he has learned about writing in the pieces he crafts. He is able to use techniques which show rather than tell his readers some aspect of the character or the situation, use conversations in the stories he tells, and use graphic organizers (webs) to help him organize ideas for writing.

3. Needs additional help with noticing how and where authors use figurative language in their pieces. Focusing on this aspect of writing will help D.J. write even better pieces.

4. Needs to widen his spectrum of writing. He especially needs opportunities to experiment with writing essays and poetry.

In addition, when I asked D.J. what he learned about himself as a reader and writer from putting his portfolio together, he said:

> I learned from putting together this portfolio that I like to read and write about things I can relate to, things I know about. It is from these things that I can write about and describe best. I like strong words like verbs that build up what you are describing.

D.J.'s comments about what he learned about himself tells me that he understands that writers use their knowledge and experiences to write; that unless he knows his subject, he probably will not be able to weave as good a tale as he may like.

When discussing goals for himself, D.J. said that he would like to read more books, learn how to read quicker, but still be able to understand the meaning expressed by the author. Another goal is to spend more time writing in his journal, to put more effort into making his pieces the best they can be, and to keep trying to excel in writing.

When I think about how much I learned about D.J. as a reader and writer from having him put together a portfolio, it makes me realize how little I knew about my students before I used this technique. I also learned how portfolios can not only help the teacher develop instructional plans, but how portfolios can help students reflect on their own literacy development and set goals for themselves. Probably, the most important reason for having students put together portfolios is to help them evaluate themselves and in the process discover what it is they do well and areas where they need help, and then to set goals for themselves. In this way, evaluation is put where it belongs, in the hands of our students, and it is we, their teachers, who benefit. As Tierney, Carter, and Desai (1991, p. 42) state, "Portfolios offer a new framework for assessment — one that facilitates student reflection in conjunction with reading and writing — a framework that responds to demands for student empowerment, the changing nature of classrooms, and a new consensus regarding the need for revamping testing practices."

The one area that I didn't have the foresight to have students include in their portfolios concerned data about their reading. I should have had my students:

1. Keep track of the many books, magazines, new articles, and so forth they read. This activity would have given us (students and me) interesting insights into their reading diet.

2. Copy quotes, sayings, phrases, and so forth from books that caught their fancy. This activity would have given us information about the settings my students pay attention to when reading.

3. Write their thoughts about those books which really made an impression on them and why. This activity would have given us wonderful data about the ways in which books influence them.

Observing Students

> The best alternative to testing comes from direct and, in most cases, informal observation of the child in various situations by the classroom teacher. (Y. Goodman, 1989, p. 119)

Once I learned how to be a kid-watcher, my teaching became more relevant. But what kinds of things are most useful for teachers to notice? Every day provides many opportunities to collect data about our students' literacy development. I have developed two simple guidelines which have helped me become a better observer of students.

1. Notice what students say about their own and each others' reading and writing.

2. Notice how students use reading and writing in their everyday lives.

Noticing what students say.

When I started paying more attention to the literacy events in which students engage and what they said about one another's reading and writing, I learned a lot about them. For example, here is part of a conversation that occurred when several students had a conversation with undergraduate students about their reading.

Adult:	Have any of you read *The Chronicles of Narnia* (1982)?
Silas:	Yes, but I don't like reading science fiction. But, Sean Griffith, a third grader in our class, really likes them.
Lucas:	What about Sean Kaley?
Silas:	Oh yeah, Sean Kaley really likes them too; he read all of them last year.
Adult:	How do you get ideas for your stories?
Emily:	For my story, "The Electric Dream," I got the idea from a book I read about sound waves. In the book, it said that sound waves have arches. So I used this information in my story.
Silas:	I like to read before I write. It helps me when I can't get into my writing.
D.J.:	I got the idea for how I was going to organize a story from a book that Yvonne read. The book had a story-within-a-story plot. After we discussed it, I decided to try it out.
Adult:	Do you guys read at home?
Emily:	That's the first thing I do when I come home from school every day. I love to read.
Lucas:	I always read before I go to bed.
Silas:	Me too. I read before I go to bed and also when I get home from school.
D.J.:	I read every day. I always read before I go to bed.
Adult:	How do you choose books to read?
D.J.:	I like to read books by favorite authors. And my mom reads a lot, and she gives me books to read that she thinks I might enjoy.

Silas: I read the blurb on the book jacket. Sometimes I ask other people if the book they're reading is interesting. There's not too much I don't like. I just like reading.

Emily: If I couldn't read, I'd be bored.

Lucas: I like to read any books about animals and nature. I love animals. Sometimes my friends will tell me to read a book because they know I might like it.

D.J.:   When I read *Hatchet* I wanted to rewrite the book. It was so good. Practically every fifth and sixth grade boy read that book, because it was so good. We kept passing it from person to person. Everyone wanted to read it. Remember, Yvonne, you couldn't read it, because everyone else wanted to read it.

This conversation astonished me. I knew my students enjoyed reading. But, I was surprised at their knowledge of each other's tastes in reading and the influence reading had on their writing. I also was pleased to know that my students enjoyed reading so much that they chose to read outside of school.

Noticing how students spontaneously use reading and writing for personal reasons.

There are many occasions for engaging in reading and writing that occur throughout the day. The ways in which our students spontaneously take advantage of these opportunities tell us whether or not they view reading and writing as useful and powerful tools. Here are three examples of the ways my students, on their own, used writing to try to influence others.

Halloween was on a Monday. Several children in my class were upset because they had to go to school the next day. So these children took it upon themselves to write individual letters to the President of the School Board expressing their dissatisfaction with this policy. To the delight of the children, the Board President even wrote back.

Another occasion presented itself when a guest speaker came into the class to talk about the depletion of the rain forests and the possible consequences of this current situation. After the guest speaker left, Lucas was so bothered by the apparent lack of concern about this serious condition, that he wrote a letter to Colombia (see Figure 7.5).

At the mountain schoolhouse where I previously taught, the enrollment has slowly increased over the years. Because of the greater numbers of children, there was less room on the school playground to play active running and catching games safely. Even though the land adjacent to the school sits vacant, the children are not allowed to play on it — it is private property and not landscaped properly for play. Frustrated with not having enough playground space, several students decided to write a letter to the owners of the land requesting that they sell it to the School District.

These kinds of literacy events showed me that my students are empowered writers. They understand the power of the written word and use their knowledge of writing to inform, persuade, and communicate their ideas and feelings to others. For them writing and reading are not filling in blanks, drawing lines to, or circling. My emphasis on creating authentic reasons for using reading and writing has empowered my students to read and write for their own reasons, not mine. Consequently, they read and write more, and in the process they learn about the strategies and skills literate people use to help them learn.

Figure 7.5

May 10, 1989

Dear Columbia,

I was wondering if you could stop cutting down your rainforests, because if you don't we will have the green house affect.

Our ozone is almost gone. Do you want to dye? If you cut down the rainforest, you will be killing yourself and everyone else too, plus animals and some of the most endangered animals. I would not mind living in a rainforest. You are very lucky to have so many different trees from America, and if you cut down the trees we will have less oxygen. Because trees give us air. Trees are living things.

And when you use your chainsaw it pollutes the air. It is all up to you to save everyone's lives not just yours. Do you know you don't have to have live stock to get money or wood? You could sell fruit from the trees.

An I bet you would get a lot of money from fruit. I really hope you don't cut down all the trees.

Well, I hope you will write to me.

From,
Lucas Albrighton
4th grader at Jamestown
School in Colorado

Noticing How Students Use Literature to Inform Their Writing

Students who write, read differently. They read not only for the information and experiences contained in books, but to learn how the authors used language and design to craft their works. Students who notice how authors crafted their pieces, often make use of this information in future pieces they write. For example, when D.J. was reading a novel written by Tony Hillerman, he noticed that Hillerman drew vivid images about his main character. Whenever D.J. came upon passages which did this, he would point them out and read them to me. Two weeks later, when D.J. was getting ready to write his next piece, he asked, "Yvonne, how do you develop characters in writing?" Astonished by this question, I responded with, "Why in the world would you want to know how to do that?" D.J. simply stated, "In the books I read I've noticed that the authors develop their characters... That is what I want to do in my next piece."

Because I couldn't help D.J. I said, "I can't help you. I don't know how to do that. But who can help you learn how to develop your characters since I can't?" D.J. insightfully responded, "From the authors who develop their characters." D.J. immediately gathered books that did a good job of developing characters and perused them. After that, he wrote "The Season," the piece he chose as his best (see page 163) where he felt he did a good job of showing what his character is like.

When students read as writers and actually use the information learned from reading in their writing, we know they are reading at a high level and are truly critical readers. So notice how students use what they learned in reading to craft the pieces they write.

Other Resources

Besides this book, there are other sources on the market which address holistic literacy assessment and evaluation. The following ones have been helpful to me and other teachers.

General Information on Evaluating Literacy: *Evaluating Literacy, A Perspective for Change* by Anthony, Johnson, Mickelson, and Preece; *Windows Into Literacy: Assessing Learners K-8* by Rhodes and Shanklin; *Literacy Assessment: A Handbook of Instruments,* edited by Rhodes; and *The Whole Language Catalog: Supplement on Authentic Assessment,* edited by Bridges, Goodman, and Goodman.

<u>About Portfolios</u>: *Portfolios and Beyond: Collaborative Assessment in Reading and Writing* by Glazer and Brown; *Portfolio Assessment in the Reading-Writing Classroom* by Tierney, Carter, and Desai; *Writing Portfolios, A Bridge from Teaching to Assessment* by Sandra Murphy and Mary Ann Smith.

<u>About Using Response Journals and Logs</u>: *Response Journals* by Les Parsons.

Each book is "teacher-friendly" and offers theoretically sound advice and concrete suggestions that help teachers find answers to their own particular assessment questions about their students' literacy development.

Becoming Literate

Being literate means more than being able to read, write, and pass standardized tests. Unfortunately, I have encountered too many individuals who know how to read and write, and who passed standardized tests, but who choose not to read and write. These individuals are friends and students in my university classes who have told me that they haven't selected a book to read for personal reasons in years, and that they feel insecure about writing and dislike it immensely. When I pressed them to discuss the reason for this negative attitude toward reading and writing, many related that they did not have experiences that engaged them in authentic literacy events where reading and writing were used for personal reasons, nor were they involved in examining and evaluating their own progress in reading and writing.

Despite current and past criticisms about our youngsters' ability to read and write, the problem is not that test scores are dropping, but that test scores are overemphasized. Holistic techniques for collecting data about how students do in reading and writing can not only help teachers plan meaningful instruction, but also provide a powerful tool for helping students honestly evaluate themselves as readers, writers, learners, and thinkers.

As Dr. W. Edwards Deming, in Walton (1986, p. 93), the genius who revitalized Japanese industry, said about running a company on visible figures alone (for which he credits Lloyd S. Nelson of Nashua Corporation), "...the figures that are 'unknown and unknowable' are even more important."

References

Anthony, R.J., Johnson, T.D., Michelson, N. & Preece, A. (1991). *Evaluating literacy, A perspective for change.* Portsmouth, NH: Heinemann.

Bird, L.B. (1989). The art of teaching evaluation and revision. In K.S. Goodman, Y.M. Goodman, & W.J. Hood (Eds.), *The whole language evaluation book* (pp. 15–24). Portsmouth, NH: Heinemann.

Brown, R. (1989). Testing and thoughtfulness. *Educational Leadership, 46,* 31–33.

Cochrane, O. (Ed.). (1992). *Questions & answers about whole language.* Katonah, NY: Richard C. Owen Publishers.

Costa, A. (1989). Re-assessing assessment. *Educational Leadership, 46,* 2.

Farr, R. (1989). A response from Roger Farr, director, Center for Reading and Language Studies, Smith Research Center, Indiana University, Bloomington, Indiana. In Questions & answers: Portfolio assessment, edited by K.S. Jongsma. *The Reading Teacher, 43,* 264.

Glazer, S.M., & Brown, C.S. (1993). *Portfolios and beyond: Collaborative assessment in reading and writing.* Norwood, MA: Christopher-Gordon.

Goodman, Y.M. (1989). Evaluation of students: Evaluation of teachers. In K.S. Goodman, Y.M. Goodman, & W.J. Hood (Eds.), *The whole language evaluation book* (pp. 3–14). Portsmouth, NH: Heinemann.

Hiebert, E.H., & Calfee, R.C. (1989). Advancing academic literacy through teachers' assessments. *Educational Leadership, 46,* 50–54.

Interview with Jane Hansen. (1989). *The Colorado Communicator, 12,* 1, 21.

Jaggar, A. (1985). On observing the language learner: Introduction and overview. In A. Jaggar & M.T. Smith-Burke (Eds.), *Observing the language learner* (pp. 1–7). Newark, DE: International Reading Association.

Murphy S., & Smith, M.A. (1992). *Writing portfolios, A bridge from teaching to assessment.* Portsmouth, NH: Heinemann.

Parsons, L. (1990). *Response journals.* Portsmouth, NH: Heinemann.

Pikulski, J.J. (1989). The assessment of reading: A time for change? *The Reading Teacher, 43,* 80–81.

Reif, L. (1990). Finding the value in evaluation: Self-assessment in a middle school classroom. *Educational Leadership, 47,* 24–29.

Rhodes, L.K. (Ed.). (1993). *Literacy assessment, A handbook of instruments.* Portsmouth, NH: Heinemann.

Shepard, L.A. (1989). Why we need better assessments. *Educational Leadership, 46,* 4–9.

Teale, W.H., Heibert, E.H., & Chittenden, E.A. (1987). Assessing young children's literacy development. *The Reading Teacher, 40,* 772–777.

Tierney, R.J., Carter, M.A., & Desai, L.E. (1991). *Portfolio assessment in the reading-writing classroom.* Norwood, MA: Christopher-Gordon.

Valencia, S., & Pearson, P.D. (1987). Reading assessment: Time for change. *The Reading Teacher, 40,* 726–732.

Walton, M. (1986). *The Deming Management Method.* New York: Dodd, Mead & Company.

Children's Books Cited

Babbitt, N. (1975). *Tuck everlasting.* New York: Bantam Skylark.

Bauer, C.F. (1981). *My mom travels a lot.* New York: F. Warne.

Brown, M.W. (1949). *The important book.* New York: Harper & Brothers.

Charlip, R. (1964). *Fortunately.* New York: Parents' Magazine Press.

Lewis, C.S. (1982). *The chronicles of Narnia.* New York: Caedmon.

Numeroff, L.J. (1985). *If you give a mouse a cookie.* New York: Harper & Row.

Paulsen, G. (1987). *Hatchet.* New York: Bradbury Press.

Chapter 8

Whole Language Assessment and Evaluation: A Special Education Perspective

Hilary Sumner Gahagan

Introduction: The Gnawing Dilemma

Assessment and evaluation for the special educator is a fact of life. For the holistic teacher it is the gnawing dilemma of coping with local, state, and federal regulations while orchestrating an authentic, purposeful, child-centered program. Ken Goodman (1989) writes that whole language has been a grass-roots movement motivated by teachers who are knowledgeable about the learning process and language development. Whole language teachers believe that evaluation must occur in authentic, meaningful ways within the natural context of a student's learning environment. Most traditional evaluation is inappropriate and often underestimates a child's growth in the functional use of language. Goodman explains that whole language teachers represent a courageous group that rejects imposed teaching methods and narrow curriculum. They rebel against behavioral objectives and traditional evaluation, especially standardized tests, because they are contrived, synthetic, confining, and dated. Whole language teachers, instead, engage in on-going, interactive assessment as part of their "whole" program.

Holistic special educators are no exception. We believe that in order to assess learning appropriately, we need a clear understanding about the natural learning process. We need an instructional environment that enhances meaningful, interactive learning. We need confidence that our assessment methods actually assess what we are looking for and in turn inform our instruction. Our assessments are a gathering of data that is ongoing, authentic, and integrated naturally within our instruction. Above all, we believe that our assessments must lead to some kind of improvement for our students.

So how does the special educator, whose belief system embraces holistic learning theory, deal with the shackles of differing definitions, questionable instructional and assessment practices, Individual Educational Plans (IEPs), and federal, state, and local regulations? It's not easy, but IS well worth it!

The purpose of this chapter is to explore this dilemma. We will look at the legal definitions and regulations as they relate to holistic theory. We will focus in on the special education students most commonly found in our classrooms, those identified as having learning disabilities. We will review both past and current beliefs and practices of instruction and assessment for these children. And we'll explore some innovative avenues which remain in legal compliance while still promoting programs that instruct, assess, and evaluate special needs students' development in holistic and relevant ways.

IDEA: The Guiding Force of Special Education

The field of Special Education encompasses a broad range of mildly to severely handicapping conditions. As a result of much litigation, the United States Congress passed a compulsory education law called the *Education For All Handicapped Children Act of 1975* (U.S.O.E., 1977). This act has been revised and amended, and is now known as the *Individuals with Disabilities Education Act*— IDEA (Federal Register, 1992). IDEA is designed to assist states in meeting the special educational needs of children with disabilities. States are responsible for ensuring that all children with disabilities have available to them a free, appropriate public education. It was intended to guarantee that all decisions regarding special education were made in a fair and appropriate manner. The law specifies that each identified special education child should have an individualized educational plan (IEP), designed by the school and the child's parents, including annual goals and short-term instructional objectives. The IEP must be based on a comprehensive individual assessment by a multidisciplinary team (MDT). The IEP must specify the student's present levels of functioning, the goals and objectives to help the student benefit from his special education program, the when and where of the services that will be provided, and the means by which a student's progress will be evaluated. To insure that the student is educated in a setting that maximizes his opportunities to interact with his non-handicapped peers, IDEA mandates that he be placed in the least restrictive environment possible to meet his special needs. For many mildly disabled students this is the regular classroom with additional support services.

Children addressed in this act are those defined as having mental retardation, hearing impairments (including deafness), visual impairments (including blindness), speech or language impairments, serious emotional disturbance, orthopedic impairments, autism, traumatic brain injury, other health impairments, specific learning disabilities, deaf-blindness, or multiple disabilities. Congress includes specific provisions in the law regarding assessment for these children::

1. Tests and other evaluation materials are provided and administered in the child's native language or mode of communication, unless it is clearly not feasible to do so.

2. Tests and other evaluation materials have been validated for the specific purpose for which they are used.

3. Tests and other evaluation materials are administered by trained personnel in conformance with the instructions provided by their producer.

4. Tests and other evaluation materials used include those tailored to assess specific areas of educational need, and not merely those that are designed to provide a single general intelligence quotient.

5. Tests are selected and administered so as best to ensure that when a test is administered to a child with impaired sensory, manual, or speaking skills, the test results accurately reflect the child's aptitude or achievement level or whatever other factors the test purports to measure.

6. No single procedure is used as the sole criterion for determining an appropriate educational program for a child.

7. The evaluation is made by a multidisciplinary team or group of persons, including at least one teacher or other specialist with knowledge in the area of suspected disability.

8. The child is assessed in all areas related to a specific disability, including — if appropriate — health, vision, hearing, social and emotional status, general intelligence, academic performance, communicative status, and motor abilities.

IDEA stipulates that in interpreting evaluation data and in making placement decisions, each public agency shall draw upon information from a variety of sources. IDEA describes the short-term instructional objectives as milestones and general benchmarks for determining progress toward meeting the goals. These objectives are to be projected so as to be accomplished over an extended period of time.

Interpreting IDEA

The provisions do not mandate specific assessment tools, nor do they require the reductionistic view of evaluation that has been so prevalent in special education in the recent past. They DO require equity, validity, and nondiscrimination. They repeatedly refer to *"tests and other evaluation materials and procedures."* They stipulate a team assessment approach, multi-measure decisions, and an evaluation based on specific educational needs. Furthermore, the last provision noted actually mandates a look at the "whole child." In passing IDEA, Congress has assisted the states in meeting the special needs of children with disabilities in a fair and appropriate manner.

Unfortunately, many special educators have narrowly interpreted the public law. They have reduced assessment to the measurement of discrete, fragmented parts in an attempt to be scientifically objective and controlled. The public law does not require that assessment be limited to isolated subskills. Nor does it suggest that instruction focus on the remediation of those skills by less-than-meaningful, repetitive tasks. The law does not exclude subjective assessment; in fact, it requires classroom observation as part of the identification process. The law clearly leaves the choice of assessment methods up to the educator, and stipulates that objectives on a student's IEP serve as milestones for measuring progress toward meeting the annual goals. Our dilemma is not one brought about by conflicting law, but more one caused by our misinterpretation of it.

The LD Child: The Most Common Disability Teachers Face in the Classroom

One of the most difficult conditions in the field of special education to define and assess is the group of individuals identified as having learning disabilities. This is also the most common disability regular education teachers face in the classroom. IDEA defines "specific learning disability" as:

a disorder in one or more of the basic psychological processes involved in understanding or in using language, spoken or written, which may manifest itself in the imperfect ability to listen, think, speak, read, write, spell, or do mathematical calculations. The term includes such conditions as perceptual disabilities, brain injury, minimal brain dysfunction, dyslexia, and developmental aphasia. The term does not include children who have learning problems which are primarily the result of visual, hearing, or motor disabilities, of mental retardation, emotional disturbance or environmental, cultural, or economic disadvantage.

(IDEA, Federal Register, 1992, p. 44802)

From "Dyslexia" to "Learning Differences"

This condition, now known as "specific learning disability," in the past was commonly referred to as "dyslexia." Bartoli and Botel (1988) report that historically dyslexia was believed to be organic in nature: the result of a neurological defect, either genetic or induced by minimal, nonobservable brain trauma. Since the mid-1950s "dyslexia" has never been clearly defined, nor has any etiology, or cause, ever been shown to be conclusively valid. Moreover, the instruction which was based on the motor and perceptual deficit theories of dyslexia has not proved particularly effective in the teaching of reading. Since it is usually not possible to distinguish organic causes from other causes for the basis of a reading disorder, the academic term "learning disability" seems more appropriate to many professionals than the medical term "dyslexia." In fact, some even prefer the term "less-developed" (Bartoli and Botel, 1988). It is not uncommon to hear teachers refer nowadays to L.D. as "learning differences," for these terms seem more consistent with current developmental learning theory and the belief in the potential for these students to become more efficient readers and writers.

Has Reductionist Theory Served the LD Child?

Speculation about the causes of learning disabilities has primarily focused on conditions intrinsic to the child (Rhodes, 1988). This is a very convenient explanation for most of our more severe reading failures. Typically the children, not the curricula, instructional practices, or the assessments are seen as the problem. Poplin (1988) reports that the field of learning disabilities has struggled to transform from the early medical definitions. She reviewed the popular models of learning disability theory that have developed over the past forty years. Although each model defines learning disabilities differently, they all are similar in their "reductionistic learning theory." Poplin explains that reductionism is the process by which we break ideas, concepts, and skills into parts in an attempt to understand and better deal with the whole.

The teaching and assessment methods many practitioners have used with learning disabled children are examples of the misconception that a complex whole such as "human learning" can be systematically broken down and separated into its component parts. This task analysis was done in a genuine attempt to design more effective instruction and assessment. But, in fact, this separation of "subskills" and the subsequent, isolated "drill and practice" has fragmented and disrupted the natural learning process for LD students. In contrast to what is now known about natural language acquisition and holistic learning, the earlier models of learning disability theory have several things in common.

1. Learning was segmented into discrete parts. These parts were then taught and assessed in isolation, out of context.

2. Instruction was believed to be most effective when it was tightly controlled and directed by the teacher, leaving the learner basically passive.

3. Instruction usually focused on students' deficits rather than their strengths.

4. Each model held that there was one "right" way to learn something, which revealed a basic distrust of students' minds and natural learning.

5. Each model held the belief that natural learning would not develop without direct instruction.

6. Teaching and learning were considered uni-directional; in other words, the teacher alone knew what was to be learned and the student was expected to learn it.

Constructivist Theory and the LD Child

We have learned a great deal about cognition and the natural learning process over the past decade. Learning is a complex, multi-faceted, and very individual process of perceiving and "constructing" knowledge. It does not happen in isolation. It is not discrete and uni-directional. It is not passive. And there is not one right way of doing it. Learning is an intricate orchestration of making personal meaning of one's environment. It is intimately connected to the learner's background knowledge, experiences, and emotional state. It is a continuous process of interacting. Individuals identified as having learning disabilities are not exempt from "natural learning." Quite the contrary! But these learners need support in trusting and organizing the complex connections among their perceptions. Perhaps more than any learners, they need a meaningful context in which to confirm their predictions, the opportunity to interact with their environment and, reaffirming assistance to make sense of their world. Many mildly learning disabled students are not even identified as being different until they hit the mainstream of public school.

A Whole Language Environment Empowers the LD Student

LD students are a diverse group and it is not easy (or particularly useful) to generalize them into distinct categories of deficits. It is more productive to describe what they CAN do. The majority of LD children are intellectually quite capable. They are survivors. They go through elaborate strategies to try and make sense of their worlds. They are individuals who learn differently, but do indeed learn. They often need to be physically involved, to speak out, to "do it their own way." They have varying strengths and learning styles. Some learn visually and have great difficulty processing auditory information and using it effectively. Some have very strong "voices" but have difficulty using oral and written language effectively. Other confuse visual stimuli (reversals, directionality, etc.) but do quite well when they can hear something explained and get to verbally respond to it. Some need to "move," to physically interact in order to make sense and to store information. Most use a combination of many learning styles, depending on the context.

Learning disabled students, by their very nature, need a learning environment that responds to their individuality and their varied developmental stages. They need instruction that is relevant to their current world and built upon their background experiences. They need the opportunity to interact. They need guidance and motivation to self-reflect on their own learning, to set their own goals, to assess themselves in order to become responsible and independent learners. *Whole language classrooms provide this environment and support.* They need both freedom and structure. They need the freedom to choose what is relevant and meaningful to them and the structure that provides a framework within which they are safe and valued. Structure does not mean a rigid, barren classroom. It means a classroom community in which children are encouraged to learn in the modes they are most successful using. The varied physical arrangements, instructional and curricular opportunities, classroom expectations that empower children to learn in their own way, and the collaborative respect of a whole language classroom provides this structure. As long as instruction and assessment in special education continue to adhere to dated theory, the natural language and learning processes of LD children will continue to be disrupted, perpetuating our gnawing dilemma.

How Does a Holistic Resource Program Accommodate the LD Student's Learning Needs?

The Whole Language Resource Program is based on the belief that all children learn by the process of constructing meaning. They do this through the interaction of what they already know, the context of the situation, and the new experience (Poplin, 1985). Learning in the Resource Program is an active process which is controlled by the student, not the teacher. The role of the resource teacher is that of a facilitator who supports this interactive process, who is acutely aware of the LD child's unique learning strengths and special needs, and who provides an integrated blend of appropriate curriculum, instruction, and assessment.

Learning disabled students often encounter a mismatch among their new experiences, the context of their new learning, and their background knowledge. This can occur because the children are not developmentally ready for the new learning and may need help organizing the new information so they can relate it to what they already know. The mismatch can occur because the children's background knowledge is insufficient for the experience to be meaningful. Classroom activities are designed to provide varied, hands-on experiences to build that missing background knowledge. The mismatch can occur because LD children have difficulty processing new information to connect and store the experiences. They need activities that stimulate them visually, auditorily, and kinesthetically. They need to be taught strategies which encourage them to make predictions, to justify them based on their personal knowledge, and they need the opportunities to demonstrate their learnings in a variety of ways. Since LD youngsters have a greater difficulty making the connections, the resource program is adapted to each individual.

A holistic resource program should encourage literacy through the constant interaction of the students' listening, speaking, reading, and writing experiences. Thematic units, using real-life materials, authentic children's literature, and cooperative learning activities are particularly successful ways used to create this interaction. They not only accommodate LD children's background knowledge, learning styles, and developmental stages, but they invite discovery, experimentation, and collaboration. This type of active participation with their classmates is critical for LD children who need help making the meaningful connections. A thematic, literacy-based approach to instruction is profoundly more appropriate for learning disabled students than the typically controlled, remedial skills-based approaches used in the past. Unfortunately, too often the LD child's learning has been incomplete, not solely because of deficits within the child, but because the teaching process, assessments, and the classroom environments were not responsive to their developmental learning needs.

Multiple Assessment Audiences in Special Education

The resource teacher's gnawing dilemma has a great deal to do with the type of assessment data that is needed in a resource program. Even with a program carefully crafted to accommodate the LD children's unique learning needs, we are still required to assess and document student progress for many different audiences. Each of these audiences or stakeholders has a different purpose for the assessment data wanted and each may have a different understanding of student learning and evaluation. The policymakers are looking for evaluations that comply with state and federal regulations and support the eligibility and IEP processes. Parents often want the assessments to tell them how their child is doing in relation to other kids. We want our evaluation data to meet the legal requirements AND effectively communicate with our parents. We are also looking for an ongoing validation that our students are becoming more efficient readers and writers. Are the strategies we're teaching relevant and do they transfer to the regular classroom? Does our curriculum and instruction invite discovery and self-assessment? Are our students becoming more engaged, responsible, and independent learners?

The key to coping with the gnawing dilemma is for us to find a balance among our assessments. We are the professionals who are experienced and knowledgeable about the needs of our special students.

We are supported by the law and given the latitude to make responsible choices about our assessments and evaluations. We take this seriously and we choose measures that honor our students' literacy.

Multi-Dimensional Assessment in Special Education

As special educators, we engage in multi-dimensional assessment. Before a student is served in our programs, we are responsible for assessment and evaluation related to the referral, eligibility, and IEP processes. A closer look at IDEA revealed that the law clearly supports a team assessment approach, multi-measure decisions, and an evaluation that looks at the "whole child." What does that look like in our programs from a holistic perspective? The following is a scenario that demonstrates those processes. A third grade teacher is seeking support for one of her special students and initiates a special education referral for evaluation.

Scenario:
3rd Grade Classroom Teacher Refers Student for SPED Assessment
(a look at the "whole child")

Mrs. Tsugawa comes to the Resource Room to ask Ms. Mardi (the Learning Disabilities Specialist) about one of her students. She wants to come to the M.D.T. to discuss Dimitri's special needs and his frustrations in the classroom. Mrs. Tsugawa has tried everything she can think of and nothing seems to help. Dimitri is making very little progress in reading and writing and has become rather disruptive in class. She met with the *Teacher Assistance Team* several months ago. They helped her with a student tutor and parent helpers in class. She has been trying a variety of new strategies that the team recommended in her classroom but she feels he needs more. Dimitri's parents have been very supportive and Mrs. Tsugawa is in close communication with them. Together they have tried home-school contracts, homework plans and rewards. They are frustrated too. What can they do? How can they help him? They worked on the same issues with last year's teacher. Does he have a disability, are they overlooking something, or is he just being lazy?

Ms. Mardi spends some time talking about Dimitri with Mrs. Tsugawa. When did she first notice his difficulties? Is there a specific time of day, activity, situation when it is more pronounced? What, specifically, are his parents' concerns? What does the teacher who taught Dimitri last year say? Is this frustration new? What has she tried to modify in the classroom to help

Dimitri be successful? Is there anything in his school records that relates to the problems she's experiencing? Ms. Mardi writes some preliminary anecdotal records about their conference and asks Mrs. Tsugawa to complete a prereferral form explaining her concerns and how she has tried to help him.

This prereferral asks for a brief, specific summary of the problem. It asks for Dimitri's present levels of functioning in all core subjects and the ways Mrs. Tsugawa assesses Dimitri to determine this. It asks about what strategies the teacher and the parents have tried together. It includes questions about Dimitri's general health and attendance. What were the interventions the teacher has tried in the classroom to improve the situation and the results?

How well does Dimitri function in different learning situations (individual, pairs, small group, cooperative groups, whole groups) and what curricula does she use with him? Finally, Ms. Mardi asks Mrs. Tsugawa what information she is seeking from the M.D.T. With this information the team hopes to develop a complete picture of Dimitri's strengths, difficulties, and his environment. She also is validating Mrs. Tsugawa's ability to "kid-watch" (Goodman, 1978) and is helping her to become aware of the importance of looking at the "whole picture" of Dimitri's learning.

Ms. Mardi and Mrs. Tsugawa present their concerns at the next multidisciplinary team meeting. Based on the prereferral information (and the efforts she has made prior to referring to special education), the team decides a formal referral is appropriate to determine if Dimitri is qualified for special education services. The M.D.T. determines the areas of concern and assigns the appropriate specialists for the evaluation (i.e., the Learning Disabilities Specialist, Speech & Language Pathologist, School Psychologist, Motor Development Team, School Nurse, etc.).

It is important that the teacher make every effort in the classroom and with the parents long before a student is referred for a special education evaluation. If teachers were willing to take a look at instructional and curricular modifications, and individual learning styles more often, fewer students would be referred to special education.

It is however, every student's and parent's legal right to have a full evaluation to determine eligibility for special education services. If the child is found eligible, he or she then has the right to an individualized educational plan and all appropriate services.

Ms. Mardi, Mrs. Tsugawa and the parents then conference about Dimitri's needs and the process of the evaluation is explained. The parents are required to give written permission for any special assessment. Ms. Mardi interviews the parents to learn as much as possible about their expectations and Dimitri's history. Once she has permission, and background information about Dimitri, Ms. Mardi reviews the interview data and his student records to learn about his health, his attendance, progress reports, and any other relevant information that might have an impact on his present learning situation. Then Ms. Mardi visits Dimitri's classroom to observe him within the context of the whole class. As she watches and notes his involvement, she also records the activity of the whole class and that of another student. Without this comparative information, Ms. Mardi might record an unfair picture of Dimitri. If the whole class is active and perusing the classroom, then Dimitri is not off-task or inappropriate if he is also up and about. Ms. Mardi's observation also includes information about the lesson she is watching, the size of the learning group, and the types of interactions Dimitri has with the teacher and other classmates. An appropriate observation needs to consider the entire academic and social interactions in which the student is engaged.

After Ms. Mardi visits in the classroom, she meets with Dimitri. She asks him to tell her about school. She asks him what is "best" about school. It's important to focus on his strengths before they discuss what help he might need. Then, with all the information from the parents, the classroom teacher, and from Dimitri himself, Ms. Mardi can responsibly *begin* to evaluate his academic needs.

Eligibility

Ms. Mardi's school district uses a discrepancy formula to help determine Dimitri's eligibility for special education in the area of learning disabilities. She and the School Psychologist administer a variety of standardized tests to evaluate whether Dimitri shows a significant discrepancy between his cognitive ability and his academic achievement. To support the standardized testing, Ms. Mardi takes a look at Dimitri's literacy in other ways. In the past, parents and other teachers were interested in grade level equivalencies. They wanted to know just how many months behind their child was. Ms. Mardi prefers to assess what Dimitri CAN DO. She has Dimitri read from a selected children's book, into a tape recorder, and administers a Reading Miscue Inventory so she can analyze the quality of his miscues and the efficiency of his reading strategies (Goodman, Watson, Burke, 1987).

She might have Dimitri write a short, independent piece on a topic of his choice. She would ask him to take some time to think about his writing first, then write it the best he could on his own. It is important that he have no time limit (if possible) to get a full picture of his writing processes. Ms. Mardi asks Dimitri to choose several pieces from his classroom Portfolio to show her — maybe a "best piece," a favorite piece, and a rough draft (as an example of his revising and editing). She is interested in his self-reflections on the pieces that were chosen from his Portfolio. She wants to see why he picked them and what he says they represent about him as a learner.

Ms. Mardi asks Mrs. Tsugawa to gather classroom work samples over time and in different contexts to balance the assessments (journal entries, reading responses, content area projects, his portfolio, assignments in general that show his strengths and needs). She wants to build a complete picture of Dimitri's literacy as close to his natural school environment as possible.

As part of the prereferral process, Mrs. Tsugawa had gotten information from other staff members that came in contact with Dimitri regularly (i.e., the P.E. and Music Teachers, the playground staff, the principal, the secretary, the Media Specialist, instructional aides, etc.). They often have valuable information about how he functions in other subjects, in social situations, with peers. Perhaps they have known Dimitri for some time. Are his learning problems generalized (are they noticeable in most contexts), or are they specific to his class?

By the time the M.D.T. meets to determine eligibility, Ms. Mardi is well prepared to discuss Dimitri's cognitive assessment, literacy, present achievement, and schoolwide interactions. She has a profile of the student from many sources, and the team is then much better equipped to decide his eligibility for special education.

Two of the most difficult things to decipher, when making eligibility decisions, are the effects of the classroom and home environment on a child's school achievement. We know how powerful the learning climate is. We also know how delicate the subject of change is. It is unfortunate, but not surprising that special education has focused on interchild deficits rather than change in the learning environments.

Individualized Educational Plans

The Multidisciplinary Team does determine that Dimitri is eligible for Learning Disabilities services in Language Arts (Reading and Written Language). An individualized educational plan (IEP) is designed by the teachers and parents.

IDEA describes that the IEP includes a statement of the child's present levels of educational performance, annual goals, and instructional objectives with "criteria, evaluation procedures, and schedules for determining (on at least an annual basis) whether the short-term instructional objectives are being achieved." The annual goal statements are designed to "describe what a child with a disability can reasonably be expected to accomplish within a twelve month period in the child's special education program." The objectives are intermediate steps between the child's present levels and the annual goals — they "serve as milestones for measuring progress toward meeting the goals." The objectives are written as benchmarks projected over a specified period of time (i.e., an entire school quarter or semester) and are not meant to be as detailed as daily or weekly classroom instructional plans.

Table 8.1 presents examples of the individual annual goals and short-term objectives the IEP team designs for Dimitri to help him become a more efficient reader and writer. They are based on his "present levels of performance" from the assessment data.

Balancing and Integrating Authentic Assessment

As discussed at the beginning of this chapter, we holistic special educators engage in ongoing, interactive assessment as part of our whole programs. We use assessments that are authentic and integrated naturally within our instruction. As we design goals and objectives for our students, we choose evaluation methods, criteria, and schedules that do not disrupt our programs for "testing day" but are intricately woven into our programs. What do we mean by "authentic, integrated assessment" and how do the "portfolios" we've talked about help us to balance and integrate our programs?

Authentic Assessment in the Resource Program

Our authentic assessments involve the processes of observing, recording, and documenting student work. It includes both the work children do *and* how they do it as the basis for the educational decisions we make that affect our special kids. Authentic assessment in our programs is balanced and integrated, because it is:

1. centered in our classrooms
2. centered around the goals and objectives specific to *each child* and is directly linked to appropriate curriculum and instruction for *that child*.

Table 8.1: Sample I.E.P. Goals & Objectives

Dimitri A. Reader   *Grade 03*   *Language Arts*

Annual Goal — Reading

Dimitri will use a variety of strategies to become a more efficient and independent reader.

Short-term Instructional Objectives

1. Dimitri will skip words or substitute meaningful synonyms when he comes to words he does not know, 80% of the time, while maintaining comprehension.

   Measurement Method: Oral testing/Measurement Schedule: End of 1st & 2nd quarters

2. When orally reading, Dimitri will make meaningful substitutions for unknown words, showing attention to beginning & ending sounds, for 75% of his sound-symbol miscues.

   Measurement Method: Oral testing/Measurement Schedule: End of 1st semester

3. Dimitri will self-correct miscues which affect the meaning of a text he is reading by backtracking, re-reading, or reading-on to get more information, for 80% of his miscues.

   Measurement Method: R.M.I./Measurement Schedule: End of 2nd quarter

4. Dimitri will retell a text he has read including characters, setting, story events in a logical order, plot and theme, with 75% accuracy.

   Measurement Method: R.M.I./Measurement Schedule: End of quarters

5. Dimitri will create a story map after reading a text, including characters, setting, problem, and resolution to teacher satisfaction and classroom criteria.

   Measurement Method: Work Samples/Measurement Schedule: Quarterly

Annual Goal — Written Language

Dimitri will write, revise and edit a draft for presentation or publication.

Short-term Instructional Objectives

1. Dimitri will use semantic mapping strategies to organize and write a rough draft with a clear beginning, middle, and end to teacher satisfaction and classroom criteria.

   Measurement Method: Work Samples/Measurement Schedule: End of 1st semester

2. Dimitri will revise his rough draft by adding, deleting, or reorganizing his information independently and with peers, to classroom criteria.

   Measurement Method: Student-teacher conference/Measurement Schedule: End of semester

3. Dimitri will use a proofreading checklist to edit his rough draft for word choice, syntax, spelling, capitalization and punctuation, for 70% of his mechanical errors.

   Measurement Method: Student checklist/Measurement Schedule: Monthly

4. Dimitri will record his ideas or concepts he has learned in a journal or learning log when assigned by the teacher, according to classroom criteria.

   Measurement Method: Student journal/Measurement Schedule: Weekly

5. Dimitri will write an evaluative response about a completed piece he has written, showing self-reflection about the writing process, his effort or growth as a writer.

   Measurement Method: Portfolio Review/Measurement Schedule: Quarterly

3. consistent with our knowledge about how these children learn.

4. a profile gathered OVER TIME.

5. QUALITATIVE and QUANTITATIVE.

6. focused on our professional judgment because we are closest to the learners.

7. interactive: a collaboration of both the teacher and the student.

Portfolio Assessment

We achieve this balance and integration with the help of portfolios. Portfolio assessment represents the belief that learning is developmental and that development is an ongoing and interactive process. It represents the range of our students' learning while allowing for their individual differences. Portfolios offer meaningful demonstrations of their growth and developing responsibility in the classroom. With portfolios, we are better able to communicate about our students' progress with parents, with other educators and, most importantly, with the students themselves. Portfolios are as unique as the children who create them. There is no RIGHT kind of portfolio. They do, however, have several characteristics in common:

> *A portfolio* is a purposefully chosen collection of evidence:
> * that represents a child's growth over time
> * through collaborative selection
> * criteria & standards
> * and student self-reflection
> (Paulson, Paulson & Meyer, 1991)

There has been growing concern that "portfolios" are looked at as the panacea for all of the inadequacies of standardized testing. Donald Graves (1992) warns us that we must be careful not to overpromise portfolios and lose their obvious long-term potential. They will not (and should not) satisfy all of the purposes for which we assess. As teachers, we need to consciously consider our own purposes for moving to portfolio assessment and ask what that "obvious potential" is for the children in our programs.

* What is my purpose for using portfolios in my classroom with my students? What do I hope to accomplish?

- What do I want my students to learn from the process of developing their own portfolios?

- What do I want to communicate to the parents, other teachers, and my administrators through our classroom portfolio system?

- Who will own the portfolios in my classroom?

- What gets included in the portfolios? How are the contents chosen and organized? How often? By whom?

- What are our standards and criteria for choosing the contents?

- And probably the question most wrestled with today in our movement toward authentic assessment: "How are the portfolios to be evaluated while still retaining their authenticity?"

As we struggle with the balance between the multi-dimensional purposes of assessment, it helps to realize that a portfolio is not a static, single entity. To the contrary, the "portfolio" can be viewed as a three-tiered vehicle with several purposes. Consider the possibility of an assessment system in your classroom in which there are three separate but intimately related levels of "portfolio":

- the child's working folder(s),

- the teacher folio, and

- the Student's *Showcase Portfolio.*

These levels address the differing purposes of assessment. Two of these levels are already in place in most classrooms. Students have *"working folders"* in many forms (reading & writing folders, content area notebooks, journals, etc.). Teachers record and document student growth in *"teacher folios"* as they collect and analyze student work on a daily basis. These may take the form of files, grade books, computer data systems, parent communications, tests, surveys, work samples, anecdotal records, IEPs, and the like. The most common missing element is the student's *"Showcase Portfolio."*

The *Showcase Portfolio* is the student's opportunity to choose favorite examples of who he or she is as a learner. From the varied pieces saved in the working folder and special memorabilia from the regular classroom and outside school, the child picks representative selections. These pieces are purposefully chosen based on specific criteria that are determined by the child and his or her teacher. If we were to allow the children undisturbed ownership of their Showcase Portfolio and used this primarily as a vehicle for student self-assessment, the purity of its authenticity could be retained. Students would choose pieces without the fear of traditional grading, and based on their personal reflections about what it means to them.

We can develop the *teacher folio* as our vehicle for evaluation. Within that we can include those selections (or copies) of authentic work we wish to grade under whatever standards and criteria we need. The *teacher folio* offers child-centered assessment, profiles over time, qualitative as well as quantitative documentation, is interactive, and is based on the professional judgment of the teacher. These assessments can include reading and writing benchmarks (checklists with numerical indicators if desired), analytical trait scorings, literacy profiles, developmental report cards, test protocols, reading miscue inventories, reading and writing response records, IEPs, etc. The possibilities are numerous. But the final goal is to keep assessment authentic, compatible with instructional improvement, and fully integrated within our programs. Table 8.2 shows examples of possible contents of *Showcase Portfolios and Teacher Folios,* and Table 8.3 describes the many assessment opportunities of the three levels of this portfolio system.

Table 8.2: Sample Contents of Showcase Portfolios and Teacher Folios

Showcase Portfolio	Teacher's Folio
Projects and thematic units that show cross-curriculum work	Anecdotal records from observations and conferences
Favorite rhymes, poems, songs	Literacy Profiles
Samples that illustrate variety of writing styles (persuasive, narrative, expository, descriptive)	Developmental checklists
	Surveys, interviews and interest inventories
Literature logs, scripts for drama (reader's theater), webs, clusters, charts, murals	Rough drafts and final copies that demonstrate "Writing As A Process"
Student records of books read	Parent correspondence
Periodic audio tapes of reading and video tapes of performances	Reading Miscue Inventories
Writing responses to literary components: plot, setting, character development, theme	Tests
Writings that demonstrate analytical trait development (ideas and content, organization, voice, word choice, sentence fluency, writing conventions)	Report cards
	Copies of Special Education IEPs with goals and objectives
Evidence of the stages of WRITING AS A PROCESS	Copies of student work — graded with rubrics and/or evaluated with self-reflections
Art, photos, memorabilia	Student goal-setting

Table 8.3: Balancing Multi-Dimensional Assessment

The Working Folder: everyday work in progress.

*Evaluation includes the child's
informal reflections about:*

- what has been accomplished

- what still needs to be done

- what finished pieces might go into the Showcase Portfolio

The Showcase Portfolio: the "gems"

Evaluation can include the child's:

- Self-Reflections

- Best pieces, rough drafts and special favorites
(not necessarily best work)
√ some scored for analytical traits

- Memorabilia, art, etc.

- Student Portfolio Evaluation letter/form
√ scored holistically using class criteria

- Parent reflections following
Student-led Portfolio Conferences

The Teacher Folio: the teacher's file of evidence to inform instruction, support report cards, and enhance parent communication.

Evaluation can include:

- Observations and anecdotal records

- Student submitted best pieces (and rough drafts)
  Student-scored (holistic and/or analytical traits)
  Teacher-scored (holistic and/or analytical traits)

  Samples of student self-reflections

- Literacy profiles & developmental checklists

- Reading miscue inventories

- Developmental or traditional report cards

- Records of student/teacher/parent conferences

- Student and parent surveys

- Student tests and project evaluations

Earlier in this chapter we explored the benefits our special students, experience in a holistic resource program. Using portfolios offers them the individuality, relevance, and motivation to engage in their learning. They feel empowered and accepted at whatever level they might be. Our students have often felt programmed and powerless in school. Portfolios provide the structure and freedom they desperately need to begin to feel valued as learners. As they begin to evaluate themselves, they learn how to self-reflect, how to set goals, and they start to take responsibility for their own development.

Self-reflection is probably the single most important element in the portfolio process and the foundation for life-long learning. It can be done in many forms, and should be done for every piece that is chosen for a student's portfolio. Only the owner of a portfolio knows why a piece is chosen and what it represents about him or her as a learner.

Tables 8.4 to 8.7 give examples of student and parent portfolio evaluation forms, practical formats for written reflections, and sample special needs students' responses.

Table 8.4: Student Portfolio Evaluation Form

Name: _____   Date: _____

Teacher: _____

$\boxed{\sqrt{}}$

1. I have organized my portfolio and I am ready for my parent conference _____
2. I have a complete, updated Table of Contents   _____
3. All the work in my portfolio is dated   _____
4. My portfolio contains a variety of things like:

Stories	_____	Tapes	_____
Letters	_____	Book Lists	_____
Poems	_____	Photos	_____
Journal	_____	Literature logs	_____

   Projects from:

Writer's Workshop	_____	Reader's Workshop	_____
Math	_____	Social Studies	_____
Science	_____	Art	_____
Home	_____	Other	_____

5. I have self-reflections on each piece I put in my portfolio   _____
6. I think this portfolio deserves a score of _____ because I _____

   _____

   _____

   (Use our holistic classroom rubic to score)
7. I have conferenced with my teacher and presented my portfolio.

   I am ready for my parent conference   _____

| _____ | _____ |
| Student's initials | Teacher's initials |

Table 8.5: Parent Survey — Student-led Portfolio Conference

Dear Parents,

Thank you for coming to school for your conference. We enjoyed sharing your child's portfolio with you. Please take a few minutes with this survey and let us know your thoughts about the portfolio.

1. What new things did you learn about your child after sharing in the student-led portfolio conference?

2. What parts of the portfolio and the conference did you like best?

3. Did anything in the portfolio surprise you?

4. How was this portfolio helpful in showing you about your child's growth and development?

5. Did you find this experience more informative than traditional report cards? Why or why not?

6. What do you want to know more about?

7. Questions? Suggestions? Comments?

As we think about planning our resource programs to meet the special needs of our students and to instruct and assess in an integrated fashion, the gnawing dilemma goes beyond the legal constraints and the designs of our whole language pullout programs. How integrated can we be while our students' school experience is that of two separate worlds? Many regular classrooms offer whole language programs that promote choice, responsibility, and independence. Many classrooms enhance student development through the use of portfolios and authentic assessment. Should our students create *showcase portfolios* in our resource rooms as well as their classrooms?

The last part of this chapter explores how we offer special education services to our students and the effects of those services on them. If we really value integrated programs, perhaps we need to look beyond the walls of our resource rooms.

Table 8.6: Practical Formats for Written Reflections

Practical Formats for Written Reflections

Written reflections come in many forms. A student could write a *lengthy description* about all the ways he or she has grown.

A+ I lernd how to speel better.
A+ I lemd where you put marks.
A+ I lerndathat it dosint mater if your on a slopy copy.
Toremeber to put perids at te ending of a sentice

November 2, 1992
11-2-92 Shelby
I learned to write in cursuf And I know ho to spell a lot more. Here are son of my storys that I did. . . The Lion and The B My WonderFul Summer and The scary rides. I like to write a lo

I am strugaling with Knowing were ito put thea her end of the word But I am doing ok

I have writen longer storys. Beacuse at the first of the year I skip a line when I write my storys. But now I write long storys to the bottom of the page.

My next goal in writing is a very long to the back of the page. And my other goal is that I write a Chapter book.

Teachers can provide *Reflection Sheets* which focus on the reading, writing and the portfolio processes.

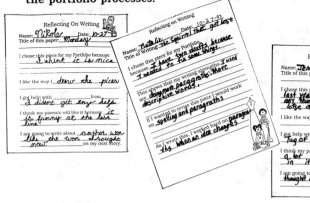

Table 8.7: Sample Responses of Special Needs Students

Post-it notes are an easy, non-threatenting way for students to reflect on their writing. Younger or less-able writers might prefer to *dictate* a reflection to the teacher, an older student buddy, or a parent helper.

Colorful post-its, or ones with fun shapes are very motivating for kids. Likewise, special pens (neon, rainbow, etc) liven up written reflections.

The physical format of the reflection is not what is most important. *The timeliness is.* Children, at best, have short attention spans. Their passion for a project and their effort can soon be forgotton (or at least lose momentum). The sooner the children can reflect, the better. They will be more in touch with their needs and achievements if they reflect promptly.

Special Education Service Delivery

Each school serves special education students differently, depending on the needs determined by their IEPs. Some resource models pull children from the regular classrooms and instruct them in small groups or individually. In some programs, specialists go into the classroom and assist the children in their regular environments. Some Learning Disability Specialists serve as consultants and team teachers with the regular classroom teachers. Most programs involve a combination of these models. Inclusion of special needs children in the regular classroom, with in-class special education services, is gaining increased national attention. Proponents of inclusion are concerned about:

- student stigma and lowered self-esteem with pullout programs
- minimal transfer of strategies and skills taught outside the regular classroom
- fragmented programs and scheduling
- unrelated curriculum and instruction
- rising drop-out rates for special education kids
- dwindling school resources
- parental demands for inclusion
- classroom teachers' need for training and in-class support during the rest of the school day

Inclusion is most often used to describe programs for students with disabilities, but it also pertains to students from different cultures whose first language is not English, students at-risk of failure because of substance abuse, and other special needs children. The aim is to integrate them with their non-disabled peers into the classroom communities and value them for their abilities and for who they are (Friend & Cook, 1993).

Successful inclusion of special needs children in the regular school community is truly our final goal. The overriding mission of IDEA is to assist these children to benefit enough from their special education so that they are able to be integrated into and succeed in the mainstream. Special educators can be very influential in making this succeed. It takes patience, flexibility, and commitment. Not only do we need to fully understand our special students, we must be sensitive to the special needs of our colleagues.

What Can Make "Inclusion" Successful?

- Compatible philosophies about learning
- Common beliefs about:
  - authentic assessment
  - integrated assessment and instruction
  - child-centered classrooms
- Common commitment among colleagues to:
  - schedule cooperatively
  - plan collaboratively
  - team teach
  - stay flexible
  - honor each other's teaching and learning styles
  - pursue training about special student needs

Inclusion is not for every special needs child nor is it appropriate in every classroom. The IEP will determine the extent to which a child can effectively be served in his regular classroom. The classroom environment, the regular and special education teacher's belief systems, and the special education teacher's ability to consult and collaborate will ultimately determine the success of inclusion.

Trying Inclusion in a Holistic Resource Program

We have discussed the law. We have looked at how a whole language environment empowers learning disabled students and accommodates their special learning needs. We have considered the many audiences and purposes of assessment and visited in-depth the value of authentic assessment — especially portfolios. How can we facilitate these components of our holistic resource programs outside of the "pull-out" models we are accustomed to?

- Start small!
- Be sure the classroom teacher is willing and eager to include the child and YOU within his or her classroom.
- Ask: How can we best provide an educational program for "this child" in "this classroom" to promote his or her school success?

- Ask: How do we define success?
- Predetermine how you will assess both this child's growth related to the IEP and general well-being.
- Be sure you have parental support.
- Cooperatively plan and schedule.
- Stay open, be flexible, and adjust as concerns arise!

One of the easiest ways to try an inclusion program is in the area of language arts. Regular classrooms that provide a Reader's or Writer's Workshop format are child-centered communities which, by design, honor developmental evaluation and process learning. Students have opportunities for personal choice, cooperative peer interactions, varied instructional groupings, individual student-teacher conferences, goal-setting, and self-reflections. In many of these classrooms students create portfolios as part of their assessment systems. Special education inclusion in this type of classroom environment can be very successful. It's an excellent place to start. The following section presents a design for such a program format and describes how it is applied in Scenario #2.

Designing a Language Arts Inclusion Model

- Schedule Language Arts cooperatively among like-classrooms.
  * Grade levels
  * Splits
  * Blends

- Teach Language Arts in a *Writer's Workshop* format.
  * Writing As A Process
  * Student-response groups
  * Student-teacher conferences
  * Varied instructional groupings to meet developing student needs… (whole-group, small-group, individual)

- Include specialists as *team-teachers* in the regular classroom.
  * Specialists can work with all students, but their primary responsibility is to monitor IEP students.

- Group students heterogeneously for student-response groups.

* Classroom teacher *and* specialists facilitate these groups.
* Regroup these students every four to six weeks.

- Classroom teachers and specialists teach whole-group lessons, small-group lessons, and individual lessons as student instructional needs develop.

- Include specialists in parent conferences.

- Set up your *Portfolio System.*

- Teach the students how to present their portfolios during student-teacher conferences. Then hold student-led parent conferences.

- Assess the students using a variety of authentic measures to accommodate all students' individual needs:
  * portfolios
  * observation & anecdotal records
  * holistic & trait rubrics
  * developmental literacy checklists/profiles
  * student self-reflections

Scenario #2:
Inclusion in Language Arts (Regular Classroom Writer's Workshop)

After the M.D.T. determined that Dimitri was eligible for special education services for learning disabilities, Mrs. Tsugawa, Ms. Mardi, Dimitri's parents, and the school psychologist meet and design his IEP. Mrs. Tsugawa has strong concerns about how they will implement his special program. Her classroom has a large percentage of special needs children this year, and she is worried about the fragmentation of her classroom community if a pullout program is used. Dimitri's parents are likewise concerned about what he might miss if he leaves her room and the stigma he might feel if he is away from his peers.

Mrs. Tsugawa and Ms. Mardi have heard a lot about inclusion lately. They discuss the pros and cons of this approach in relation to Dimitri's needs. Both teachers have been working together to set up Mrs. Tsugawa's portfolio system in her classroom. They decide that Dimitri and several other of her IEP students would benefit from being included in Writer's Workshop with the whole class. Writer's Workshop (like Portfolios) allows the students to work at their own levels, to work cooperatively with their peers, and promotes student responsibility, independence, and self-evaluation.

Ms. Mardi and Mrs. Stroup, the Speech/Language Pathologist, have been interested in working with some of their joint special education students in the regular classroom setting for some time. The three teachers feel that their philosophies about learning and developmental evaluation are similar and they want to try it.

Mrs. Tsugawa is still required to assess her students with the district and state standardized tests and to use district report cards. But the teachers are also eager to see how their developmental evaluation methods compare with traditional assessments. They suspect the alternative assessments will greatly enhance their communication with parents and in fact make it easier to "grade" the students through performance-based outcomes instead of letter grade percentages. Ms. Mardi is excited because this model is compatible with her assessment of Dimitri's needs and his IEP goals and objectives. The teachers meet and plan and schedule the program together.

Portfolio-Supported Inclusion through Writer's Workshop

10:30–10:50 a.m.
Each day Mrs. Tsugawa begins Writer's Workshop by recording "status of the class" (asking the students to identify which stage of the writing process they are working in that day, such as: prewrite PW, drafting D1 or D2, Revision R, Editing E, etc.). She records this on an attendance sheet overhead which takes about 2–4 minutes. With this introduction the students are responsible for identifying their work for the day and she knows immediately who might be ready for a conference. It also identifies who needs to work in the "quiet areas" and who will be revising or editing with friends in the "quiet talking" areas of the room. Then she teaches a mini-lesson, reinforces a skill, or reviews the writing process with the whole group. After the lesson, the students go to work on their writing and portfolios.

10:50–11:30
Ms. Mardi, the LD teacher, joins the class on Mondays, Tuesdays, Wednesdays, and Thursdays. Mrs. Stroup, the Speech & Language teacher, comes in on Mondays and Wednesdays. The specialists and the teacher work with *all* of the students on their

writing (research, organizing information in webs/clusters, paragraphs, revision, editing, reflecting on pieces chosen for their portfolios, etc.). The IEP students are monitored closely. The teachers conference individually with the students on a regular basis. Near the end of each quarter as the students organize their portfolios, the teachers help them prepare for their student-led parent conferences.

Each Wednesday they group the students heterogeneously for Author's Circle. The children choose a writing draft to share and get feedback from their peers and the teachers. The students are regrouped every four to six weeks during the year.

The three teachers cooperatively assess the students throughout the term using authentic measures of both processes and products.

Observation of processes:
- students engaged in the stages of the writing process
- student responses during "Status of the Class"
- student response groups (reflections & peer feedback)
- student reflections during conferences
- student portfolio efforts
- literacy profiles & developmental checklists
- miscue inventories
- surveys & interviews

Assessment of products:
- student portfolio contents
- trait rubric assessment of student writing
- literacy profiles & developmental checklists
- student journals and logs
- classroom designed rubrics to evaluate portfolios as a whole

During common planning times:

The teachers together prepare modified and traditional district report cards and share conferences with the parents of the IEP children. In the winter and spring they hold Portfolio Evening Open Houses.

The teachers meet to plan and evaluate the program at varied times, as their busy schedules allow (before school, just after Writer's Workshop, during lunch, PE or after school.)

All three teachers attended the IEP meetings and any multi-disciplinary team meetings when their students are discussed.

Inclusion of special needs children in language arts, as described above, can be very successful and rewarding for all. The overriding intention is for the specialists to provide assistance, modifications, and support for the IEP students so that they can be fully participating and contributing members of the classroom community. This model additionally benefits the regular education students as well. The three teachers are able to share the responsibility for mini or whole-group lessons. They also share the individual student conferencing, and they learn from each other's expertise. The class as a whole gains from the additional teacher contact, from the cooperative learning with their peers, and from the opportunities to share and get feedback during student-response groups. Everyone gains from the experience of creating portfolios.

The movement toward inclusive education is gaining momentum rapidly. It is not an all-or-nothing concept. There will always be some special needs that require individual attention, but the majority of "learning differences" are being recognized as a normal part of our school (and real-world) societies. It is no longer "OK" to exclude these children from the opportunities their peers enjoy. We special educators can make a significant difference. We are well advised to start small, be creative, be flexible, talk with each other, and see what wonders we can accomplish.

From "Gnawing Dilemma" to "Innovative Opportunities"

Johnston (1990) reminds us that the functional goal for all education is optimal instruction for ALL learners. We need to look toward instruction and assessment in terms of responsibility, rather than accountability. We have the responsibility to provide our students with learning opportunities that are relevant, engaging, and inclusive. We have the responsibility to evaluate our students in such a way as to honor their processes and celebrate their products. We have the responsibility to take great care in making eligibility decisions which will affect these youngsters for the rest of their lives. We have the responsibility to comply with the legal mandate to educate our children, and also to educate the community and policymakers about authentic, relevant schooling. They need to know what we know about the natural learning process.

IDEA was the result of a lengthy, concerted effort by parents advocating for the rights of their special kids. It is in all respects a human rights document. Education and assessment have indeed changed as a result of community pressure and court litigation. If we are really looking for a universal shift in belief about the learning process and the ways we evaluate it, then we need to reframe our thinking so that we are not just coping with the "gnawing dilemma" but instead are welcoming the "innovative opportunities" of educating all kids in holistic and relevant ways.

References

Bartoli, J. & Botel, M. (1988). *Reading/learning disability: An ecological approach.* New York: Teachers College Press, Columbia University.

Federal Register. (1992, September 29). *Individuals with disabilities education act (IDEA), Assistance to states for the education of children with disabilities program.* Department of Education, Vol. 57, #189.

Friend, M. & Cook, L. (1993, November/December). Inclusion. *Instructor.*

Gahagan, Hilary Sumner. (1993). *Portfolios: Assessment that honors student literacy: An educator's handbook.* Portland, Oregon: Gahagan & Sumner Associates.

Goodman, K.S., Goodman, Y.M., & Hood, W.J. (1989). *The whole language evaluation book.* Portsmouth, NH: Heinemann.

Goodman, Y.M. (1978). Kid-watching: An alternative to testing. *National Elementary School Principal, 57*(4): 41–45.

Goodman, Y.M., Watson, D.J., & Burke, C.L. (1987). *Reading miscue inventory: Alternative procedures.* New York: Richard C. Owen Publishers, Inc.

Graves, D. (1990). International Reading Association Convention, Atlanta, Georgia.

Hasselriis, P. (1982, January). IEPs and a whole language model of language arts. *Topics in Learning and Learning Disabilities,* 17–21.

Johnston, P. (1990). International Reading Association Convention, Atlanta, Georgia.

Johnston, P. (1987). Teachers as evaluation experts. *The Reading Teacher, 40,* 744–748.

Jongsma, K.S. (1989). Portfolio assessment. *The Reading Teacher,* 43(3), 264–265.

Paulson, L., Paulson, P., & Meyer, C. (1991, February). What makes a portfolio a portfolio? *Educational Leadership.*

Poplin, M. (1988). The reductionist fallacy in learning disabilities: Replicating the past by reducing the present. *Journal of Learning Disabilities, 21*(7): 389–400.

Poplin, M. (1985). Reductionism from the medical model to the classroom: The past, present and future of learning disabilities, *Research Communications in Psychology, Psychiatry, and Behavior, 10* (1, 2): 37–70.

Rhodes, L. & Dudley-Marling, C. (1988). *A holistic approach to teaching learning disabled and remedial students.* Portsmouth, NH: Heinemann.

Salvia, J. & Ysseldyke, J.E. (1985). *Assessment in special and remedial education* (3rd ed.). Boston, Mass.: Houghton Mifflin Co.

Sumner, Hilary M. (1993). Portfolio assessment: The grading debate intensifies. *Northwest Journal,* Oregon Reading Association.

U.S. Department of Education, Office of Special Education. (1980, May 23). *Individualized education programs (IEPs).* OSE Policy Paper.

U.S.O.E. (1977, December 29). *Assistance to states for education of handicapped children: Procedures for evaluating specific learning disabilities.* Federal Register, 42.

Valencia, S. (1990). A portfolio approach to classroom reading assessment: The whys, whats and hows. *The Reading Teacher, 43*(4), 338–340.

Chapter 9

Assessment and Evaluation in Bilingual and Multicultural Classrooms

Dorothy King

Overview

Whole language multicultural and bilingual classrooms are rich environments in which students and teachers learn from one another. The attitudes of whole language teachers, including sensitivity to individual differences and joy in diversity, are critical to effective multicultural and bilingual programs. The principles and forms of evaluation and assessment that one finds in whole language classrooms apply to multicultural and bilingual classrooms. Evaluation is intentional and expansive to help teachers, students, and the community facilitate learning as curriculum is created to take into account variations in interactional, communication, and behavioral standards.

Tomacita is five years old and attends a bilingual/biliteracy school in the Navajo Nation. One morning her mother called the teacher aside and told this story:

> As Tomacita ate with her family, she spied a jar of dill pickles on the table and asked what they were. Her uncle told her that the jar contained prairie dog. Tomacita had seen many prairie dogs and protested that the jar did not contain prairie dogs. Her uncle told her that when prairie dog is cut up, salted and preserved, it looks like that. Tomacita tentatively conceded. When the label was turned toward her

she said, "Oh, dlóó," and pointed to the word "dill" with satisfaction. (Dlóó is the Navajo word for prairie dog.)

When Tomacita's teacher heard this story, he was thrilled. He had been working very closely with the parents of the children in his class so that they would be able to recognize the evidences of their children's literacy learning. He was happy to add this incident to Tomacita's evaluation folder as an example of Tomacita's growing awareness of print. Tomacita's response was a perfect example of a reader getting meaning and then looking to the print to confirm that meaning. She demonstrated that she expects print to make sense in its context (Harste, Woodward and Burke, 1984).

> During recess, the student teacher talked to Devon about ways to make the playground safer. When the kindergartners gathered for a class meeting after recess, she called on Devon. "What would you do to make the playground safer, Devon?" Devon sat and looked at the floor. She asked again and he remained silent. The teacher smiled and said, "Let's get into groups and talk about what we can do to make the playground safer." The children got into their current teams and started talking. Devon talked quietly with the others. Later the groups presented their ideas and Devon was the reporter for his group.

The teacher explained to the student teacher that Devon's family held traditional ideas about behavior and that Devon would do nothing intentionally to call attention to himself as an individual; he would be quiet, reserved, and anonymous. At five and a half, Devon is already concerned that he be part of his larger society. Among his Navajo classmates, Devon's behavior is appropriate. The teacher and student teacher began to evaluate the classroom environment and their plans for the year to specifically include experiences that would help the kinder-gartners realize that the larger culture values behaviors that may differ from their own.

Like all whole language teachers, Tomacita and Devon's teacher is a dedicated and proficient kidwatcher (Goodman, 1978), fascinated by his students' language and social learning and eager to learn from his students. Most of his students begin schooling with Navajo as their first language or with Navajo English as their predominant dialect and they come from families that have traditional Navajo values and standards of conduct. As they learn to speak and read and write in English and Navajo, and as they learn about other ways of social interaction, he finds many things to be excited about. Collecting language stories and behavior anecdotes is a vital and integral part of the ongoing evaluation which whole language multicultural and multilingual teachers use to inform the curriculum they and their students create. Whole language accepts learners and builds on their strengths.

Ken Goodman (1986) summarizes these teachers' beliefs and goals for their classrooms:

> Schools should build on the language development children have attained before they start school, and on the experiences they have outside school. Whole language programs respect the learners: who they are, where they come from, how they talk, what they read, and what experiences they already had before coming to school. That way there are no disadvantaged children as far as the school is concerned. There are only children who have unique backgrounds of language and experience, who have learned to learn from their own experiences, and who will continue to do so if schools recognize who and where they are. (p. 10)

Bilingual and Multicultural Classrooms

The United States has a long history of trying to assimilate and homogenize its peoples; the "melting pot" metaphor is a familiar one. Recently a general, though not unopposed, attitudinal change toward recognizing the fundamental values of cultural and linguistic diversity has occurred. This change is partly responsible for legislative and funding support for bilingual and multicultural programs.

The term bilingual simply means "being able to speak two languages." Programs labeled "bilingual" in schools show a great variety. Bilingual may mean that the language of instruction or the language favored for instruction is different than the students' first language. Some classes begin instruction in the first language while teaching another language and by the middle grades phase the first language out of instruction. Other classes and schools may support the first language by conducting part of daily instruction in the first language or by supplementing the language of instruction with explanations of concepts in the first language. Some schools have the goal of having all students proficient in two languages (Zintz and Maggart, 1984; Tenorio, 1990). Because of the relationship of language and culture, bilingual classes should be multicultural, though in practice some are not.

Multicultural classrooms are those in which a conscious effort is made to make the cultures of the students an integral part of instruction, and to promote understanding, appreciation, and acceptance of cultural differences. Multicultural education is based on the unwavering belief that all people's social, ethnic, cultural, and religious backgrounds are valid and of value. Multicultural education is predicated on the concept that all learners can be enriched by perceiving different ways of viewing the world. There is no inferiority or superiority of language or people; there is appreciation of diversity.

Multicultural classrooms show infinite variety. A multicultural class may consist of a teacher and students from mainstream culture and one student from Viet Nam; it may consist of a majority of students from diverse cultures from many parts of the world; or the teacher may be the class member who is from the divergent culture.

Monocultural classes — those in which students are seemingly homogeneous in terms of culture — may also be multicultural if instruction has a pluralistic focus.

If all the subcultures of any country are taken into account, then all classes could be considered multicultural.

Language and Culture

The system of a language reflects the entire culture of the people who create and use it. Language reflects the interpretation and perceived relationships of phenomena and experience for members of that culture. Culture defines ways of feeling, thinking, and behaving. It provides the concepts for determining and shaping the view of the world that the people in that culture hold. Cultural differences in language practices represent very different ways of understanding the world and human beings' place in it. Culture defines what is logical, what is reasonable, what is appropriate, what is true. Language reflects all these (King and Goodman, 1990).

Children learn the rules of the language(s) around them without explicit instruction. They learn the language and the cultural rules for use of that language because they have a need to communicate in various settings and for various purposes. Immersion in language settings that provide for real and authentic transactions among language users fosters the intense and personal involvement in language use necessary for language learning.

This authentic language use — in a child's first, developing, and other languages — is a strength of whole language bilingual and multicultural classrooms. The ways people use oral and written language are inextricably bound up with patterns of cultural belief and conceptual principles characteristic of their culture (Heath, 1983). Multicultural classrooms display a variety of learning activities meant to build on diverse learning styles and patterns of social interaction. All languages are accepted as legitimate for instruction and learning, for creating and expressing meaning. The classrooms capitalize on research findings that academic and linguistic gains are made when curriculum integrates and expands the languages and experiences of learners (Tikunoff, 1984).

Evaluation and Whole Language Bilingual and Multicultural Classrooms

Evaluation and assessment in whole language multicultural and bi- or multilingual classrooms serve the same purpose they do in whole language classrooms that do not have the designation. Evaluation and assessment help students and teachers plan how to learn and to find out if they are accomplishing what they want. Evaluation is an integral part of the curricular and decision-making process.

As in other whole language classrooms, evaluation in multicultural and bilingual classrooms is intentional. Teachers, students, and the community are consciously aware of what they are doing and why they are doing it. They observe, analyze, and make decisions based on knowledge of themselves in particular and of learners in general. Learners are evaluated in real situations during authentic acts. Because the acts are authentic, the language chosen by the learner is valued and its use becomes a part of evaluation.

The Importance of Whole Language Evaluation to Linguistically and Culturally Diverse Learners

Misleading and inaccurate ideas about linguistically and culturally diverse learners have dominated educational thinking because these learners have not been dealt with fairly. They have been asked to play in games for which they do not know the rules. They have been judged by standards that make no sense to them. As a result they have been labeled "disadvantaged" or "deficient" or a number of other labels which say "You don't fit; you can't make it." A situation in which one is considered inferior, where self-confidence is threatened, where one is expected to perform "correctly" without the requisite linguistic and cultural knowledge, can hardly be supportive of learning.

Phenomena and practices that occur in non-whole language classrooms and lead to false pictures of students' abilities and performance are precluded by the very nature of a whole language classroom. These phenomena have to do with teacher attitude, school and classroom climate, instructional practices, and the kind and purpose of evaluation used.

Teacher Attitude

Whole language teachers believe in learners and in every learner's ability to learn language and behavior in accordance with what he needs and wants to learn. They understand that the intent to learn is always determined by the learner (Smith, Goodman, and Meredith, 1976). They view their task as helping the learner decide to learn by providing contexts in which learning is useful and meaningful. They also respect the learner's decision about whether something is useful to learn at any particular time; learners may offer alternatives. For learners of diverse language and culture, the faith in their ability to learn and succeed and regard for the time it may take to understand the usefulness of learning something are important considerations.

Whole language teachers understand the relationship of language, culture, and development. They are committed to appreciating cultures and understanding them at more than a surface level. They know that culture is far more than how groups dress, the words they use, their recipes, or their ways of acting. They actively seek to ready themselves for how students think and perceive the world. Teachers who have this kind of motivation will be avid consumers of research about specific cultures; they will read autobiographies and biographies of people from cultures with which they interact; they will read literature from the culture; they will be careful observers and questioners of learners' reactions and interactional patterns, and their questioning will be based on the belief that behavior is purposeful and reasonable; they will study perspective-perceptual sources such as music, poetry, literature, religion, folklore, and other cultural expressions (Gold, Grant, and Rivlin, 1977). Because whole language classrooms operate as part of the larger community outside the school, teachers will learn from their natural participation with community people in their cultural value systems and socializations. Teachers will observe colleagues who are successful in multicultural settings and note body language, attitudes, and rapport-building procedures used (Zukowski/Faust, 1988).

Whole language teachers have made a conscious commitment not to diminish existing ways of knowing or explaining. They know that the farther a teacher is from the culture of the students, the more alert and sensitive she or he must be.

Whole language teachers interpret the agenda of the wider culture to students and, at the same time, support the ways of knowing and the knowledge which are already valuable to the learners. They are constantly sensitive to the need of all people to maintain their home language and an identity with their community, its history, and aspirations. Teachers are committed to finding out about their students' ways of viewing so that they can better understand them and so that they can help their students expand their perceptions and views of the world to include those of other cultures, including that of the larger general society.

Whole language teachers value the languages learners use, accept their use of all their languages in learning, and actively support efforts for learners to become more proficient in all chosen languages.

Because of whole language teachers' sensitivity to culture and individual beliefs, the phenomenon called "cultural discontinuity" (Garcia, 1988) is less likely to occur. Discontinuity occurs when experiences in schooling and classrooms do not accommodate or are not compatible with cultural backgrounds of students. For example, children from communal cultures of the South Pacific are likely to find that the idea of earning money for individual material gain is incongruous with what they know about social relationships and their idea of "goodness" in people (LeSourd, 1990). Children from Puerto Rican backgrounds may have difficulty accepting mainstream American society's preoccupation with systems and organization because their culture places paramount value on human relationships (Gold, Grant, and Rivlin, 1977). Whole language teachers evaluate responses in light of cultural understandings.

Zukowski/Faust (1988), Hall (1989), and others discuss several areas in which diverse perceptions and interactions may be apparent. These include:

- time; pacing; emphasis on past, present, and future
- self-reliance, independence, and competitiveness
- voice level and non-verbal communication
- directness of communication
- standards of conduct
- personal space
- authority, control, and power

Consideration of each of these phenomena and patterns will help make evaluation more accurate.

School and Classroom Climate

In whole language bilingual and multicultural classrooms differences among learners are valued; diversity of background is viewed as an asset and as a powerfully enriching resource for all class members. Language and experience are accepted and used as the bases for learning. Accommodation and understanding of all learning and social interaction styles is a goal. Because classrooms may consist of learners from several different backgrounds who vary widely in terms of perceptions, whole language teachers and students may start out by mutually developing rules which will allow them to work together and learn about each other. These rules are developed initially with the understanding that as class participants learn more about each other, the rules will change or be interpreted to be as compatible as possible with all the cultures represented in the class. An attitude that "we are all different, but the differences among us are what make us interesting" is established (Zukowski/Faust, 1988). The intellectual and social advantages of multilingualism (Diaz, 1990) are continuously presented, discussed, and demonstrated as development in all of a learner's languages is fostered.

The classroom community is tied to the larger communities from which students come. In this way, the artificial differences in learning in school and out of school are reduced. Barrera (1992), among others, has emphasized that for learning to occur in bilingual classrooms, it must relate to the real cultures in which learners live every day.

Community resources and people are an integral part in instruction and evaluation. For example, Lucia's grandparents returned from a month's visit to relatives in Palermo, and were invited by the seventh grade to talk about their visit and the similarities and differences they perceived in the "old country" Italian community and their own Italian-American community. Several students decided to do sociological studies and their grandparents were involved in the projects.

When communities are part of education, then the resources for cultural understanding and for learning and evaluation are multiplied. Community members can provide insights into behavior and interaction and language use, as well as be sources for materials in first languages. They may also act as advocates for a school's securing first-language materials for the library and classrooms.

Part of the integration of culture into evaluation involves the recognition of various standards of child development within the cultures from which students come. Different cultures focus differently on developmental characteristics according to what the culture values. Children from cultures which emphasize cooperation, communalism, and mutual aid — for example, those from African-descent cultures — conform to different expectations than children from cultures which stress individualism (Gold, Grant, and Rivlin, 1977). Whole language evaluation takes into account the different views of what is considered "normal" for different cultures.

Instructional Practices

Evaluation and instruction are inextricable. For too long linguistically and culturally diverse students have been subjected to instruction in which they have had little chance of success. Knapp and Shields (1990) raise questions about the value and appropriateness of the instruction which many linguistically and culturally diverse children receive, for example, skills-based, sequentially ordered, teacher controlled. MacDonald, Adelman, Kushner, and Walker (1982) point to "a largely behaviorist pedagogy [in which] language is divorced from its cultural contexts of meaning and use, componentized and taught as abstraction. This is arguably the most difficult way yet devised to promote literacy and the least responsive to the student's cultural resources."

When a language is destroyed it becomes harder for anyone to learn it. It is especially hard for learners from cultures and languages that are different from a language being learned because these learners don't have the background to guess at what the pieces could mean. Fragmented language is without meaning. Unable to deal with the meaninglessness of their instruction, many children are considered to be deficient. In a whole language bilingual or multicultural classroom, the competence of learners is already accepted and the environment supports, respects, and builds on the language and experience learners have.

When learners are evaluated in environments in which there are multiple opportunities to express ideas in a variety of ways and time is provided to work on a variety of topics for many purposes, to reflect on ideas, express feelings, present information, entertain with a story or dance or drawing, narrate events, and express opinions to a variety of audiences, their learning is obvious (Rigg and Enright, 1986; Franklin et al., 1989).

Purpose and Kinds of Evaluation

Whole language strives to make evaluation fit the learner, not to make the learner fit a preconceived evaluation model. For this reason, evaluation is purposeful in facilitating learning and it exists to help learners as they engage in authentic situations and acts. It does not disrupt what is going on, but is an integral part of the ongoing activity and learning. Each language sample or anecdote is viewed from many perspectives.

Evaluation is expansive, not reductionist. Teachers and students seek to expand and get meaning from their actions, not narrow the focus to one particular item. And when different languages and cultures are involved, the rich information used and gained in making evaluations is a learning asset.

A part of this expansiveness includes evaluating the context. Whole language teachers always consider the context of the classroom and look for conditions which may serve to constrain what students and teachers can accomplish. Cultural knowledge of the students is integrated into the evaluation.

Slaughter (1988) suggests that four kinds of context are important to assessment: the physical situation (is it familiar or unfamiliar? is it a group discussion or a one-to-one conference? and so forth), the linguistic and paralinguistic context (how what is expressed relates to what was communicated before and what is yet to be communicated), the social context (the social meaning of the communication, the status and relationship of the speakers, the cultural expectations held for the encounter), and the invisible context (the assumptions of each participant about background information and what is known and shared about the topic).

Because whole language bilingual and multicultural classrooms are part of communities and consider contexts, evaluation takes many forms. Whole language classrooms allow for all kinds of evaluation. For example, some cultures may not emphasize auditory and visual expression; students from these cultures may prefer tactile and kinesthetic presentations of their learning and express themselves better through art than through reading and writing. These expressions of learning are unquestionably valid.

Learners in whole language bilingual and multicultural classrooms have a stake in their own learning. A large part of evaluation is self-evaluation, that is, learners decide if they are doing what they want and if and how to do better. After listening to fellow students discuss a draft of his report on Samoan legends, Aisa decided that he had not communicated what he wanted and revised the organization and language usage so that his points were clear.

Short and Burke's (1991) vision of evaluation as a combination of perspective on learning (who is doing the evaluating — self, collaborative others, or larger society) with what aspect in the process will be evaluated (learner intent, engagement, or artifact) is especially important in multicultural classrooms. Such a schema for evaluation reminds the participants that multiple perspectives and assessments are necessary to learners' success. Evaluation from everyone making up the classroom community or having a stake in it is valued.

A Cautionary Word

Whole language teachers may find that some of their own most cherished stances and approaches are challenged in a bilingual or multicultural classroom. Some behaviors in whole language classrooms may initially upset students from other cultures. For example, whole language teachers see themselves as fellow learners and this stance does not lead to being an authority figure. Some students expect teachers to be authorities and evince obvious leadership in terms of telling others what to do. In another example, students from Japanese backgrounds may have a strong cultural taboo against directly opposing someone else's view (Livingston, 1985), whereas a whole language teacher may genuinely crave thoughtful discussion and questioning, the evidences of the inquiry that results in learning (Watson, Burke, and Harste, 1989). Whole language teachers will accept these differences and willingly work with students so that both teacher and student needs are met.

Some Examples of Evaluation in Bilingual and Multicultural Classes

Evaluation in whole language bilingual and multicultural classrooms will take the same forms as it does in other whole language classrooms. Teachers will use evidence of learning intention, engagement, and artifact in regard to language, content, interaction, and behavior. Evaluation and assessment instruments and procedures mentioned elsewhere in this volume will be used. Always the evaluators (teachers, peers, self, or others) must keep in mind the perceptions and development of the students as they interact and create in the classroom.

The following are examples of evaluation in multicultural and bilingual classrooms. These examples are the authentic evidence that learning is occurring.

Observational Records

Students and teachers may keep track of their language and interactions in a number of ways. One of the basic ways is through anecdotal records.

> 11/2/88   Robin said, "Teacher, I thank you very much from me." I think this is the first time he has used the generic English "you." In his language in Ceylon he would never use a familiar form to a teacher, but would use a formal form of "you" which English doesn't have. He seems to be showing willingness to accept that English doesn't need to express such differences.

> 11/7/89   Carletta and Mary were writing a play. Dorothy (the student intern) was taking dictation. Carletta said, "He be working" and Dorothy wrote "He's working." Carletta said, "Shanelle say he coming" and Dorothy wrote "Shanelle say he coming." Carletta said, "That not right. Spell it right." Dorothy wrote "Shanelle said he's coming." Both Carletta and Mary said, "Alright!! Don't do that no more," and laughed. They demonstrated that they do know Standard English, but in the informal situation prefer their Black dialect. They are proud of their play and want it written in Standard English so that others can read and appreciate it.

It is usually helpful to organize observations. This serves the purpose of helping the evaluator look at the many facets of a particular sample or evidence of learning. One way is to use lists of potential indicators of learning. The following example has proven useful in multicultural and bilingual classrooms.

The "Evaluation of Basic Reading and Writing Processes" was developed by Stephen Kucer (1988) for use in a bilingual (Spanish/English) classroom. Originally intended as a way to help teachers make change — that is, to show that if the evaluation instrument is changed, the curriculum changes to match it — the grid presents a way to organize anecdotal observations as well as keep track of the reading and writing processes which students are using. Below is an excerpt from one such record (see Figure 9.1).

Figure 9.1

Evaluation of Basic Reading and Writing Processes

Student's Name: Marquis   Grade: 6th

Age: 12   Evaluator: M.S.

Writing Processes	Yes	Somewhat	No
1b. Generates and organizes major ideas or concepts.	1/6		
2b. Expands, extends, or elaborates on major ideas or concepts.	1/6 "Home" is good example		
3b. Integrates meaning into a logical and coherent whole.		1/6 starting to take peer advice	
4b. Uses a variety of linguistic cues -- textual, semantic, syntactic, graphophonic.		1/6 see above	
5b. Uses a variety of text aids -- pictures, charts, graphs, sub-headings, etc.			
6b. Uses relevant background knowledge.	1/6		
7b. Predicts/plans upcoming meanings based on what has been previously written.		1/6 see above	

Written Language Samples

Keeping track of written language samples over time can reveal what students are working on in language development and their progress toward standardization and convention. As described elsewhere in this volume, writing samples may be evaluated for sense of story or genre convention, for example, parts of a letter; sense of audience; growth in syntax; and orthographic conventions — spelling, punctuation, spacing, and legibility (TAWL, 1984). Written language samples can also reflect developing other language proficiency.

When asked to tell a story to accompany Tomie DePaola's wordless book *Pancakes for Breakfast* (1978), six-year-old Manny responded "Casa" to the first page of the book, which shows a house in a countryside covered with snow at sunrise. Five months later, Manny wrote a story on blank strips of paper clipped to each page of the same book. Figure 9.2 shows his first page.

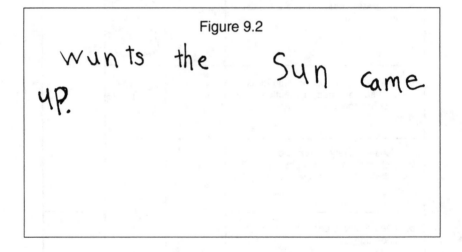

Figure 9.2

wunts the Sun came up.

We know that Manny has developed confidence in English usage, expresses his understanding of story grammar, and is experimenting with graphophonemic relationships in English as he creates a spelling for "once."

In the written conversation between Rafael and his teacher (see Figure 9.3), the teacher noted that when he was in a hurry to convey his ideas and experiences, Rafael preferred his first language. His teacher, who is bilingual, accepted his use of Spanish in genuine conversation and proceeded with the belief that he would soon come to use English with the same proficiency when the situation called for it.

Figure 9.3

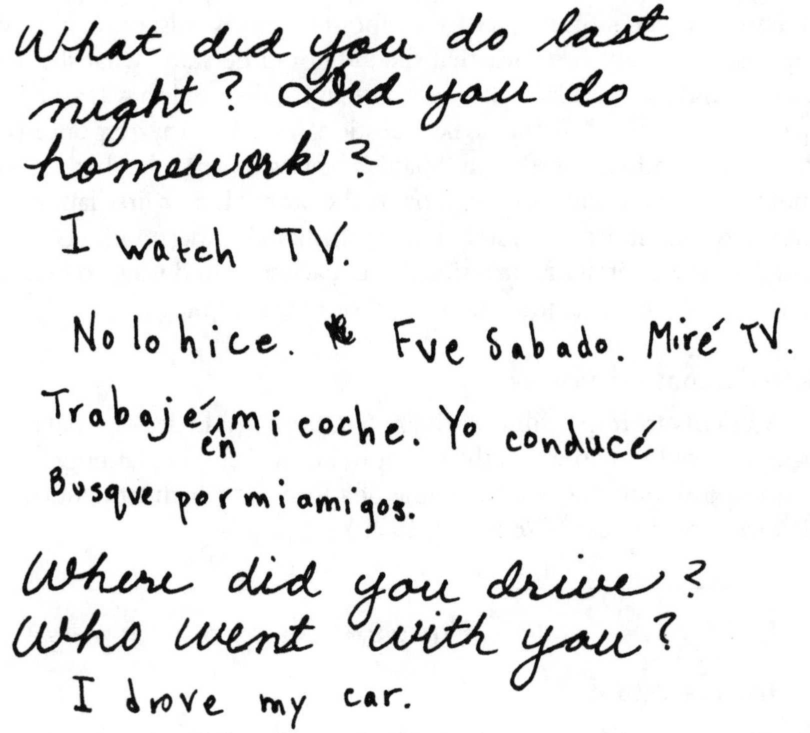

What did you do last night? Did you do homework?

I watch TV.

No lo hice. & Fue Sabado. Miré TV.

Trabajé en mi coche. Yo conducé

Busqve por mi amigos.

Where did you drive?
Who went with you?

I drove my car.

Retellings in First Languages

In addition to the miscue analyses, reader profiles, and interviews described elsewhere in this volume, teachers in bilingual classrooms will take advantage of their students' multilingualism to check on reading proficiency.

A very useful way to check on readers' understandings of what they are reading (and to evaluate classroom procedures) is to allow students to retell or respond to questions and probes in a their first languages. Moll and Diaz (1987) report that readers who are multilingual frequently understand more of what is read or heard in English than they can retell in English.

When readers are permitted to do retellings in their first language, their comprehension of a story may be more accurately reflected. For example, after a reading lesson in English, one of the students, Sylvia, was asked to respond to the question of why the children in the story thought a classmate was lost. Responding in English, Sylvia gave a brief, hesitant, rather confused response of about twenty words. From observing this, one might conclude that she did not understand what she had read in English. Right after her response in English, Sylvia was asked in Spanish to respond to the same question. Her lengthy response (of almost a hundred words) in Spanish showed that she had easily understood the events and actions in the story. Using first-language retellings may more accurately reflect students' understandings. The results of these retellings also signal the teacher to find ways to extend first-language abilities into the second or other language.

Self-Evaluation Forms

Students are responsible for their own learning and decide what they want to know and how well they want to know it and of planning what to do next. Figure 9.4 is an example of a form on which students may plan what to do next (Crenshaw, 1990).

Figure 9.4

Today I learned:

_____

_____

I have a question:

_____

_____

I worked on:	Mon	Tue	Wed	Thu	Fri
Math	___	___	___	___	___
Science	___	___	___	___	___
Social Studies	___	___	___	___	___
Reading	___	___	___	___	___
Writing	___	___	___	___	___
Computers	___	___	___	___	___
___	___	___	___	___	___
___	___	___	___	___	___

Summary

Teaching in a whole language bilingual or multicultural classroom is one of the best experiences on earth. It is challenging and the rewards are great. One is constantly alive and alert because there is so much to learn and feel about language, culture, and individual perception. There are always questions to be asked and answered about relationships, teaching, learning and evaluation, and making the world a better place.

References

Barrera, R., Crawford, A., Mimms, J., & Silva, A. (1993). Un pequeno ruido: Libro del maestro. Boston, MA: Houghton Mifflin Co.

Crenshaw, S. (1990). Encouraging students to self-evaluate. Presentation at NCTE Spring Conference, Colorado Springs, CO.

DePaola, T. (1978). Pancakes for breakfast. New York, NY: Harcourt, Brace and Janovich.

Diaz, R. (1990). The intellectual power of bilingualism. *SWCOLT Newsletter, 6*(1), 2–6.

Franklin, L., Franklin, K., Tullie, V., King, D., & O'Brien, K. (1989). Second language learning through writing process. *Journal of Navajo Education, 6*(2), 21–28.

Garcia, R. (1988). The need for bilingual/multicultural Indian education. In J. Reyhner, (Ed.), *Teaching the Indian child.* Billings, MT: Eastern Montana College.

Gold, M., Grant, C., & Rivlin, H. (Eds.). (1977). *In praise of diversity: A resource book for multicultural education.* Washington, DC: Teacher Corps and Association of Teacher Educators.

Goodman, K. (1986). What's whole in whole language? Portsmouth, NH: Heinemann.

Goodman, Y. (1978). Kidwatching: Observing children in the classroom. *Journal of National Elementary Principals, 57*(4), 41–45.

Hall, E.T. (1989). Unstated features of the cultural context of learning. *The Educational Forum, 54*(1), 21–34.

Harste, J., Woodward, V., & Burke, C. (1984). *Language stories and literacy lessons.* Portsmouth, NH: Heinemann.

Heath, S. (1983). *Ways with words: Language, life, and work in communities and classrooms.* Cambridge, MA: Cambridge University Press.

King, D., & Goodman, K. (1990). Whole language: Cherishing learners and their language. *Language, Speech, and Hearing Services in Schools, 21*(4), 221–227.

Knapp, M., & Shields, P. (1990). Reconceiving academic instruction for the children of poverty. *Kappan, 71*(10), 752–758.

Kucer, S. (1988). Evaluation of basic reading and writing processes. Inservice for Nazlini Boarding School, Ganado, AZ.

LeSourd, S.J. (1990). Curriculum development and cultural context. *The Educational Forum, 54*(2), 205–216.

Livingston, M., & Abe, H. (1985). Japanese students and the learning of English: Cultural and other sources of frustration. In S. Johnston & D. Johnson, (Eds.), *Rocky Mountain Regional TESOL '85: A collection of papers.* Phoenix, AZ: AZ-TESOL.

MacDonald, D., Adelman, C., Kushner, S., & Walker, R. (1982). *Bread and dreams: A case study of bilingual schooling in the U.S.A.* CARE Occasional Publication #12. Norwich, England: University of East Anglia, Center for Applied Research in Education.

Moll, L. C., & Diaz, S. (1987). Change as the goal of educational research. *Anthropology and Education Quarterly, 18,* 300–311.

Rigg, P., & Enright, S., (Eds.). (1986). *Children and ESL: Integrating perspectives.* Washington, DC: TESOL.

Short, K., & Burke, C. (1991). *Creating curriculum: Teachers and students as a community of learners.* Portsmouth, NH: Heinemann.

Slaughter, H. (1988). A sociolinguistic paradigm for bilingual language proficiency assessment. In J. Fine, (Ed.), *Second language discourse: A textbook of current research.* Norwood, NJ: Ablex.

Smith, E., Goodman, K., & Meredith, R. (1976). *Language and thinking in school,* 2nd ed. New York, NY: Holt, Rinehart and Winston.

TAWL (Tucsonans Applying Whole Language). (1984). *A kid-watching guide: Evaluation for whole language classrooms.* Tucson, AZ: University of Arizona.

Tenorio, R. (1990). A vision in two languages: Reflections on a two-way bilingual program. *Rethinking Schools, 4*(4), 11–12.

Tikunoff, W. (1984). An emerging description of successful bilingual instruction. Executive Summary of Part I of the *Significant bilingual instructional features studies.* San Francisco, CA: Far West Laboratory.

Watson, D., Burke, C., & Harste, J. (1989). *Whole language: Inquiring voices.* New York, NY: Scholastic.

Zintz, M., & Maggart, Z. (1984). *The reading process: The teacher and the learner,* 4th ed. Dubuque, IA: W.C. Brown.

Zukowski/Faust, J. (1988). The multicultural classroom. *Arizona English Bulletin, 30*(3), 18–22.

Chapter 10

Record Keeping in Whole Language Classrooms

Jean Church

It was 8:30 A.M. Bright paintings, like the sunny September morning, adorned the walls of the kindergarten room. Eyes sparkled from the faces of the lively five- and six-year-olds as they scurried for a place on the carpet close to Mrs. Rogers. She was about to read a story entitled *Cookie's Week*. With each disaster caused by Cookie, the kitten, the kindergartners would laugh. Some of them rolled back with delight and others squealed their predictions of what Cookie would do next. At the end of *Cookie's Week,* cheers and applause arose from the tiny students. Animated conversations followed.

Teacher: What did you like about this book?
Child: I liked Cookie when he knocked over the flower pot.

Teacher: How did you figure out that something would happen each day of the week?
Child: I just knowed after the Monday and Tuesday part. I just thinked it would be that way.

Teacher: How do you think the author got the ideas for this story?
Child: Maybe he has cats.

Teacher: Do you think we could write a story like this?

All the time, Mrs. Rogers referred to the children as such good readers, such good writers, such good thinkers. Ideas poured forth, were talked over, were recorded on the chalkboard. All the time, the students were deciding upon the words to be used, deciding upon how they might be spelled, deciding upon what pictures were needed, and so forth. The classroom just described is a whole language classroom — where

- children really read,
- children make choices about reading and writing,
- children are responsible for learning,
- children develop confidence in their ability to learn,
- children are assumed to be literate and treated as such,
- teachers help and collaborate,
- teachers are learners too,
- teachers and children are excited about learning,
- teachers and children work together to build a community of learners,
- children are immersed in countless opportunities to learn language, learn about language, and learn through language for real purposes.

No doubt readers of the opening paragraphs will agree that learning is taking place, and we agree with Frank Smith (1993) that we don't think children need to be tested or assessed to find out if they are learning. However, until the ideological issues surrounding the nature of teaching and learning are more widely understood, we feel compelled as teachers to seek viable, credible, authentic ways to document student progress over the standardized and behavioristic measures so prevalent in our world. Dillon (1990) sadly acknowledges that there still seems to be a tremendous preoccupation with evaluation as an end in itself rather than as an ongoing, integral part of teaching and learning. And at almost every inservice, workshop, or gathering of teachers, one of the first questions that is asked is, "But how do you grade that?"

Three years ago, when I wrote the last lines of this record keeping chapter, I stated that our story was far from being finished with the close of the chapter, but rather just beginning. What follows with the second edition of this work, is our story — part two. Like a useable portfolio, this chapter has become an ever-changing, continuous representation of our learning. Some of the old chapter remains and some gives way to newly acquired understanding.

As we continue to journey into this new realm of understanding of learning and at the same time take responsibility for representing that learning to our students, our parents, ourselves, our colleagues, and our community, we need to focus on (1) purposes of record keeping, (2) what kinds of records provide needed information and, finally, (3) what needs to be recorded. Evaluation involves two steps. First, collecting data, and second, making value-laden judgments and decisions about all aspects of teaching and learning — process, product, and attitudes.

Purposes of Record Keeping

To present evidence of learning, careful documentation of systematic observations of and interactions with children as they learn language, learn about language, and learn through language must be kept. Records provide the data from which interpretations, value judgments, and evaluations can be derived. Record keeping, assessment, and evaluation can no longer be the sole responsibility of the teacher, but must be a responsibility shared by teachers, students, parents, and administrators. Although the data may be presented in a variety of different ways for a variety of different audiences, it will still be the same data. Therefore, it is important that teachers understand for whom the data is intended and for what purpose it will be used. Record keeping should (1) help students make self-evaluations, (2) construct a history of the learner's development, (3) guide interactions and instruction, and (4) serve as a means to communicate with parents and other stakeholders.

Helps Students Make Self-Evaluation

"The foremost goal of evaluation is self-evaluation, that is, the analysis of our own attitudes and processes so that we can use the information to promote continued growth and learning. The purpose of self-evaluation is the purpose of education — to enable an individual to function independently, intelligently, and productively" (Routman, 1991).

As we have shifted paradigms from a behavioristic model to a model of constructivism, the importance of the learner sharing responsibility for his own learning has become a basic belief undergirding our classroom practice. Often in the past, learners have been left out of the process of record keeping, evaluation, and establishing future learning. The teacher would collect the assignments, mark the errors, return the papers, and go on to the next lesson. Just as we have found it essential, as we change our teaching, to keep asking ourselves, "What are we learning?" it is also essential for the students to continually be challenged to think about and express what they are learning. This helps them begin to build internal standards for judging what constitutes good work.

Constructs a History of the Learner's Literacy Development

Within the traditional orientation to assessment, students were often tested for acquisition of isolated skills. Language was assumed to be learned in a hierarchical, sequential manner. Learning was defined by a score or letter grade on these assessments and students were compared to these predetermined standards. However, with the advent of the notion that learning is an active, constructive process and that literacy emerges over time, it is crucial to collect documentation that describes children's personal understandings of the forms and functions of language and other curricular areas as they go about using language in the classroom. Through such a collection, students, teachers, and parents can reflect on where the learner has been, where the learner is now, and where he or she needs to go.

Guides Interactions and Instruction

When we began to view curriculum as a collaborative, creative, learning-centered process (Short and Burke, 1991) rather than a fixed, static set of materials or topics to be covered, the focus of record keeping became indeed to inform our interactions and our instruction. As we thought across the curriculum about the unit tests, the workbook pages, the reading level placements, the math homework, and so forth, we used to administer, we realized that these were decontextualized fragments of information. They told us nothing about the child's reading strategies; they told us nothing about the processes the child used; they told us nothing about the child's attitude toward reading and writing; they told us nothing about understanding of mathematical concepts or of his or her reasoning ability. In fact, they did little to guide interactions and instruction. For records to be valuable, data must be collected in the context of children using language, science, math, or any other subject of the curriculum. Knowing something means being able to use it in purposeful ways.

Communicates to Parents and Other Stakeholders

Another purpose for selective record keeping is to inform parents and others who have a share in the education of our nation's children. Careful thought must be given to the kinds of data collected and deliberate plans need to be made to include the parents so that all involved will understand and recognize how learning is reported.

Kinds of Records

Brian Cambourne (1988, page 122) states that

> "one continually builds up a store of knowledge about each child's literacy development. In this sense, the teacher becomes like a classical anthropologist. Like an anthropologist, she alternates between participant observer, detached observer, and collector of artifacts. At times she observes the "members of the tribe" from a distance, recording her observations for later analysis. At other times she asks questions of various informants about what they know and think and about the ways they produce their artifacts, all the time recording their responses. Her records become her store of knowledge. From this store of knowledge she tries to construct what reality is for the tribe or culture she's observing. In the case of the teacher building a store of knowledge about literacy development, the reality she is trying to construct is how each one of her pupils' knowledge and skill in literacy and all that it entails is changing and developing over time.

As Cambourne suggests, an anthropologist doesn't just record some events, but records a range and depth of experiences of the culture. Likewise, the teacher and students must view all classroom events as opportunities to sample learning. However, to be effective and manageable, teachers and students must be selective and reflective. Anthony, Johnson, Mickelson, and Preece (1991) suggest there are four categories of data to be considered: observations of process, observations of children's products, classroom measures, and decontextualized measures. The age level of the students and the purposes for the assessments determine the amount of information appropriate in any one of the four areas.

Proceeding from the premise that assessment and evaluation is a shared responsibility, we now understand that record keeping, which had formerly belonged to the domain of the teacher, is carried on by teachers and students with input from parents. "Time that was previously spent on scoring, computing, recording, averaging and justifying grades was now spent collecting, saving, discussing and reflecting upon kids' real work" (Zemelman, Daniels, and Hyde, 1993). Listed below are some examples of records which might be kept by the various participants.

Teacher Records	Student Records	Parent Input
belief statements	reading/writing folders	parent profile
anecdotal records	daybooks/notebooks	parent goal setting
interviews	reading response logs	parent response
conference notes	individual goals and plans	parent observation
status of the class	self-assessments	
teacher journals	portfolios	
	work records and summaries	

In rethinking the keeping of records and the reflection process, we have come to the understanding that this really is an integral part of instruction. As teachers and students confer together, much sharing of information, teaching, and learning takes place. No longer is the majority of record keeping completed after the students have gone home as it was when we primarily viewed our role as that of assignment checker. Even though we have listed several ways in which data can be collected, teachers did not use all these as separate records; for example, some teachers placed conference notes in the anecdotal record, whereas others combined interviews and conference notes. In short, the way in which the teacher organized the classroom heavily influenced the way in which the data was collected and organized.

Belief Statements

Of all the lessons we have learned over the past three years, the primary one is that significant change can come about only when teachers critically examine their belief systems and make sense of their theoretical positions. Unless we understand the differences between the transmission model of learning and the transactional theory, there is danger that portfolios, anecdotal records, conference notes, or any other form generally associated with whole language may become little more than a "basalized" approach to evaluation.

In order to plan for learning and to be confident in their ability to talk to parents and others about their classrooms, some teachers in our district spend time completing a belief statements form (see Figure 10.1). Because one's teaching practices are much like a liquid, in that they take the shape of their belief container, it is important that teachers reflect upon their beliefs about how children learn. Once these beliefs are articulated, then the community or environment, the events or daily instructional happenings, and the ways in which growth is recorded and evaluated will be consistent.

and not even... "I believe this class or this child learn best when... ?

Figure 10.1   Belief Statements

I believe children learn best when...	Because of these beliefs, these learning opportunities occur in our classroom:
• they have time to wonder and to think, ponder and reflect	• blocks of time for students to formulate questions and carry out inquiry
• they have opportunity to collaborate with the teacher and with their peers	• time for students to work together with their peers and with the teacher... conferencing, discussing, sharing
• they are involved in planning the work	
• they are encouraged to take risks to try new things; approximations are expected and respected	• goal setting and planning sessions... sometimes whole class, sometimes individual
• they are actively involved in tasks and encouraged to construct meaning	• regular daily times to read and write about self-selected topics
• they perceive the work as being purposeful and meaningful	• regular times for teacher support... mini-lessons, guided reading and writing, discussion groups, science and math investigations
I believe evaluation:	Therefore progress may be documented by:
• must include the learner	
• is part of curriculum	• anecdotal records
• focuses on process, product, attitudes	• conversations and discussions
• is continuous and ongoing	• notebooks, journals
• uses data collected in context	• work plans and summaries
• uses the learner as the instrument of measurement	• conferences
• serves as a guide for individual and group instruction	• portfolios
	• student-kept records
	• student projects, or presentations

Anecdotal Records

Anecdotal records are dated notations about student behaviors. The purpose is to try to capture the child's literacy development. It is generally descriptive in nature and, by asking the following questions, teachers seek to look at learning from the child's perspective (Taylor, 1990).

What does this child know?

What can this child do?

How does this child use language to gain membership in the classroom?

What control does this child have over oral language? over printed language?

How does this child go about problem solving?

How does this child plan, organize, and go about completing tasks?

What kinds of questions does this child ask? Are they relevant?

How does the child use language (listening, speaking, reading, and writing)?

What kinds of comments or remarks does she or he make while working?

Questions such as those listed above give insights into student behavior in a variety of contexts and contribute to a developing profile of each learner. Over the course of time, other focus questions help teachers record specific kinds of knowledge about the students in their classrooms (Comber, 1991).

What kinds of grammatical conventions does this child use when editing?

Does this child use prediction as a reading strategy?

Does this child demonstrate comprehension through retelling?

Does this child know how to formulate inquiry questions and carry out the gathering of information?

Does this child understand place value?

Does this child record simple observations as a strategy to make sense of science?

Teachers use a variety of techniques to help themselves keep track of all students in their charge — selecting a small group of students to focus on each day, observing for specific behaviors, focusing on evidence that students are using strategies which have been studied. They also use a variety of methods to make quick notations: post-it notes, index cards, clipboards, tabbed notebooks, and so forth.

Interviews

Drawing upon the example of the anthropologist again, the teachers have learned to inquire of the children about their work. They listen for the child's process, his or her line of reasoning. One of the teachers remarked in her own journal that the more she listened, the more she learned about her students. She wrote that her teacher talk had always dominated the classroom, but now she hears the voices of the children. Yetta Goodman (1989) taught us that as we reflect on the learning of the student we can reflect on our own professional development as teachers.

Jane Hansen (1987) and Nancie Atwell (1987) believe that young students as well as those in the middle grades are quite capable of talking about their work and helping to plan their next steps in their language learning. Both researchers used interviews to gain information from children. Questions which Hansen asked the children were:

1. What's something new you've learned to do in writing?

2. What's something you would like to learn so you can be a better writer?

3. What's something new you've learned to do in reading?

4. What's something you would like to learn so you can be a better reader?

Likewise, Atwell conferenced students about their reading and writing by using the following three discussion topics:

1. The main thing they hoped to learn during the grading period.

2. The main thing they did learn.

3. One thing they intend to do because of what they learned.

In the following examples from a fourth grade class, the teacher took the self-evaluation forms of the students and added interpretive comments for the parent. Parents often times look at all the "stuff" but need help from the teacher in understanding what it means. The examples in Figures 10.2 and 10.3 represent the range of Mark Church's fourth

Figure 10.2

Third Quarter Self-Evaluation March 19, 1993	Teacher Response
Name _____ Sarah _____	Sarah's responses show, to a great extent, the amount of reflection she does as a writer... obviously she's made a connection between the time she spends thinking and the quality of the work she produces.
What do you like most about your writing? I like the way I try to explain my stories and the setting of them. I also think that I try to put excitment and slightly scary or funny parts in my stories. I think that parts of stories can be imagined or related to the reader's personal experiences.	
In your opinion, what makes a good writer? A good writer writes for the reader they need to think about what the reader would like or how to make the reader love the story. A writer should make sure that he or she keeps the interest of whoever is reading.	Sarah demonstrates an awareness for her audience. This guides her word choice and is highly valued.
What are some of the things you want to try in your writing this next quarter? I would like to try non-fiction stories or maybe stories with a message. Maybe I'll try writing some poems.	Sarah's writing has been mainly fiction. I'm glad she's branching out to other genres.
What are some new things you've learned lately? I've learned how to make really interesting stories, more interesting than before. I think I'm writing stories more people will like. I've also learned about the history of Indiana and the people that lived here.	She's really learning from the investigations she conducts. She has seen the need for research, not because I have assigned it. The inquiry is within her and the responsibility she demonstrates is quite mature.
What do you want to learn about this next quarter? I want to learn about some historic places in Indiana, and maybe about endangered animals.	Mr. Church

Figure 10.3

Third Quarter Self-Evaluation March 19, 1993	Teacher Response
Name ~~RoBeRt~~	Robert has advanced in his maturity as can be seen by his responses. He no longer speaks in general terms, but can identify specific details about the quality of his work. Robert's desire to produce writing which has a "point" or a "moral" is valued. This shows he is beginning to use higher order thinking.
What do you like most about your writing? THey HaVe a PoN't a MoRal	
In your opinion, what makes a good writer? SomewonWoh Can Get a adeints	Robert is aware of audience, thus he must consider himself a writer. Isn't that exactly what we want from him?
What are some of the things you want to try in your writing this next quarter? NeW StoPPy Fonny storry	
What are some new things you've learned lately? math art music Stience	Robert has some general direction as to where he wants to go with his learning. I'll continue to lead him as needed. I was especially pleased with the work he did on his play. He is definitely improving
What do you want to learn about this next quarter? a lof lieKHOWTHesun rotat around THe earth	mr. Church

grade class, yet they demonstrate the fact that children of all abilities can reflect on their work and participate fully in a reading/writing classroom. Statements by the teacher demonstrate how one can focus on the growth of each child and give the parent a perspective of the child's work.

As we continue to consider the many aspects of assessment, the field of mathematics has greatly contributed to our use of interviews. Marilyn Burns (1992) has taught us to probe for children's understanding by asking:

Why do you think that?

Why does that make sense to you?

Can you explain that?

Writing is being used more and more in our math classes for students to explain their thinking. We have found *Mathematics Assessment, Myths, Models, Good Questions and Practical Suggestions* (NCTM, 1991) to be a valuable source for learning how to keep more authentic records in this area.

Conference Notes

With the abandonment of the three reading group model, reading and writing conferences take place on a regular basis. As the student conferences with the teacher about his reading, writing, or content area project, the teacher makes notes. Most of the teachers add these conference pages to the student's section in the anecdotal record notebook. Included here is an example of one of the reading conference forms used (see Figure 10.4). Depending upon the level of the students and the objectives of the teacher, the specific indicators varied.

In addition to individual conferences, teachers often keep notes on literature discussion sessions. Small groups of children read the same book or piece and then discuss it. One of our fourth grade teachers, in an attempt to include the learners in curriculum planning and to develop responsibility, discusses with his class at the beginning of the year the nature and purpose of the book clubs. He simply asked the students, "Why do we have reading in school?" After the initial silence, since they had never considered this before, the students agreed that it was so they would become better readers. Next, the teacher asked, "How do you get to be a better reader?" The teacher charted all the suggestions and added his guidance.

Figure 10.4   Conference Notes

Name _____   Date _____

Title of Piece_____   Type of Piece _____

Attitudes/Interests/Background

Comprehension

Fictional Text
• main ideas
• details
• setting
• characters
• inferences

Informational Text
• facts
• concepts
• vocabulary

Strategies Used

Further reading or extension project

Student suggestions:
    We get better by...
    • reading faster.
    • knowing more words.
    • understanding what the
      story is about.
    • remembering when one book
      is like another.
    • reading different kinds of stuff.
    • knowing stuff the author
      just meant.

Teacher's responses:
    Teachers call that...
    • fluency.
    • vocabulary study.
    • comprehension.

    • comparison.

    • genre study.
    • inferential thinking.

Next the teacher asked, "Alright, if we have book clubs in this class, what kinds of things will you do in your groups to let me know that you are getting better at reading?"

Student suggestions:
    We can...
    • write down new words and use them when you listen and in our
      writing.
    • talk about how this story is like another.
    • talk about parts of the book we don't understand.
    • try to write like the author in our own writing.
    • can practice reading.

In this way the students "owned" the literature circles and were part of the goal setting. They were also better able to discuss their growth in reading ability. Figure 10.5 is an example of a book discussion form teachers use while listening to student discussion groups. Of course teachers change the elements at the top to help them focus on specific strategies or indicators which they and the students have been studying.

In our classes, the lines that once separated reading and writing have now blurred. From Shelley Harwayne's (1992) work, we began to learn about the power of using literature in the writing workshop. She inspired us to become passionate about literature, to implement writer's notebooks (for ourselves and our students), to rethink our use of mini-lessons, and to use authors and ourselves as mentors. But most of all, her work has encouraged us that the best conferences are those where we listen and respond in wise and gentle ways. In helping students become

Figure 10.5   Book Discussion Notes

Title of Book _____ Date _____

Student Names:

Comments: (Record student responses which indicate ability to elaborate, justify, explain, communicate, or express feelings.)

writers, conferencing is done sometimes with whole-class discussions. At other times conferencing is offered in small-group settings and at still other times in one-on-one settings.

As teachers in our district struggled to develop a global understanding of how to help kids become better writers, we considered how we might improve at (a) observing for writing growth, (b) planning mini-lessons or topics for study, and (c) promoting growing control over conventions.

Observing for Writing Growth

Teachers began actually looking at young children's writing to establish a broad framework or continuum from scribbling (preconventional) through more fluent behaviors. They examined how they organized the school day. How many opportunities really were afforded the children to use writing for authentic and expressive purposes? Using notes, cards, letters, recording thoughts, making lists, modeling by the teacher, committee work, and so forth were all deliberately planned. For example, one of the kindergarten teachers formed research committees. She talked with the children about the fact that in school much of what we do is to find out about things. During work time, those who signed up for the "cat" committee met. Questions such as what do we know about cats, what do we want to find out, where can we find that information, and how can we share our learnings formed the framework for the pint-sized researchers. Classroom work such as this yields rich examples of authentic student reading and writing and helps teachers build a framework of writing growth.

classroom time for research committees [handwritten margin note]

Planning for Mini-Lessons or Topic Study

Harwayne (1992) has helped us to rethink purposes for direct instruction in supporting developing writers. She has helped us come to expand the notion of mini-lessons from that of giving short little lectures on procedures, mechanics, technique, or style to that of using writing as a way of thinking, learning, working, and living. We think about our demonstrations of the options and techniques we want kids to try. We carefully consider when to step in, when to offer direction, or when to allow the students to struggle.

We now actively seek literature which demonstrates those techniques we want kids to experience, such as:

effective use of language — imagery, metaphor, simili, personifi-
cation, alliteration, idioms, mood, feeling, tone, symbolism,
irony, etc.

techniques — flashbacks, repetitions, foreshadowing, dialog,
rhyme, satire, etc.

story elements — plot, setting, characterization, theme, conflict,
climax, resolution, etc.

genre — folktale, fable, myth, biography, short story, novel, etc.

types of writing — narrative, expository, persuasion, etc.

In this way we, ourselves, become better readers and writers and plan for
longer periods of study and experience with these topics.

Promoting Growth in Conventions

In helping children gain control over conventions, our teachers have
agreed that the most critical of Brian Cambourne's (1989) conditions
for learning — assuming that countless demonstrations are a natural part
of the classroom — would be that of responsibility and use. Figure 10.6
is an example of a form used by some of our upper grade teachers.

Pat Bringman's second graders keep daily learning notebooks across
the curriculum. In an effort to help children gain control over conventional spelling, she has the students keep responsibility statements in
their notebooks. Since the purpose for spelling is written communication, it is important that children in the elementary school learn to use
conventional spelling for high frequency writing words, learn to use
knowledge of phonics to approximate words not frequently written, and
learn to find conventional spellings of unknown words when the piece
is for written communication.

Dear Mrs. Bringman,

    I am responsible for the high frequency writing words that I have
highlighted on the list. I can spell these words without having to even
think about them. You will find them spelled correctly in all my written
work, first draft or final copy. These are my personal words that I can
spell correctly.

Date_____

Signature_____

These second graders have responsibility for selecting their specific
words, as well as how many words they want to become responsible for.
Pat works very hard at helping the children understand that the goal is

Figure 10.6   Author's Considerations

Name _____ Date_____

Title of your piece _____

Type of writing _____

Directions: Read your piece and think about each area listed below. Make notes for items you need to rethink or revise in your work. When you are satisfied that your piece is ready for final copy, place it along with this sheet in the final file.

Meaning/Content	Notes
Does your writing make sense? Have you used clear expression? Are your ideas fully developed? Are all your ideas relevant to the topic? How have you tried to make your writing interesting to your readers?	
Structure Is your piece organized? Do all ideas fit together? Is the sequence logical and does it build? Does it have a beginning, middle, and end?	
Conventions Spelling Punctuation Grammar Vocabulary use Penmanship	

for these words to really become automatic for them and not to have big long lists of words that they spell right once on a test, but then don't use in written work. The rigor in this type of spelling program is in the writing program and not in memorizing for spelling tests.

Many of our teachers use the forms found in *Literacy Assessment: A Handbook of Instruments*, edited by Lynn K. Rhodes (1993).

Status of the Class Check

Even our primary teachers have found Nancie Atwell's (1987) status of the class check helps students focus on the work period with a plan (see Figure 10.7). Pat Bringman's second graders utilize the media center as a natural extension of the classroom. No longer are her students scheduled in the media center for a once-a-week session on library skills in isolation, but they are continually in and out searching for information for their work. One requirement, however, is that during the status of the class check, they need to state what they are working on and how the media center would be the most appropriate place to accomplish their goals. Pat reports that occasionally students go just to browse. Since she often browses in libraries and bookstores, she counts this as valued behavior.

Figure 10.7   Status Of The Class Check

Date _____

Student Names:	Plans for the Day	Materials or Resource Persons Needed	Comments
Sarah	*Continue work on River City Gazette (Newspaper project)*	• *Working with Mardee and Michele* • *Will interview local historian*	*Girls are well planned and focused. Check on interview questions.*
Jason	*Starting research on fishing industry*	*Will need to go to media center*	
Michele	*See notes on Sarah*		*Make sure Michele gets opportunity to call Mrs. Clark to set up interview.*

Tim Moss regularly uses this technique to keep track of his students and to help them focus their work period. Tim says the comment column helps him focus himself during the work period as well as sometimes serves as an anecdotal record. Tim has been experimenting with making weekly status of the class checks and then having the students reflect and summarize their work at the end of the week.

Teacher Journals

Recently when Don Graves spent some time with us, he inspired us to write daily for ourselves, to develop our own literacy. Daily reading and writing needs to be a lifestyle for us. Then when we show this to children, it becomes an authentic literacy lesson. The teachers and principal at one school involved in a grant project to study our Wabash River have begun to keep personal daybooks. On a daily basis, the teachers and principal try to capture thoughts, perceptions, images, insights into the teaching/learning situation, things they would like to learn, and so forth.

Goals for this project were (1) teachers and principals would learn more about collaboration among teachers, administrators, students, parents, and community members; (2) they would learn more about how a guided research or theme project could form the basis of student/ teacher work rather than work organized by traditional subject areas or disciplines; and (3) they would learn more about working with children in multi-aged, multi-ability grouped settings. In addition to these project goals, each staff member was to generate some personal goals. At the end of the project, the staff selected pieces from their journals that demonstrated their learnings about each of the goals.

At first, it almost seemed an additional chore that had to be done. However, within a few weeks, the teachers were amazed at how much broader they seemed to view the classroom, their own lives, and the world. One teacher commented that "it feels good to look at that log book. It represents my work and my learning. It's great to hold learning in your hands."

Writing and Reading Folders

Collections of student writing are kept by the children. Patterned after the work of Graves (1982) and Harste (1988), they contain all the pieces the children are working on. In the case of our emerging authors, much of their work is completed in one or two writing sessions. However, these young learners are quite capable of stamping the date on the piece with their teacher's date stamp and filing them under their own names arranged alphabetically. By keeping track of the date stamped on the work, it becomes apparent that a pattern of growth emerges over the course of the year. Older students might have several pieces in progress, but they too need to be able to see their own growing control over the form and function of written language.

Students keep track of the reading they are doing. Sometimes this is merely recorded on a reading log (see Figure 10.8); at other times written responses might be collected in a folder. Many of the intermediate teachers write letters back and forth with the students about their reading (Atwell, 1987). The letter has proven to be a natural way in which the teachers and students can carry on book conversations. In the early primary grades, the students generally just keep track of the books they are reading and make simple comments or recommendations.

Figure 10.8   Reading Log

Name _____

Name of Book/ Article/Poem	Date Started	Comments or Recommendations	Date Completed

Portfolios

From their reading and writing folders, students are asked to build a portfolio that represents their learning. Much of what we know about portfolios as documentation of the learner's knowledge can be attributed to Donald Graves during his time with us and through the writings of others (Routman, 1991; Tierney, Carter, Desai, 1991; Graves and Sunstein, 1992). He helped us to view the portfolio as an ongoing, ever-changing artifact as the students pass from one layer of learning into the next. The basic assumption is that the student selects those examples that best demonstrate his learning, his knowledge, and his growing control over language.

In selecting material for their portfolios in the river grant project, the teachers and students decided that their selected pieces should be related to their personal goals, as well as those of the project. In some cases, the students wanted to present their learnings in the form of a media presentation; others wanted to include their art work; and still others had constructed some models of bridges, barges, and paddleboats and wanted to include those. It was finally agreed that "artifacts" as well as written documentation would be appropriate.

Some of the goals for the project included that

- students would become familiar with real, fictional, or legendary river characters
- students would gain familiarity with historical figures of our Wabash Valley
- students would build an understanding of the importance of the river in the settlement of the valley
- students would become familiar with art and music that pertains to rivers
- students would gain an understanding of environmental concerns.

Examples of what students and teachers might select for the portfolio based upon these goals could include

- samples of questions prepared to interview the city's mayor pertaining to the future plans for the river and the final text of the interview along with the student's comments
- a script written for an historical drama about the establishment of Fort Harrison, along with bibliographies of resources used

- drawings and paintings done at the river
- a musical presentation using dulcimers and other early instruments
- original folktales written by the students, including draft copies
- a full dress portrayal of Mark Twain, written material compiled by the student
- a videotape documentary pertaining to environmental concerns about the pesticides being used in the watershed
- constructions of model bridges, boats, or barges, along with the plans for the constructions and the procedures
- maps and charts made of the Native Americans of the area.

As we presented, displayed, explained and shared our learnings with the parents and interested persons in the community, we felt that they did indeed receive us as learners. The teachers expressed the need to continue to work with this kind of data as an alternative to the traditional methods of testing at the end of a unit.

During the time since the river project and a visit with Jane Hansen, portfolios have become more commonplace in our classrooms. Abbi Pell's fourth grade students view their portfolios as a place to demonstrate who they are as people and as learners. Abbi and her students agree upon some common elements that all students would place in their portfolios over a specified reporting period which would demonstrate achievements in what they are studying in class. For example, it might be agreed that each student would have:

a letter of introduction
class goals for the reporting period → *individual goals too?*
documentation of achievement of goals *Maybe they come*
rationale for selection of artifacts *under)*
audiotape of reading
math task cards
projects
future directions

In addition to these, students are encouraged to place items of special significance to them in the portfolio. At regularly scheduled times, Abbi and her students host a "Portfolio Parent Night."

Parent Profile

As David Dillon (1990) states, "It's also sad seeing educators taking on all the burden of evaluation themselves… when they could be sharing that responsibility with learners and their parents." In our district, when children enter kindergarten, we have parents complete background cards. We had always checked addresses, phone numbers, guardianship, health information, siblings, and so forth, but had not until recently asked about anything that pertained to early literacy development. Figure 10.9 shows our first attempt at seeking parent input and partnership from the beginning of the child's school career.

Figure 10.9

Parent Profile for_____
                                                    Student Name

Date_____

Welcome to our school. Since parents are the first and best teachers the child has, we can learn much from you. Please help us help your child.

Does your child seem interested in school?	☐ Yes	☐ No
Does your child retell stories you have read to him/her?	☐ Yes	☐ No
Does your child show a desire to use written language?	☐ Yes	☐ No
Does your child pretend to write or copy or trace print?	☐ Yes	☐ No
Does your child enjoy music and art?	☐ Yes	☐ No
Would you say your child is willing to try new things?	☐ Yes	☐ No
Does your child respond to environmental print such as signs, labels, etc.?	☐ Yes	☐ No
Do you have a set time for reading to your child? If so, when and about how much time?	☐ Yes	☐ No

_____

Comments:

Parent Goal Setting

At the beginning of the school year, several of our teachers invite the parents to think about and write goals for their children for the year. This inclusion of the parent in goal setting enables us to assure the parents that the children are acquiring those characteristics deemed important by the parents and further shares the responsibility. Across the grade levels, the majority of parents respond with similar goals. Overwhelmingly parents want their children to gain confidence, to learn to work with others, to become responsible, to become problem solvers and thinkers, to become better readers, writers, speakers, and listeners, to develop understanding and facility with mathematical concepts, to learn where to find information, and to enjoy school.

The following example from Tim Moss's second grade demonstrates the thought that parents put into this when teachers genuinely seek parental input (see Figure 10.10).

Figure 10.11 is an example of a parent response sheet for portfolios.

Once again, Dillon (1990) states that he believes that if parents were involved in understanding that viable evidences of literacy learning can be documented, they would perhaps serve as allies with us to influence policymakers as we search for better assessment and evaluation procedures.

What to Record

In our medicalized education system (Taylor, 1990), the typical procedure is to test or check for specific isolated skills and then prescribe the cure. We traditionally examine the learners for what they can't do rather than what they can do. The basic assumption underlying this model is that language learning consists of a series of skills acquired in a linear fashion; therefore, teachers should look for missing parts, supply those, and it will result in reading. But with our shift in philosophy from a fragmented view of language learning to an integrated whole, what to record from our observations of learners becomes a central issue. Like Cambourne and Turbill (1990), we found that what to record became a "value-laden enterprise." What the teachers recorded in their anecdotal records and conference logs was influenced by what they knew and understood about language learning and it changed from one marking period to the next as the teachers built different understandings of learning. This continual change, at first, was uncomfortable. Pat Bringman wrote in her journal that, "just when I think I have a system for marking the students or a routine established, one of the students will do or say

Figure 10.10   Goal Setting
Teacher + Students + Parents

Dear Parents: Please read the goals that your child and I have written for this year. Please think about two or three goals you would like for your child to accomplish in second grade and write them in the parent space below.

Teacher Goals for this Year:

1. The students and I will work together to make our classroom a learning environment where each person is a valued member of our community.
2. We will enjoy reading, writing, singing, and laughing together.
3. We will learn about spelling strategies and become responsible spellers.
4. We will learn about our city, state, country and the world.
5. We will use mathematics to solve many interesting problems.
6. We will investigate science topics and health issues.
7. We will be kind and considerate of others and will absolutely, positively love second grade.

Student Goals for this Year:

1. one of my goals is to learn about deer.

2. Another one of my goals is to learn about horses.

3. Another one of my goals is to learn division.

Parent Goals for this Year:

1. Learn to work as a member of a team to problem solve and accomplish goals because in today's society it is necessary to be successful in life.

2. To be a conceptual thinker (or at least get a start on concepts).

3. MOST IMPORTANT
   HAVE FUN WHILE LEARNING !!! ☺
   I believe learning can be fun for all ages.
   Thanks for asking !

Figure 10.11

Parent Response to _____ Portfolio
Student Name
Date _____

List of goals set by student for this period	Parent Comments
1. Correct spelling of high frequency words on a consistent basis	*What do you notice about your child's developing control over spelling of high frequency writing vocabulary?*
2. Use more action packed verbs in written pieces.	*Please comment on Joey's use of verbs.*
3. Math …	
4. Social Studies…	

something that causes me to change all over again. But when I think about this, language learning is not systematic or routine and neither should teaching be systematic or routine."

Taylor (1990) states that observational teaching and instructional assessment cannot be packaged, for this is problem-solving teaching. Sometimes, when observation forms and checklists are devised, an overly simplistic view of the complexities of language arises. Each teacher must find his own ways to portray his students'evidences of developing literacy. Checklists do not yield helpful information unless they are designed to meet the needs of your specific students.

However, Cambourne and Turbill (1990) suggest that there are certain "markers" of natural growth and development which parents use intuitively to determine the progress of their children. Likewise, teachers, through years of experience working with young children, develop signposts of literacy development. Although specific examples and emphasis change over the grade levels, the following broad categories seem to be recognized as important:

1. developing control over the conventions, skills and mechanics of language

2. comprehension and understanding of both printed and oral language

3. using language for a variety of purposes and audiences

4. social behaviors and thinking skills

5. attitudes and interests

6. amount of time engaged in reading, writing, speaking, and listening

As we consult with the learners about how we as teachers can know that students are learning, we find that they suggest that we

1. "look at the things we make or do"

2. "listen to what we say or talk about"

3. "pay attention to how our thinking changes as we investigate topics."

Once again the idea that we must trust the children to learn is apparent.

As we discussed the categories we had generated and what the students had said, it became clear that students must set many of their own purposes for reading, writing, and learning. One of the teachers recently had enrolled in a computer class at the local vocational technical school. Her purpose was to learn to operate the new equipment at her school and to be able to apply these skills in her classroom. However, the instructor's course agenda intended for the students to become experts in computer terminology, understand some programming, etc. She remarked to the group after her first test, "he tested me on the things I didn't know and never let me show him all the things I did know. I guess that must be the way our students feel when we don't include them in on planning how they can demonstrate their learning."

What we record then must be based on the aims and objectives of the teacher, students, and parents. Although, according to Cambourne (1988), "there is no definitive, conclusive set of standards or levels which can be applied universally to each grade level or age group," data which permit one to draw conclusions about the learner's attitude and the learner's developing control of language must be recorded.

Figures 10.12 and 10.13 are some examples of what the teachers utilized. These lists and examples were intended to sharpen the teachers' observational and listening skills rather than serve as the kind of checklist tool we used to use to determine whether the child measured up or not.

learner's attitude
learner's development

What we record reflects our values —
what is important in learning / teaching /
life.

Figure 10.12   Early to Beginning Stages

Name_____ Dates	1st	2nd	3rd	4th

Indicators of Developing Control and Comprehension
Code: M = Most of the time   S = Sometimes   N = Not yet

Talking and Listening   Code   Comments

	1st	2nd	3rd	4th	Comments
– Communicates with others about own activities					
– Explains ideas clearly					
– Uses expanded vocabulary related to classroom activities					
– Communicates in a group setting					
– Repeats nursery rhymes, chants, poems, etc.					
– Responds to and talks about stories					
– Sings songs					
– Dictates stories, personal messages					
– Listens attentively to class activity					
– Listens and responds in community talk					
– Talks about reading and writing					

Reading

	1st	2nd	3rd	4th	Comments
– Displays interest in books					
– Chooses to spend time with books					
– Asks for rereading of favorite stories					
– Anticipates and joins in on repetitive phrases					
– Displays sense of story					
– Understands environmental print					
– Possesses knowledge about letters					
– Pretend or memory reads					
– Recognizes some words					
– Focuses on deriving meaning from text					

Writing

	1st	2nd	3rd	4th	Comments
– Displays interest in print					
– Pretend writes and attaches meaning					
– Spends time writing					
– Attaches print to art work and other work					

Figure 10.12 (continued)

Writing (con't)

– Understands a variety of purposes and kinds of writing				
– Uses inventive spelling				
• random letters				
• some representative letters				
• phonic spelliing				
• correct spelling of high frequency words				
– Writes on own for personal communication				
– Patterns writing after literary structures				

Indicators of attitudes and social behaviors

– Is willing to be challenged				
– Is productive and involved during work periods				
– Expresses enjoyment as a result of hard work and achievement				
– Cooperates with others				
– Contributes to group work				
– Displays sensitivity and respect for others				
– Learns from watching others				

Indicators of thinking skills

– Articulates ideas clearly				
– Generates solutions and ideas to solve problems				
– Considers suitable resources				
– Differentiates between relevant and non-relevant information				
– Considers other points of view				
– Spends time reading, writing, constructing, researching, reflecting, etc.				
– Talks about information discovered				
– Explains, shows or helps others to understand learning				
– Asks worthwile questions				
– Plans, organizes and carries through on tasks				
– Understands not all problems have simple solutions				

Figure 10.13   Developing to Independent Stages

		1st	2nd	3rd	4th
Name_____	Dates				

Indicators of Developing Control and Comprehension
Code: M = Most of the time   S = Sometimes   N = Not yet

Talking and Listening

	Code				Comments
– Expects what is heard to make sense					
– Monitors understanding of spoken language by asking questions, seeking clarification, etc.					
– Uses a variety of speaking patterns to adjust to audience					
– Speaks confidently before a group and within the community					
– Communicates clearly and effectively					

Reading

– Selects reading material with confidence					
– Reads for literary experience					
– Reads to be informed					
– Reads to perform a task					
– Constructs meaning, develops interpretation and makes judgments					
– Compares and contrasts, makes application					
– Understands story features—irony, humor, organization, point of view					
– Uses a variety of strategies—prediction, rate, background, information, etc.					
– Rereads for different purposes					
– Displays an expanding vocabulary					

Writing

– Initiates writing for specific and personal purposes					
– Incorporates models from literature					
– Participates in writing conferences by asking questions and giving comments					
– Is aware of voice, sense of audience, sense of purpose					
– Displays control over mechanics • punctuation					

Figure 10.13 (continued)

Writing (con't)

• grammatical constructions					
• spells high frequency words correctly					
– Pieces are well developed and organized					
• style					
• characters					
• setting					
• detail					
• logical progression of events					
– Informative pieces are well developed					
– Displays research skills					
– Edits and proofreads					
– Talks confidently about writing					

Indicators of attitudes and social behaviors

– Is willing to be challenged					
– Is productive and involved during work periods					
– Expresses enjoyment as a result of hard work and achievement					
– Cooperates with others					
– Contributes to group work					
– Displays sensitivity and respect for others					
– Learns from watching others					

Indicators of thinking skills

– Articulates ideas clearly					
– Generates solutions and ideas to solve problems					
– Considers suitable resources					
– Differentiates between relevant and non-relevant information					
– Considers other points of view					
– Spends time reading, writing, constructing, researching, reflecting, etc.					
– Talks about information discovered					
– Explains, shows or helps others to understand learning					
– Asks worthwhile questions					
– Plans, organizes and carries through on tasks					
– Understands not all problems have simple solutions					

The information on our observation forms is in no way to be considered universal or the most important behaviors to be noted. These indicators are merely representative of the complexities of language learning. The forms and lists will change as we become more informed about how children acquire and use language. Teachers should look for global behaviors and overall patterns in the move toward literacy.

The work of Don Holdaway (1980) contains important print-related learnings which could serve as a base to develop your own lists. In addition, the work of Anne Forester and Margaret Reinhard (1989) is most helpful with young students. Another recommended resource would be The Primary Language Record (1988), published by Centre for Language in Primary Education, London, and available in the United States through Heinemann Educational Books Incorporated.

Concluding Remarks

ONE MUST LEARN
BY DOING THE THING; FOR THOUGH YOU
THINK YOU KNOW IT
YOU HAVE NO CERTAINTY, UNTIL YOU TRY
— Sophocles

Nancie Atwell (1991) began her book, *Side by Side,* with the above quote and I would like to end this chapter with Sophocles' words. For until we become students of our own and others' teaching, until we seek to become aware of our own learning, we really can't know teaching and learning. Teachers must take the risk and try more authentic forms of assessment and evaluation if we ever hope to propel ourselves into a new realm of understanding.

References

Anthony, R., Johnson, T., Mickelson, N., & Preece, A. (1991). Evaluating literacy: A perspective for change. Portsmouth, NH: Heinemann Educational Books, Inc.

Atwell, N. (1987). In the middle: Writing, reading, and learning with adolescents. Portsmouth, NH: Boynton/Cook, Heinemann.

Atwell, N. (1991). Side by side: Essays on teaching to learn. Portsmouth, NH: Heinemann Educational Books, Inc.

Bouffler, C. (Ed.). (1992). Literacy evaluation: Issues and practicalities. Portsmouth, NH: Heinemann Educational Books, Inc.

Burns, M. (1993). Mathematics: Assessing understanding. White Plains, NY: Cuisenaire Company of America, Inc.

Cambourne, B. (1988). The whole story: Natural learning and the acquisition of literacy in the classroom. Auckland, N.Z.: Ashton Scholastic.

Cambourne, B., & Turbill, J. (1990). Assessment in whole language classrooms: Theory into practice. *The Elementary School Journal,* 90(3).

Comber, B. (1991). The learner as informant. In E. Daly (Ed.), *Monitoring children's language development: Holistic assessment in the classroom.* Portsmouth, NH: Heinemann Educational Books, Inc.

Dillon, D. (1990, March). Editorial for *Language Art,. 67*(3).

Forester, A., & Reinhard, M. (1989). *The learner's way.* Winnipeg: Peguis Publishers.

Goodman, Y. (1989). Evaluation of students. In K. Goodman, Y. Goodman, & J.W. Hood (Eds.), *The whole language evaluation book.* Portsmouth, NH: Heinemann Educational Books, Inc.

Graves, D. (1982). *Writing: Teachers and children at work.* Portsmouth, NH: Heinemann Educational Books, Inc.

Graves, D., & Sunstein, B. (1992). *Portfolio portraits.* Portsmouth, NH: Heinemann Educational Books, Inc.

Hansen, J. (1987). *When writers read.* Portsmouth, NH: Heinemann Educational Books, Inc.

Harste, J., Short, K., & Burke, C. (1988). *Creating classrooms for authors.* Portsmouth, NH: Heinemann Educational Books, Inc.

Harwayne, S. (1992). *Lasting impressions: Weaving literature into the writing workshop.* Portsmouth, NH: Heinemann Educational Books, Inc.

Holdaway, D. (1980). *Independence in reading.* Toronto: Ashton Scholastic.

Rhodes, L. (1993). *Literacy assessment: A handbook of instruments.* Portsmouth, NH: Heinemann Educational Books, Inc.

Routman, R. (1991). *Invitations: Changing as teachers and learners K–12.* Portsmouth, NH: Heinemann Educational Books, Inc.

Short, K., & Burke, C. (1991). *Creating curriculum: Teachers and students as a community of learners.* Portsmouth, NH: Heinemann Educational Books, Inc.

Smith, F. (1993, January). The never-ending confrontation. *Phi Delta Kappan, 74* (5).

Stenmark, J. (Ed.). (1991). *Mathematics assessment: Myths, models, good questions, and practical suggestions.* Reston, VA: National Council of Teachers of Mathematics.

Taylor, D. (1990, February). Teaching without testing: Assessing the complexity of children's literacy learning. *English Education.*

Tierney, R., Carter, M., & Desai, L. (1991). *Portfolio assessment in the reading-writing classroom.* Norwood, MA: Christopher-Gordon Publishers, Inc.

Ward, C. (1988). *Cookie's Week.* (Illustrated by T. dePaola.) Scholastic.

Zemelman, S., Daniels, H., & Hyde, A. (1993). *Best practice: New standards for teaching and learning in America's schools.* Portsmouth, NH: Heinemann Educational Books, Inc.

Chapter 11

Assessment: Re-Visioning the Future

William P. Bintz and Jerome C. Harste

> **Knowledge**
> I've got it all figured out
> by the time I'm an old man
> I'm going to know almost
> everything about everything
> but I'll bet on my ninety-fifth
> birthday
> some little girl will
> come up to me and say
> Mr. Nathaniel why doesn't
> the such-and-such do
> so-and-so
> and I'll have to say
> I don't know
>
> — Eloise Greenfield (1988)

In the first edition of *Assessment and Evaluation in Whole Language Programs* (Harp, 1991), we described a vision for the future of assessment in whole language classrooms. This vision was a specific response to recent calls by reading educators to reform reading comprehension assessment, as well as a general proposal for a theory of assessment based on the best we currently know about language, language learning, learning, and schooling (Harste & Bintz, 1991). Since then, we have engaged in many conversations with colleagues, students, and each other which have significantly challenged and pushed our thinking about assessment. The purpose of this chapter is to build on and continue these conversations by describing our current best thinking on the future of evaluation in whole language classrooms. Our aim is to update and further refine our theory of assessment. Our hope is to propose a re-vision that will help shape and guide the future of assessment into the 21st century.

To this end, we start with a critical examination of the theoretical assumptions underpinning the assessment reform movement. In this section we argue that recent efforts to reform assessment are inadequate because they are based on a model of education that privileges verification over inquiry, and a theory of learning that highlights sameness over difference. Then, we describe a re-vision for the future of assessment based on a model of education that supports inquiry, and a theory of learning that highlights difference, not consensus. We conclude by inviting readers to join us in continuing this conversation by asking, "Where does this re-vision get us?"

Assessment As Verification

We introduce this chapter with the voice of Nathaniel because we believe that what he learns about knowledge is a metaphor for what we as educators need to admit about learning, namely, that we don't have learning all figured out. What we have figured out is that learning is not tidy and orderly, but messy and unpredictable, and that there will be instances when our current best theories of learning won't be able to give an answer to "Why does the such-and-such do so-and-so?" We have also figured out how critical these instances are for interrogating and outgrowing our current theories of learning, given the fact that the potential of any theory is greatest when it doesn't work (Burke, 1992). We believe a good starting point for thinking differently about the future of assessment, then, is to interrogate our current assumptions about the nature of learning.

Over the past several years the assessment reform movement has created a new set of "buzz words," or more accurately "buzz phrases," in the field of education. These phrases include real assessment, authentic assessment, process assessment, learning potential assessment, portfolio assessment, process-folio assessment, outcome-based assessment, and performance-based standards. This movement has also created a number of new "buzz groups" in the educational community, such as The Standards Project for English/Language Arts and The National Board for Professional Teaching Standards. Among other things, the aim of these organizations is to develop national literacy standards, national educational goals, and national curriculum standards, as well as explore the efficacy of using alternative forms of assessment to evaluate these goals and standards.

At one level, the assessment reform movement appears to have created a wide variety of alternative forms of assessment. Moreover, these forms appear to be based on a view of learning that is significantly different than the theoretical model underlying traditional forms of evaluation, that is, formal standardized testing. In our view, however, the appearance of diverse forms of assessment is just that; it's an appearance, an illusion, if you will, rather than a real example of theoretical diversity at work. That is, the development of alternative forms of assessment have made assessment problems look different and assessment procedures appear different, but these forms represent only different variations on the same theoretical theme because they are grounded in the same theoretical model of learning. In effect, we have varied our assessment instruments and modified our assessment procedures, but we have not changed, much less interrogated, the theoretical assumptions underlying these efforts.

We believe, however, that what a theory changes tells us a lot about what a theory is (Harste, 1993). What is problematic about recent efforts to reform assessment is that the theoretical assumptions underpinning these efforts have not changed. These efforts still assume that we intuitively understand and can predict human development, still ignore the use of multiple sign systems in learning, still privilege tests over kids as curricular informants, still maintain hierarchical relationships between testers and testees, still make student learning more vulnerable than teacher knowledge, still use performance-based tasks as criteria for and proof of learning, and still perpetuate disempowering social relationships between teachers and students. Most importantly, these efforts still conceptualize assessment as verification; that is, as a tool for verifying existing theories of learning and confirming existing criteria for learning. To be sure, these attempts have created new instruments that look different, and new procedures that sound different. But these reflect instrumental and procedural changes, not theoretical shifts about the nature of learning, and therefore represent more surface level, or cosmetic, rather than substantive reform efforts.

What is also problematic is that recent reform efforts are grounded in a model of education that seeks consensus, not diversity. A consensus model of education is driven by an agenda that seeks to develop universal educational goals and universal curriculum standards, as well as universal assessment criteria to determine to what extent goals are being achieved and standards are being met. The purpose of this agenda is to develop a set of predetermined universal criteria that define what students should look like intellectually, psychologically, and emotionally at different developmental stages. The aim is to increase, if not ensure, the likelihood that students will progress through the educational system looking pretty much the same all along the way.

Concomitantly, this consensus model of education is supported by a theory of learning that highlights sameness, not difference. For example, the assessment reform movement continues to assume that our current theories of learning are unproblematic and largely a settled matter; in fact, it assumes that we've got learning pretty much all figured out. According to this rationale, the problem is not our updated theories of learning, but our outdated forms of assessment. This assumption partially explains why recent reform efforts continue to develop forms of assessment that predetermine and standardize criteria for learning. These forms see learning in terms of finding universal learning patterns and identifying specific criteria based on these patterns, and see assessment reform in terms of developing new and more sophisticated instruments for verifying these patterns and confirming these criteria.

It is important for us to note that we are not arguing against finding patterns in learning. In actual fact, we agree with Bateson (1972) who suggests that comprehension is a process of "finding patterns that connect." Similarly, we conceptualize learning as a process of finding new patterns, and intellectual growth as a process of constructing broader, deeper, and more complex patterns that connect (Harste & Burke, 1991). What we are arguing against is that the theoretical model underlying recent attempts to reform assessment fails to take into account the important role tensions play in learning. That is, by continuing to see learning solely in terms of patterns, this model fails to take note of the role that tension plays in the learning process.

An example should help. As many of you know, one of us (Harste) was involved in an extensive study of what young children know about reading and writing prior to going to school (Harste, Woodward, &

Burke, 1984). As part of this inquiry, we studied Alison's development as a writer over time (see Figure 11.1).

Figure 11.1   Signature (Alison, age 3–6)

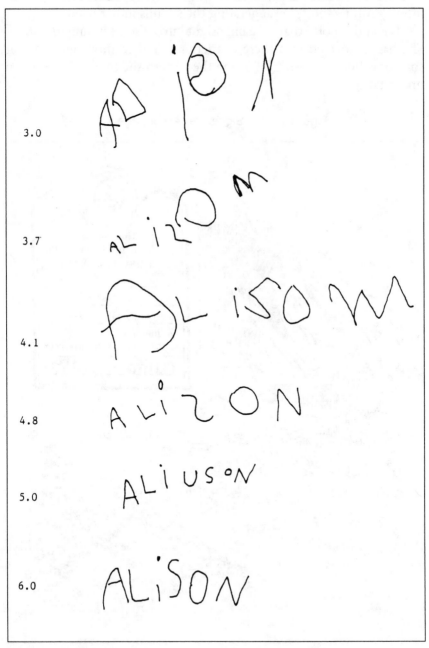

As can be seen, Alison could more or less write her name conventionally from age 3 onward. Interestingly, we really don't know anything about what is going on in her head as long as she is writing her name more or less conventionally. At age 5, however, she decided to add a "u" to her name. When we asked her, "Why?" she responded, "Well listen, /All/u/son/," exaggerating the sounds in her name.

It is at this point that we gain insight into Alison's inquiry question. She has discovered that there is a letter-sound relationship and that somehow her name isn't following the pattern she thinks she sees and understands.

Figure 11.2   Signature (Alison, age 7)

At age 7 Alison gave a book to the church library. Her mother went to the church to pick up the nameplate and to let Alison sign it. The secretary of the church — the keeper of the Methodist money, mind you — had typed Alison's name with two "l"s instead of one. Alison's mother insisted, much to the secretary's chagrin, that she change it.

Much to Alison's mother's dismay, she did the unpredictable (see Figure 11.2). Yet, it is interesting from a learning perspective. Again, unlike her conventional signatures, we have new information as to her inquiry question. Alison has noticed that various grapheme combinations placehold the same sounds in English. It is this understanding that creates a new tension for her and propels her learning.

This failure to understand the relationship between tensions and learning partially explains why assessment reform has become little more than a matter of developing new and more sophisticated instruments and procedures that verify our current theories of development, confirm our current patterns of learning, and reify our current criteria for learning.

In sum, we believe that recent efforts to reform assessment continue to view assessment as verification, a process of matching up what we already know about learning with what should be happening in classrooms. We also believe that this view of assessment is theoretically bankrupt, given the best we currently know about learning. And what we know about learning is that it is not a predictable routine, but an unpredictable experience involving anomalies, inconsistencies, and surprises which can't be predetermined or standardized. In our view, then, what is needed is a vision of assessment that highlights diversity, not consensus, and sees difference, not sameness, as the starting point for learning. To this end, we propose assessment as inquiry.

Assessment As Inquiry

Nobody rebels against exploration, only transmission (Ralph Nader).

The only thing assessment can do is help a learner or community of learners interrogate their values. It can't map development. It not only can't do what it is current assessment procedures assume they do, but it provides no useful information for short-term or long-term instructional decision making.

First and foremost, assessment as inquiry is grounded in a diversity model of education, and driven by a theory of learning that highlights difference, not consensus. Unlike consensus, a diversity model of education recognizes, values, and celebrates individual differences. It rejects the notion of education as the practice of making everyone look pretty much the same by predetermining and standardizing what students should know, and embraces instead the principle of supporting individual differences by understanding and building on what students do know, or "what's there." In other words, unlike a consensus model which starts by predetermining what learning should be there in learners and remediating those learners when it isn't, a diversity model of education starts by understanding, acknowledging, and legitimating the system of values, beliefs, and meanings students hold about the social world. This system reflects what students value and why they value it, and is central to creating curriculum in the classroom that is culturally relevant and personally meaningful.

Current assessment procedures assume that we know what inquiry questions children should be asking. They fail to allow us to identify and interrogate what lies behind children's real inquiry questions. Unfortunately, unless we can identify the intent underlying a learner's inquiry question, we have no idea how to support them instructionally.

Let's take a common occurrence in classroom. A child approaches and asks, "What's this word?" What help a teacher gives depends on the intent underlying the inquiry. If the child thinks reading is a process of sounding out words, the best response may be to help the child read ahead and use context clues to help solve the problem. Nothing is formulaic, however. If the child already views reading as a meaning-making process, but is asking for this word because she believes it is key to understanding an important message, the teacher may just decide to give the child the word. Other inquiry questions demand other responses. Assessment never gives us answers, only data on which we can make judgments.

A good evaluative device has to track a child's changing inquiry questions. Current assessments force children to answer our inquiry questions in total disregard to those the child him- or herself is asking.

Moreover, a diversity model highlights the importance of voice in education. Historically, schooling has privileged some voices over others, and in the process has silenced many students instead of hearing from them. A consensus model of education perpetuates this silence because it collapses diversity into a single, monolithic voice. A diversity model, however, breaks this silence by asserting that inclusivity, not exclusivity, is the goal of education, and by envisioning classrooms as "plurivocal" (Polkinghorne, 1983) communities of learners in which all voices get heard (Watson, Burke, & Harste, 1989). In terms of assessment, this model requires that we ask different questions of ourselves. For example, instead of asking *Does this child know what I think he or she should know?* or *Has this child mastered the content I think important?*, assessment as inquiry asks, *What does this response tell me about what the learner believes as well as what action I should take?*, *How does this response force me to change what I believe?*, *Whose voices are being heard and why?*

Assessment as inquiry is also driven by a theory of learning that highlights and supports difference, not consensus. For us, a theory of difference starts with the belief that the human mind refuses to be bored or complacent (Smith, 1986). It constantly and relentlessly seeks to construct meaning, and refuses to pursue topics it has no interest in. This partially explains why learners are not particularly attracted to what they already know, as well as why they are not specifically interested in knowing the same things as everybody else. This also partially explains why learners are not particularly attracted to formal evaluation like standardized testing. For many, including us, it represents an instance of telling, not learning. That is, it represents little more than an instance of having to prove to others what learners already know.

We believe, however, that learners are attracted to what they don't know, but especially to what they want to know more about. In other words, learners are not attracted to what is familiar to them, but to what's unfamiliar, what's new, what's questionable, what's strange, what's different, and what we haven't figured out yet. It is difference, not familiarity, that captures our eye, and engages our brain. Seeing what's different starts the inquiry process, and exploring what's different keeps the process going. That's why inquiry into what's different has enormous appeal to learners. It provides them with a different perspective on their learning, and thus creates new options to consider, new potentials to explore, new directions to take, and new questions to ask. In short, seeing and exploring what's different puts an edge on their learning (Harste, 1994).

Assessment as inquiry is an invitation to take a different perspective on the nature of learning. Specifically, it invites us to see difference, not consensus, as potential starting points for taking our learning in different directions, for different purposes, and from different perspectives. In this way, seeing "what's different" allows us to put new edges on our learning. We can only do this, however, by asking our own inquiry questions, such as *I wonder why that happened?*, *What do I want*

to know more about?, and *What is it that I haven't figured out yet?*
Inquirers know not to depend on solutions. They understand that the
secret to success is to depend on new inquiries.

As educators we will only be able to know what learners really value
and believe by helping them ask their own inquiry questions. In this
sense, we agree with Langer (1957), who reminds us that what we can
know depends on the questions we can ask. The right to ask our own
inquiry questions is what education in a democracy is all about.
Moreover, we also believe that what students can learn depends more
on their next experience, not their next skill level. In other words, the
experience of asking our own inquiry questions, rather than acquiring
a set of hierarchical and isolated skills, is what really puts an edge on our
learning.

Where Does This Re-Vision Get Us?

*Let's not put all children through the narrow eye of the same needle
(Eisner, 1991).*

We believe that in order for assessment to look different in the
future, we have to think differently about learning today. In order to do
that, we have to interrogate and change the underlying presumptions
about learning that currently drive attempts to reform assessment. In
this chapter we have argued that assessment as verification is inadequate
because it narrows what we can see, constrains what we can know, and
inhibits our ability to outgrow our present selves and our current
theories of learning. Instead, we have proposed a re-vision for the future
of assessment that is based on a diversity, not consensus, model of
education, and a theory of learning that highlights difference, not
sameness.

For us, assessment is not a tool to verify our favorite theories of
learning and confirm our preferred learning criteria. Rather, it has a
potential to unpack our favorite values and interrogate our preferred
assumptions about learning. In other words, for us assessment is an
opportunity to put our theories rather than our students continually to
the test. It has a potential for making our own knowledge as vulnerable
as our students' learning. In this sense, we see assessment as re-
assessment, the ongoing process of keeping our learning theories alive
by continuing to make them vulnerable and problematic. Only then will
we, like Nathaniel, come to understand and grow to appreciate the fact
that just when we think we've got learning all figured out, some student

will ask us, "Why doesn't the such-and-such do so-and-so?" and we will have to say, "We don't know."

References

Bateson, G. (1972). *Steps to an ecology of mind*. New York: Ballantine Books.

Burke, C. (1992). Personal correspondence.

Eisner, E. (1991). *The enlightened eye: Qualitative inquiry and the enhancement of educational practice*. New York: Macmillan.

Greenfield, E. (1988). *Nathaniel talking*. New York: Black Butterfly Children's Books.

Harp, B. (Ed.) (1991). *Assessment and evaluation in whole language programs*. Norwood, MA: Christopher-Gordon Publishers, Inc.

Harste, J. (1994). Whole language: Celebrating our successes. *Whole Language Newsletter*, 5:2, 1–8.

Harste, J., & Bintz, W. (1991). A vision for the future of assessment in whole language classrooms. In Harp, B. (Ed.), *Assessment and evaluation in whole language programs*. Norwood, MA: Christopher-Gordon Publishers, Inc.

Harste, J., & Burke, C. (1991). Planning to plan: Supporting inquiry in classrooms. Unpublished manuscript.

Harste, J., Woodward, V., & Burke, C. (1984). *Language stories and literacy lessons*. Portsmouth, NH: Heinemann.

Langer, S. (1957). *Philosophy in a new key: A study in the symbolism of reason, rite, and art*. Cambridge, MA: Harvard University Press.

Polkinghorne, D. (1983). *Methodology for the human sciences: Systems of inquiry*. Albany: State University of New York Press.

Smith, F. (1986). *Insult to intelligence: The bureaucratic invasion of our classrooms*. Portsmouth, NH: Heinemann.

Watson, D., Burke, C., & Harste, J. (1989). *Whole language: Inquiring voices*. New York: Scholastic, Inc.

Chapter 12

Supervision of Teachers in Whole Language Classrooms: What to Look For

Bill Harp

The Roles of the Whole Language Teacher

The whole language movement, as a reform movement, has defined the roles of the whole language teacher. By examining the roles of the teacher, we can begin to chart direction in the evaluation of the work of the whole language teacher. A particularly informative study on the role of the whole language teacher was conducted by Sumara and Walker (1991). The researchers spent 70 hours in one classroom and 60 hours in another observing the work of two third and fourth grade whole language teachers. Data collected included observational notes, formal and informal interviews with students and teachers, audio and video tapes of classroom interactions, collections of students' work, teachers' plans and resource materials. The major conclusions of this research are presented below.

- Whole language teachers define an empowering social structure. The teachers' collaboration with students and peers, coaching and facilitating, suggested that the teachers understood that language development needed to exist within purposeful and meaningful social contexts. The social structure desired by the teachers was created through training students in acceptable forms of social behavior — explanation of procedural matters and teacher demonstration and modeling. The teachers shared information with students and showed students how to listen and cooperate in exchanges. Once the ongoing expectations and conditions were in place, teachers assumed the role of learners, participating in the learning act with students in some way.

- Teacher control led to student choice. The researchers observed that activities were tightly planned and controlled, expectations were clearly stated and outcomes were defined. However, once these parameters were established, the control was reduced considerably (1991, page 281). Students had considerable choice over how, with whom, and where they would complete tasks, as well as choice in the selection of reading materials.

- Teachers created predictable environments. Routines and structures became points of reference for students who could then feel that at school some things did not change. The researchers observed that through the underlying structure that framed particular purposes for using language, students were motivated to use sociable language in new and innovative ways.

- Teachers' creations of authentic uses of language were situated within an understanding of what is *real* for children. Sumara and Walker say, "...the teachers became the lens through which their whole language translation of curriculum was focused. Therefore, authenticity needed to be understood through this enactment. Both these teachers demonstrated this kind of authenticity when they revealed themselves as learners, modeling what they learned, how they learned, and what they did with learning" (1991, page 283).

A second study that had a narrower focus than Sumara and Walker's was conducted to examine the work of the whole language teacher during reading instruction procedures (Watson, 1984). This research further informs our understanding of the role of the whole language teacher. Watson observed the following characteristics of the teacher's work:

- The teacher focused the children's attention on the largest unit of language suitable for the situation.

- The teacher encouraged children to construct meaning sensible to them and their lives.

- The teacher permitted deviations from text in allowing miscues.

- The teacher involved children in planning, utilized library books and other texts, and encouraged children to think about and feel what they read.

Burk and Melton-Pages (1991) have further extended the description of the roles of the whole language teacher to include a new relationship to parents of their students. About this relationship they say,

> Whole language teachers may be confronted by parents who expect their children to be taught the same way they were taught. They expect children to move systematically through a basal reading program, completing worksheets, reading in ability-based reading groups and practicing their oral reading every day. Further, they expect columns of copied words from spelling books, pages of penmanship practice, and red-inked corrections on writing. Since whole language teachers teach reading, writing, speaking, and listening through meaningful learning experiences across the curriculum, many of the products of traditional reading instruction are not available for parents' examination. (1991, page 97)

The changing relationship with parents in whole language classrooms requires careful communication so that parents know the why, what, and how of instruction. The whole language teacher helps parents understand how instruction has changed since the parents were in school, and why that change is beneficial to their children.

The work of Sumara and Walker, Watson, and Burk and Melton-Pages in defining the role of the whole language teacher will assist us in defining what to look for in evaluating the teacher's work.

The Roles of the Whole Language Teacher — Implications for Observation and Evaluation

Through carefully examining the roles of the whole language teacher, we can identify certain key elements of whole language instruction. These key elements tend to cut across grade lines, and can be found in virtually all whole language settings. Three such key elements are **choice, activity,** and **authenticity.** The notions of choice, activity, and authenticity guide the observation and evaluation of the whole language teacher (Harp, 1994).

Choice

A basic tenet of whole language instruction is that learners must exercise choice as a part of having ownership for their learning. If we believe that, it then follows that whole language teachers must be permitted to exercise choice in the evaluation process. Ownership for one's own growth as a teacher means reflective practice. Reflective practice leads to the teacher identifying his or her next learning steps — the next piece of personal growth to take. *The evaluation process for the whole language teacher must offer that teacher opportunities for choice in identifying his or her next learning steps as a teacher.*

Choice is critical to the evaluation process in another dimension as well. We have recognized that if learners are to take ownership of their learning, they must be empowered to evaluate their own learning — based on work samples they help choose and against criteria they help establish. The evaluation process for the whole language teacher must offer teachers opportunities to evaluate their own work, to offer samples of their work, and to help identify the criteria against which their work will be evaluated.

Yet another aspect of choice comes into play in the evaluation of the whole language teacher. Teachers are becoming more and more skillful at looking at their learners as readers and writers (kid watching, as Goodman [1978] called it), and in the process are beginning to ask their own research questions. The teacher as researcher is fast becoming accepted practice (Smith, 1993). As researchers, teachers ask questions, seek answers, and are potential contributors to educational theory and practice. Their classrooms become teaching and learning laboratories. The questions the whole language teacher identifies for research reflect another aspect of choice in the professional life of the teacher. The evaluation process for the whole language teacher should examine the choices that the teacher makes as a researcher. Research orientation has been used to distinguish whole language teachers from those following "traditional practice" (Bright, 1989).

Activity

The new whole language learning paradigm holds that the learner is an active participant in the learning process (Monson & Pahl, 1991). The role of the teacher is to create, in collaboration with the learner, the environment that encourages active reading, researching, experimenting, writing, thinking, speaking, investigating — all the activities that contribute to learning. In evaluating the work of the teacher, attention must be focused on the nature of the activities he or she creates for learners. The first concern is for collaboration with the learner. Are the activities created for children done in collaboration with the learner? Are students and the reading teacher partners in the creation of learning activities?

A second consideration is that of the nature of activities. Are the activities designed by, for, and with learners ones that allow the learners to behave as real readers, real writers, and real learners? Real readers often select their own reading materials to satisfy their own purposes. They write to known audiences for their own purposes, and they learn by determining what they know, what they want to know, and how they will find out. The issues centered around the activities the teacher creates are tied to issues of authenticity.

Authenticity

Just as we expect the teacher to orchestrate authentic learning activities for children, we should expect authenticity in the criteria by which the work of the whole language teacher is evaluated. *Authenticity* in the classroom context typically refers to the quality of the engagements learners have with literacy tasks. Authenticity in the evaluation of the whole language teacher means we examine the learning environment to draw conclusions about the nature of teaching and learning. We look at the nature of the environment, the activities of the learners, and the work of the teacher. Brian Cambourne (1988) has helped us define the aspects of the learning environment that foster the growth of literacy.

Guidelines for Looking at the Teaching/Learning Environment

Brian Cambourne has helped us understand that the conditions that foster learning oral language and the conditions that facilitate coming to fluency in reading are the same. The conditions that facilitate oral language learning will promote fluency in literacy. He has identified seven such conditions. Consider these conditions as the potential criteria by which we would observe and begin to evaluate the teaching/ learning environment created by the whole language teacher.

Immersion

As learners of oral language we were constantly immersed in language. Many parents talk to children while they are still in the womb. We assign intentionality to the gurgles of newborns. Just as these very young children are immersed in oral language, so must emergent readers and writers be immersed in texts of all kinds. Evidence of the existence of this condition would be a classroom in which print is used for a variety of purposes: informing, persuading, directing, controlling. The classroom library would be well-stocked and would include the publications of class authors.

Demonstration

Each time the oral language learner is immersed in language, the use of language is being demonstrated. Literacy learners need many demonstrations of how texts are constructed and used. It seems that teachers come easily to demonstrating reading. Children need to be read to many times during the day, not just for fifteen minutes after lunch. However, teachers seem to have difficulty demonstrating writing. This is probably because we have received so few demonstrations of writing ourselves. By demonstration of writing we mean actually showing children how you think through the process of writing a piece — and then demonstrating that writing.

Cambourne makes the critical point that unless children are engaged with immersion and demonstration, little learning will occur. Engagement implies that the learner is convinced that he or she is a potential doer or performer of the demonstrations, that learning these things will be beneficial, and that these new learnings can be tried out without fear of harm if the performance is not "correct."

Expectation

Parents of young children fully expect that their toddlers will make tremendous leaps toward oral language fluency, and will accomplish the task within a few years. Rarely do parents (barring unfortunate circumstances) worry about their children coming to fluency in oral language. Why, then, do some parents respond so negatively when young children spell a word the best they can at the time or make a mistake when reading orally? Whole language teachers have high expectations that children will learn to read and write, and at the same time help parents (and others) value the importance of successive approximations.

Responsibility

Parents are often grateful that they do not have to teach their children to speak. In fact, in coming to fluency in oral language children take responsibility for their own learning. They appreciate the need for clear, useful communication and modify their language to maximize its use. So children can be responsible for learning to read and write. We need to help children decide what their next learning steps are to be and how they will take them.

Use

As oral language users we practiced our control over language in very real ways —to get things done and to get our needs met. In the reading/writing classroom children need many opportunities daily to practice reading and writing in ways that are real, communicative, and authentic. Probably no one reading this text has, as an adult, drawn three rectangles on a piece of paper and then practiced addressing envelopes in the rectangles. Why? Because this is a truly inauthentic exercise. We address envelopes for the purpose of mailing something. Children need non-artificial ways to use reading and writing.

Approximation

Most families can identify certain words or phrases that a youngster approximated that were deemed so charming they have become part of that family's vocabulary. When the two-and-a-half-year-old approached with a plate at a 45-degree angle and said, "Mommy cookies all gonded, all gonded," Mommy didn't reply with, "Now, honey, that isn't the way we would say that." Mommy responded to the communication and probably enjoyed the child's approximation of standard speech. Why is it that parents who were so charmed by approximations in oral language are so disturbed by their children's approximations in reading and writing? Mistakes are a natural, developmental part of all learning. Knowledgeable teachers see the mistakes as roadsigns that lead to better understanding of the developing reader and writer. Such teachers are very careful about how they respond to approximations.

Response

Cambourne asserts that learners must receive feedback on their attempts at reading and writing that is relevant, appropriate, timely, readily available, non-threatening, with no strings attached. We must help children understand that mistakes are a natural part of learning, and the mistakes help them define what they need to learn next. The responses parents and teachers make to the child's efforts in literacy are critical factors in success. Initial classroom observations should consider the degree to which the seven conditions described above are in place. The next consideration should be the activities of the learners.

Observing the Work of Children in Evaluating the Work of the Whole Language Teacher

When principals and other supervisors visit classrooms to evaluate the work of whole language teachers they should look at the activities of the children. The learning activities in which children are engaged may be the best data source in evaluating the work of the teacher.

Children should be reading, reading, reading. One of the hallmarks of a whole language classroom is that children are frequently and enjoyably reading a variety of texts for a variety of purposes .

Authentic Texts

The children should be eagerly and freely reading texts that are authentic. That is, texts that confirm what they know about how language works rather than the dumbed-down texts that children have previously been given. Very young children come to school knowing that print communicates, and that knowledge should be confirmed by every encounter they have with print.

Books of Choice

Children should be reading books of their choice. Certainly, there will be times when the teacher is engaging a group of children in a common text through guided reading or shared reading. But there should be ample evidence of children reading good books of their choice. And such reading should be happening throughout the day, across the curriculum.

Discussion of the Reading Process

The principal should see evidence that the teacher is engaging children in discussion of the reading process. Bringing to consciousness what children know about a topic before they read, engaging them in predicting, confirming those predictions, and then integrating what they have just read with what they already know (Goodman & Burke,

1980) should all be evident. Asking children about how their reading is going, what they do when they have difficulty, helping them to monitor their own comprehension (metacomprehension) should all be evident as well (Harp & Brewer, 1991). The observer should see these discussions happening one on one with individual children, with small guided reading groups, and with larger groups doing shared reading.

Children should be writing, writing, writing. We know that just as reading is one of the best ways to learn to read, so writing is one of the best ways for children to learn to write. The classroom should be a text-rich environment, and much of that writing should come from the children.

Topics of Choice

For the most part, the things children are writing should be on topics they have chosen rather than on topics assigned by the teacher (Graves, 1983). Real writers write on topics of their choice and about subjects that they know. So should it be with children.

Invitations

Some of the best evidence that children in a classroom are emerging as real writers is their behavior toward classroom visitors. Typically, authors in reading/writing classrooms invite visitors into their literary worlds with "Do you want to see what I am writing?" or "I just published a book. Do you wanna see it?" Such invitations into children's literary worlds are clear evidence that they see themselves as writers and take pride in their craft.

Discussion of the Writing Process

Principals should examine the interaction between the teacher and students as they are writing. Is there evidence of prewriting activities in which children are invited to think, observe, experience, talk, research, and brainstorm in the process of selecting a topic? Are children engaged in thinking about purpose, audience, and form before they write? Is there evidence that rough drafts are a tentative and exploratory, recursive, and that there is the possibility that some rough drafts will not be brought to publication? Is there evidence that children engage in getting responses to their writing that lead to revision? Are provisions made for editing, in which writers get help from a variety of sources (classmates, teacher, editing committees, and so on)? Is there evidence that final drafts make their way to the intended audience, and that the classroom library houses the work of resident authors?

All of the above should be evident as the teacher engages individuals and small groups of children in conversation about their writing, how it is going, where a particular piece is in the writing process at the moment.

Children are empowered to make choices.   While there should be ample evidence that the school district curriculum goals are being met, there should also be evidence of children making choices about what they are learning and how they are going about the task.

Thematic Teaching

As the teacher introduces a thematic unit the children should be asked what they know about the theme and what they would like to learn. This way the current interests of the children are accommodated as well as the district curriculum goals. Children set their own learning goals. Themes can be very simple or very complex and can last for varying lengths of time. Some teachers use themes for enrichment activities accompanying textbook studies; others organize reading and writing programs around themes. In any event, the use of a great deal of children's literature should be evident.

Clearly, observing the work of children is important in evaluating the work of the reading teacher. Of equal importance is observing the activities of the teacher.

Observing the Activities of the Teacher in Evaluating the Work of the Whole Language Teacher

The observation criteria suggested here are based on the view of the teacher as creator of the learning environment, not the dispenser of information. Here the criteria are based on the view of the teacher as professionally knowledgeable, making instructional decisions based on the observed strengths and needs of the learner.

Teachers are set directors rather than educational technocrats.
In whole language classrooms the teacher spends more time on creating an environment in which children are free to communicate, explore, experiment, and take risks than in direct instruction. The teacher defines an empowering social structure. When the principal walks into this classroom he or she should have the feeling that the room is foremost

the children's rather than the teacher's. The teacher is responsible for what happens there, provides the structure, and then fades into the background.

Teacher Relatively Invisible

The teacher may, at first, be difficult to find when the principal enters the room. He or she is likely to be kneeling at eye level with a child discussing a writing piece. The teacher may well be on the floor working an experiment with a group of children, or doing guided reading activities. In short, the teacher is more likely to have melded into the group of children rather than be positioned in front of them lecturing. This is not to say that whole class instruction is inappropriate — it just doesn't follow the norm.

Attention Focused on Activities of Children

The attention of the principal should be drawn to the activities of the children as evidence that the classroom is student centered and teacher guided rather than teacher directed. There is a significant difference between reading a story to children and telling them to write about it as opposed to reading a story to children and asking "What would you like to do with this story now?" The second way of handling children's responses puts them in charge of their learning and leads to a far greater variety of responses than the teacher would likely ever think of on his or her own.

Teacher Creates Ways for Children to Behave as Real Readers and Real Writers

The teacher has created an environment that invites children to use reading and writing for authentic purposes: to communicate, to persuade, to inform, to entertain — both as receiver and responder. When children have read a piece, they respond the way real readers respond to literature. They don't get out the papier-mâché and create a three-dimensional representation of a character; instead they tell someone about the book, they read another book by the same author, they recommend the book to a friend, they research something that piqued their curiosity, or they do nothing. They respond to the literature the way real readers respond.

Children Behave as Real Learners

The teacher has created a learning environment that invites children to explore, to experiment, to investigate — to take responsibility for their own learning. Real learners assess what they already know, determine what they need to learn and plan strategies for learning. The principal observing the work of a reading/writing teacher should see evidence that the teacher has handed over much of the responsibility for learning to the children. Thematic and other units should begin, for example, with a discussion of what the children already know about the topic (maybe charting the information) and conclude with planning for how they will learn what they want to learn.

There should also be evidence that the teacher understands that his or her function is to create an environment that will take the child farther along the learning path than the child could achieve by him- or herself — Vygotsky's (1978) notion of the Zone of Proximal Development. Whole language teachers understand that there is a distance between what learners can accomplish on their own and what they can do with the assistance of a teacher or others. In creating a classroom environment, the reading teacher plans for cooperative/collaborative learning links from children to children and from children to teacher.

The teacher is focused on strategies as opposed to basic skills. The child-centered teacher recognizes the importance of teaching basic skills when needed, but the focus of attention is on the degree to which children are mastering strategies in a classroom that is process oriented rather than product oriented in literacy.

Knows Which Strategies Children Use

The teacher can engage the principal in conversation about the fact, for example, that Roberto is now making predictions when he reads, and that he has a strategy for rereading when he cannot confirm those predictions. The teacher can tell which children are learning to sample from the myriad of cues on the printed page to make predictions. He or she can offer evidence that children are integrating what they read with what they already know. Those children who have strategies for dealing with unfamiliar words can be identified. More and more whole language teachers keep track of the child's use of the cueing systems and reading strategies through the use of running records (Clay, 1979).

Basic Skills Are Taught in the Context of Authentic Literacy Experiences

Rather than making extensive use of workbooks or work sheets, the whole language teacher will teach and reinforce knowledge of "basic skills" as children are making real use of language to communicate. For example, the teacher might point out and discuss certain text features while introducing an enlarged text story. Review of the "short \a\ sound" might be made as the title to a story is being discussed or as a child inquires about how to spell "attic." The teacher is well aware of the basic skills that have been learned and that need to be reinforced, but those needs are met in real communicative contexts, not in artificial drill and practice lessons.

The Teacher is a Learner/Researcher

Evidence should exist in both classroom practice and professional development activities that the teacher is a learner/researcher. Teachers must operate from a solid knowledge base that is soundly rooted in language development, linguistics, psycholinguistics, sociolinguistics, anthropology, and education. Whole language teachers are professionals who carefully critique their own work, collaborate with other professionals, conduct research in their own classrooms,. and take responsibility for their successes and failures (Burk and Melton-Pages, 1991). They expect to be granted professional freedom to perform in the best ways they know, and they expect to be held accountable. Further, they are often called upon to defend their instructional practices. All of this should be taken into account in the observation/ evaluation process.

The teacher is able to engage in conversation about developmental processes. Discussions of "grade level" have given way to discussions of the use of processes and strategies. Reading/writing teachers are asking, "How can I engage this child with this text at this time?" Instead of looking at artificial grade boundaries placed over curriculum, teachers are looking at children coming to literacy in developmental ways. Whole language teachers are able to clearly articulate programs and progress to parents and other care givers.

Knows How Children Are Using the Cueing Systems

The teacher will be able to engage in conversation about children, for example, who in the fall were relying primarily on graphophonic cues with little attention to creating meaning. The teacher will now be able to describe how those children are making increasingly more miscues that have semantic and syntactic acceptability. The reading/writing teacher is an observer of children. He or she will be able to describe ways in which children are making increasingly more sophisticated use of the cueing systems in reading. Such a teacher is adept at miscue analysis.

Knows How Children Are Using the Writing Process

The teacher will be able to share writing portfolios with the principal and document ways in which each child's writing is advancing. It will be possible to document that the process of writing is being evaluated, instead of writing pieces being graded. The editing group or editing committee is the primary responder, and children write several ever-improving drafts.

The teacher can describe where each child is along a developmental continuum in the movement from emerging reader and writer to developing reader and writer to maturing reader and writer. At each phase, the teacher gives the learner feedback that is relevant, appropriate, timely, readily available, and non-threatening.

The Role of the Administrator in Evaluating the Work of the Whole Language Teacher

Just as the whole language movement has redefined the roles of the teacher and the school-life of the child, so it has changed the role of the administrator. In sum, the role of the administrator or supervisor is that of **change agent**. Whole language is about change. Teachers who wish to change from traditional practice to whole language instruction are best supported by a principal or supervisor who values the changes and the change process. Vogt (1991, page 207) has identified eight characteristics of supervisors and administrators who support change. They are individuals who

1. bring focus to the change process by tailoring their reform efforts to their particular schools;

2. maintain open communication with their students, faculty, staff, parents, and community policy makers, primarily by listening and providing opportunities to share;

3. encourage, support, and provide adequate and ongoing staff development for everyone involved in the change process, including themselves;

4. form instructional leadership teams that are involved in the collaborative planning of objectives and decision making;

5. know how to get things done even when resources are limited;

6. articulate a comprehensive educational plan for change, rather than taking a piece-meal approach;

7. create an atmosphere within the school where ideas flourish and where risk-taking and initiative are rewarded; and

8. understand and communicate the fact that change cannot and does not take place overnight, and that the role of the facilitator is ongoing.

The items above describe a very supportive administrator. This kind of support is essential if real change is to occur and equally essential if the whole language teacher is to be fairly evaluated by the administrator or supervisor.

The Supportive Evaluation Climate

It is very tempting to offer a checklist for evaluation of the whole language teacher. Vogt (1991) created a checklist that encompasses many critical elements of the classroom that should be considered in evaluating the work of the whole language teacher. Siu-Runyan, Kristo, and Crabtree (1992) have taken a more moderate, teacher-centered approach to evaluation. Instead of a checklist, they have offered a set of questions that will help the supervisor learn about the classroom, become a knowledgeable observer, and develop a collegial, collaborative relationship with the teacher.

Here is a critical point of change. Are we to evaluate the whole language teacher on a pre-determined set of criteria, or is the teacher to collaborate in determining the criteria? If we are to be true to the essential principles of whole language philosophy, the teacher *must* have a say in the criteria for evaluation. He or she must play a significant role in determining what is to be evaluated, what is to be celebrated, and what is to be changed. Therefore, we offer here a *process* of observation and evaluation rather than a checklist.

Suggested Sequence of Activities in Observing/ Evaluating the Work of the Whole Language Teacher

The following is a set of activities in which the whole language teacher and supervisor might engage in the evaluation process The list is presented here as *one* possibility; it is not to be taken as *the* list. The activities engaged in by the teacher and supervisor should be agreed upon in advance and designed to best meet the needs of the teacher. Conferences should be held at critical points along the sequence.

Step One. The teacher is asked to write a self-assessment of his or her strengths as a teacher and to identify desired next learning goals as a teacher.

Step Two: The teacher may assemble a portfolio to document strengths and from which to make conclusions about next learning goals as a teacher. As a part of the portfolio the teacher is asked to document:

1. classroom research conducted,
2. collaboration between teacher and learners in creating learning activities — a teacher/learner partnership,
3. that learning activities encourage learners to behave as real readers, real writers, and real learners,
4. that reading and writing are viewed as processes.

Step Three: The teacher joins the principal or supervisor in doing an environmental scan of the classroom, documenting evidence of the existence of Cambourne's Conditions for Literacy Learning.

Step Four: The word *value* is at the center of the word *evaluation.* Therefore, it is necessary for the whole language teacher to participate in activities that identify what is valued in readers and writers in his or her school. This dialogue should include teachers, parents, and administrators. The list of values generated through these activities should enrich or replace the observation criteria discussed under the heading "Observing the Work of Children" in this chapter. Once identified, classroom observations should document that the criteria are in place.

Step Five: Classroom observation of the whole language teacher at work should complete the process. The criteria offered under the heading "Observing the Work of the Teacher" in this chapter should be modified in consultation with the teacher and used here.

Step Six: The result of these observations should be a celebration of the successes of the classroom and the identification of the next steps to be taken to make that classroom a better place for children.

Questions to Open Dialogue Between the Teacher and the Supervisor

A valuable addition to the sequence of activities outlined above would be a frank and open dialogue about the teaching/learning process between the teacher and the supervisor. This dialogue would be held in the spirit of coaching the teacher to greater success rather than as a form of evaluation. Much more will be said about the concept of coaching in the next chapter. These questions are offered as a starting point for opening a dialogue with the whole language teacher. Both the teacher and the supervisor should add questions to the pool.

The Role of the Whole Language Teacher in the Classroom

1. How do you define *whole language* and how does that definition impact your work with children?

2. How do you define an empowering social structure in your room? How do you know children are empowered?

3. To what extent do you provide opportunities for student choice? In what arenas and to what extent do you consider student choice to be important?

4. What have you done to create a predictable environment for children? In what ways is children's use of language varied, experimental, and increasingly rich?

5. How are activities created for children done in collaboration with the learner?

6. In what ways do the learning activities you create invite children to behave as real readers, real writers, and real learners?

The Growth of the Teacher as Teacher

1. What next learning steps have you identified for yourself as a teacher?

2. How can we arrange for you best to evaluate your own work

as a teacher? What criteria shall we establish and what supporting data shall we collect?

3. What questions have you posed about teaching/learning in your classroom, what data have you collected, and what conclusions have you drawn?

4. How are you now looking at children from a developmental perspective?

Looking at the Learning Environment

1. What "artifacts" can we point to within the classroom to confirm the existence of immersion, demonstration, expectation, responsibility, use, approximation and response?

2. What ways have you employed to help children and parents better understand reading and writing as processes?

3. In what ways do children in your classroom invite others into their literary worlds?

4. How have you employed thematic teaching and what have been your results?

5. What "balance" have you struck between teaching skills and teaching strategies?

Summary

This chapter has offered a dynamic view of the observation/evaluation process with the whole language teacher. It began with a consideration of the guidelines for teacher observation. Highlighted here was the importance of the teacher having choice about the dimensions of the evaluation, the importance of self-evaluation on the part of the teacher, the value of collaborative decision making between teacher and learners, and the need for creating authentic learning activities for students.

Cambourne's seven conditions for literacy learning were proposed as the basis for an environmental scan of the classroom. This was followed by criteria through which the activities of the children and the activities of the teacher could be used to make evaluative decisions about the work of the reading/writing teacher. These criteria should be modified by the members of the learning community coming together to determine what they *value* in readers and writers.

Finally, a suggested sequence of observation/evaluation activities was proposed.

References

Bright, R. (1989). Teacher as researcher: Traditional and whole language approaches. *Canadian Journal of English Language Arts,* *12*(3), 48–55.

Burk, J., & Melton-Pages, J. (1991, Winter). From recipe reader to reading professional: Extending the roles of the teacher through whole language. *Contemporary Education, 62*(2), 96–101.

Cambourne, B. (1988). *The whole story: Natural learning and the acquisition of literacy in the classroom.* Auckland, NZ: Ashton Scholastic Limited.

Clay, M. (1979). *The early detection of reading difficulties.* Auckland, NZ: Heinemann.

Edelsky, C., Draper, K., & Smith, K. (1983). Hookin' 'em in at the start of school in a whole language classroom. *Anthropology and Education Quarterly, 14,* 257–281.

Goodman, Y. (1978, June). Kid watching: An alternative to testing. *National Elementary School Principal, 57,* 41–45.

Goodman, Y., & Burke, C. (1980). *Reading strategies: Focus on comprehension.* Katonah, NY: Richard C. Owen Publishers, Inc.

Graves, D. (1983). *Writers: Teachers and children at work.* Portsmouth, NH: Heinemann Educational Books.

Harp, B. (1992). What should principals see teachers doing when evaluating whole language teachers? *Teachers Networking: The Whole Language Newsletter, 11*(1). Richard C. Owen Publishers, Inc., Katonah, N.Y.

Harp, B. (1992). What should principals see children doing when evaluating whole language teachers? *Teachers Networking: The Whole Language Newsletter, 11*(2). Richard C. Owen Publishers, Inc., Katonah, NY.

Harp, B. (in press). Observing the reading teacher: Teacher evaluation in light of child-centered instruction. In Shelley Wepner et al. (Eds.), *The Administration and Supervision of Reading Programs.* New York: Teachers College Press.

Harp, B., & Brewer, J. (1991). *Reading and writing: Teaching for the connections.* San Diego, CA: Harcourt Brace Jovanovich.

Monson, R. J. & Pahl, M. M. (1991, March). Charting a new course with whole language. *Educational Leadership,* 51–53.

Siu-Runyan, Y., Kristo, J. V., & Crabtree, D. (1992). "HOPS: A holistic observation process for supervising whole language teachers and classrooms. *Colorado Reading Council Journal,* Spring, 9–13.

Smith, K. (1993). Meeting the challenge of research in the elementary classroom. In Leslie Patterson (Ed.), *Teachers are researchers: Reflection and action*. Newark, DE: International Reading Association.

Sumara, D., & Walker, L. (1991, April). The teacher's role in whole language. *Language Arts, 68*(4), 276–285.

Vogt, M. E. (1991). An observation guide for supervisors and administrators: Moving toward integrated reading/language arts instruction. *The Reading Teacher, 45,* 206–210.

Vygotsky, L. S. (1978). *Mind in society: The development of higher psychological processes.* M. Cole, V. John-Steiner, S. Scribner, and E. Souberman (Eds.). Cambridge, MA: Harvard University Press.

Watson, D. (1984). Two approaches to reading: Whole language and skills. A paper presented at the Annual Meeting of the International Reading Association, Atlanta, GA, May 6–10, 1984.

Chapter 13

Effective Inservice: The Key to Change

Bill Harp

In this chapter we will examine the understandings about change we have developed after years of conducting inservice workshops and sessions. We will look at the research on change and inservice training, and then draw implications from this review to propose a model for effective inservice training. Here we will use the terms *inservice* and *staff development* interchangeably.

Education in the United States is slowly gaining the status of a profession. We behave more professionally than we did thirty years ago. We now have a well-defined knowledge base that is known only by those who study and practice the profession. We have a set of instructional practices that are informed and defined by this knowledge base. We engage in continuous study of our work, with the goal of improving the performance of our clients. We demand change (at least in some quarters) as a result of this ever-growing knowledge base. Change. We have learned a great deal about change.

Our Understandings About Change in Schools

The following set of statements about change in schools is derived from thirty years of working as a change agent, conducting staff development activities, engaging in inservice education as a teacher and administrator, and examining the research. These understandings should guide the work of the educational leader in planning for change through staff development.

- Staff development activities will never have the full impact they could have or should have as long as they are "done to" teachers as isolated, disconnected efforts.

- Change is easier to achieve when teachers want to make the change instead of having the change forced on them. "Bottom-up" change is more effective and longer lasting than "top down" change efforts. Change is meaningful when is it dictated by need recognized through practice and research.

- Even when teachers want to change, the change process takes time, moves slowly, and is accompanied by some sense of loss and anxiety resulting from leaving past practices or programs and unlearning old patterns of behavior.

- Change occurs best when it is driven by a solid understanding of the knowledge base in literacy education — in this case, assessment and evaluation in student-centered instruction. Study and reflection are necessary parts of the change process.

- Commitment to innovations is achieved through putting those new practices into place and seeing that they work for learners.

- Change is facilitated best through inservice that combines consultants, resident experts, and classroom support. Peer support in the classroom, with collaborative planning and evaluation, is critical.

- Change is facilitated through administrative support that is sensitive to time constraints and needs, and focuses on changing the culture of the school rather than just a small piece of that culture.

- All change is ultimately directed at creating a better learning environment for students. Therefore, all change processes must include a research component that evaluates and validates the effectiveness of the change.

These are significant changes happening in terms of professional development practices. Seller (1993) contrasts the past image of professional development with the new image. He indicates that in the past staff development practices have been district-based with the content decided at the district or administrator level. Inservice practices were usually loosely related events targeted at a large audience, often with a limited number of formats, in a one-shot effort. The focus was often on repairing faulty practices. The new image of staff development efforts is that they are school based, planned by staff, focused on particular goals. They are designed in a variety of formats, are ongoing, and enhance effective practices.

Research on Staff Development

Joyce and Showers (1983) conducted reviews of the literature on inservice teacher training and were surprised by what they found (Showers, 1990). The trends that emerged most powerfully were that the research focused on who should select the content of the training, who should lead the training, and where and when the training should occur. They also discovered that rather than evaluating the effect of innovation, evaluation research tended to look at teachers' attitudes toward the staff development experience. In another surprising finding, they concluded that when staff development resulted in skill development for the teacher, most *assumed* that the innovation would be implemented. Often that was not the case.

Joyce and Showers conducted further research in 1980,1982, and 1988 to determine what types of training would result in effective implementation (Showers, 1990). From this research they drew several implications for inservice training. Their recommendations are:

1. Training should be designed to include theory, demonstration, and practice. Theory-only inservice results in increased knowledge on the part of the teacher, but little implementation. Teachers need to come to understandings of the theory, see multiple demonstrations of the innovation, and have opportunities to practice the innovation in the training setting.

2. Staff development training must be designed to meet several objectives, such as the following: teachers must understand the nature of the innovation, they must develop enough skill to use the innovation in the classroom, and they must apply the innovation in ways that meet the demands of the curriculum, their own needs, and the needs of their students (Showers, 1990, p. 36).

3. Teachers generally work in isolation. Schools are not necessarily collegial settings. Substantive collegial interaction — coaching — is powerful in helping implement change. In one study 80 percent of the teachers receiving coaching transferred innovations into practice compared to only 10 percent of uncoached teachers who made the change. The organization of peer coaching teams is essential for sustained implementation of change.

Drawing on the work of Siedow (1985), in which assessing staff needs was the first piece of an inservice model, Moss (1992) elaborated the concept of needs assessment as it applies to whole language staff development. She described four components of needs assessment: creating awareness, data collection, building-level needs assessment, and individual needs assessment. One could create awareness of new directions in assessment and evaluation by conducting an inservice that presented the thirteen principles defined in Chapter 3. Twelve of these same principles could be used in data collection about building-level needs and individual teacher needs. The principles could be turned into a questionnaire that asks teachers to indicate the degree of implementation they perceive in their own classroom or building-wide. An example of this follows later in this chapter.

Baker (1992) adapted an idea from Hord and others (1987) to determine the degree to which whole language program characteristics had been implemented in a school. Hord and her colleagues called the survey "Levels of Use of an Innovation in Classrooms" (LoU). These same levels of use could be built into a questionnaire to determine levels of use of critical assessment and evaluation practices. The levels of use are: *Non-use,* the teacher is doing nothing about the innovation; *Orientation,* the teacher is acquiring information about the innovation and is exploring its value; *Preparation,* the teacher is preparing to put the innovation into place for the first time; and *Stages of Use,* mechanical use, routine use, refinement, integration, and renewal. The "levels of use" concept appears to have powerful application as a kind of needs assessment.

Moss (1992) further recommended helping teachers link new information to old through the process of K-W-L originally defined by Ogle (1986). This strategy, a kind of needs assessment, asks teachers in small groups or individually to list what they know about an innovation, what they want to know (questions they have), and after the inservice to write what they have learned. Finally, Moss recommended that inservice programs in whole language follow the basic tenets upon which whole language is based. Essentially, this means inservice training should be participant-centered, move learners from the known to the unknown, and provide opportunities for teachers to try out new learnings. Such training efforts must be long-term, incremental, and address the needs of teachers.

Pahl and Monson (1992) suggest that in whole language classrooms the model of instruction is changed from the traditional transmission model to a transactional model. In the transactional model there is a focus on construction of meaning and an orientation toward process. Learning is active, student centered, and moves from whole to part. From these understandings of whole language instruction they conceive a transactional staff development model. The transactional model includes frequent opportunities for teacher experimentation, training, and collegial exchanges. They believe that through these transactional changes, belief systems will be changed and thus classroom practice will change.

In her work, Wollman-Bonilla (1991) echoes the call for linking theory and practice. She describes how in her initial work with teachers she believed that the theory had to be developed first and the "how" of the practice came second. She now sees these two facets of teaching as interdependent. "I have learned that teachers often develop an understanding of theory by trying out new practices. I have also found that teachers who are intrigued by a particular approach or materials and successfully use these then frequently want to read and discuss underlying theory." (p. 119).

Joyce (1990) made similar observations about commitment to change. He observed that commitment toward innovation follows, rather than precedes, competence. The initial appearance of commitment may be fragile. As competence in implementing an innovation rises, so does commitment to the innovation, according to Bruce Joyce.

Implementation of any innovation, however, is only worthwhile if it produces better results with learners. Short-sighted staff developers sometimes, it seems, promote an innovation for the sake of the innovation rather than for the purpose of increased performance by students. Joyce and others (1990) reported a study in which teachers were organized into study groups and trained in the use of several models of teaching. Based on standardized achievement tests, the average student in the school increased in learning rate from seven-tenths of the national average to a rate almost equal to the national average. The evaluation of any innovation should ultimately look at student performance.

In Ohio, 162 teachers responded to a questionnaire about change (Anderson, 1993). The most important reasons given by the teachers for changing instructional practice were reading the literature about whole language theory and talking with other teachers about whole language. This underscores the importance of developing understanding of the knowledge base, in part, through dialogue with other teachers.

A common thread running through the literature on staff development is the need for assistance for the teacher who is implementing change. Huberman and Miles (1984) in reviewing twelve case studies of innovation and about assistance said:

> Large-scale, change-bearing innovations lived or died by the amount and quality of assistance that their users received once the change process was underway... The high-assistance sites set up external conferences, inservice training sessions, visits, committee structures, and team meetings. They also furnished a lot of ongoing assistance in the form of materials, peer consultation, access to external consultants, and rapid access to central office personnel... (p. 273)

Shanker (1990) has drawn lessons from the experience of organizations not involved in education that have undergone drastic change. He has described four important lessons:

Lesson One: Nothing changes if the people in the organization don't change. Shanker says that this means "the creation of structures through which change can be explored and on which it can be supported. It can begin with study groups among faculties or across faculties in school districts. These groups can examine what they have been doing, look at themselves and their school(s), and ask what it is they want to be doing" (page 101).

Lesson Two: A certain amount of chaos has to be tolerated when change is taking place. He argues that people need to expect this, to be comfortable with it, and to be able to take risks.

Lesson Three: Putting aside the old ways needs to be accompanied at times with ceremony and ritual. Letting go of the familiar is very difficult for people to do.

Lesson Four: As new roles and responsibilities develop in schools, teachers and administrators are learning that they need some different skills.

Shanker argues that as a result of these four lessons, staff development will ultimately become inherent in the work of the teacher. Staff development will become an integral part of the teaching/learning process as teachers are constantly seeking to enhance student learning.

Real, significant change in schools requires rethinking staff development. Some, like Mell and Mell (1990), believe that teachers oppose change. They comment that

> Fundamentally, schools oppose change. The staff does not value change, and school organization naturally frustrates the transmission of ideas. Effective staff development requires a change in the system itself. The organization must be transformed to allow change before it can be made with any degree of certainty. Persons working in the area of staff development must find ways of creating a school culture that is able to tap the creative energy of the staff, value creativity, make it safe for staff to propose and act on new ideas, teach norms and behaviors necessary to support and be comfortable in a school open to new ideas, provide resources of time and money, and develop group consensus. (p. 232)

While admitting a lack of knowledge about the transportability of the model, Mell and Mell (1990) described the effective use of a study group model of inservice training. The study team or instructional team was composed of teachers open to change and willing to try new ideas. Members of the team took leadership in studying new ideas, implementing change, and critiquing efforts with team support. When time and money to support the study team dried up, the team continued to function because the learning needs of the members were being met. From this experience the researchers drafted some guidelines to follow as a chief facilitator of change.

1. Study the school climate and determine the orientation toward innovation. If a favorable orientation is lacking, work on the school climate before trying to implement an innovation.

2. Because change is a difficult and complicated process, be sure not to try to implement too many changes at one time. When teachers are faced with too many changes at once, they may use their feeling of being overloaded as an excuse

to make no changes.

3. District-level monetary and conceptual support are essential to effective change. Such support makes it difficult for an individual to undermine the change process.

4. Teachers who openly seek help with instructional challenges are the most likely to want to join a study team. Successful teachers who have been doing things the same old ways for years are most reluctant to join. Enlisting the support of an enthusiastic, highly regarded, long-tenured teacher may help in pulling these reluctant teachers into the team.

5. Turf battles are inevitable. Try to determine who the decision makers have been in the past and bring them into the process.

6. The chief facilitator must share power and control with the team. The study team model will not succeed unless teachers feel it belongs to them.

7. Determine the degree to which staff members will accept outside consultants.

8. Release time is necessary for the study team model to function. Initially, large blocks of time are needed for planning and determining how groups will function.

9. Parental understanding is necessary in order for there to be parental support.

10. Instructional teams require time and effort on the part of the participants. Teachers need to be provided with opportunities for special workshops and courses and with facilitator training.

One cannot examine the literature on staff development and not notice the number of researchers, administrators, and trainers who endorse the concept of peer support or coaching. It appears that coaching is considered requisite to effective implementation of innovation.

Arthur Costa and Robert Garmston (1994) have presented some critical concepts about coaching in their new book entitled *Cognitive Coaching: A Foundation for Renaissance Schools*. Using the term *cognitive coaching*, they define the process as:

...a nonjudgemental process — built around a planning conference, observation, and a reflecting conference. Anyone in the educational setting can become a cognitive coach — teachers, administrators, department chairs, or support personnel. A coaching relationship may be established between teacher and teachers, administrator and teachers, and/or administrators and fellow administrators. When a cognitive coaching relationship is established between two professionals with similar roles, or peers, it can be referred to as *peer coaching*. (p. 2)

Coaching is seen by many as a breaking away from the old labor/management model in which supervisors were in charge of bringing about change on the part of "inferiors." In coaching there is a great sense of collaboration in a school whose culture is redirected from "a place where students learn" to "a place where we all are learners." The school is seen as a place where the resources of all humans within the school are enhanced and developed. Therefore, learning by both the teacher and the coach is expected. The ultimate goal of coaching is that both the teacher and the coach will learn, and that there will be a long-term gain for the students in the school.

Costa and Garmston (1994, pp. 6–8) have identified four reasons why coaching is important:

1. Cognitive coaching enhances the intellectual capacities of teachers, which in turn produces greater intellectual achievement in students.

2. Few educational innovations achieve their full impact without a coaching component.

3. Working effectively as a team member requires coaching.

4. Coaching develops positive interpersonal relationships which are the energy sources for adaptive school cultures and productive organizations.

It is critically important in implementing a coaching model to realize the distinct differences between coaching and evaluation. Figure 13.1 makes clear the distinction between coaching and evaluation in terms of a number of attributes. Unlike evaluation, coaching can be done by a wider group of players, over the entire school year, for the purpose of improving instruction rather than the purposes of quality control. The data collected are directly related only to the teaching/learning act and are the possession of the teacher, who makes all evaluative judgments. The teacher decides the areas with which he or she wants help, and

Figure 13.1　Coaching/Evaluation Distinctions

Attribute	Coaching	Evaluation
Who's Responsible?	It is possible to delegate this responsibility to department chairpersons, peers, mentors or colleagues.	By law, only personnel holding an administrative credential may be authorized to evaluate.
Timing	Coaching starts with the first day on the job and can be ongoing throughout the year.	Districts adopt policies and deadlines by which teachers must be evaluated.
Purposes	Improve instruction, curriculum, and student learning.	Quality control and meeting contractual requirements.
Sources of Criteria	The teacher determines what the coach shall look for as criteria for excellence in terms of student behavior and teacher behavior.	Quality teaching standards are usually developed, negotiated, adopted and made public on forms which are used in the evaluation process. While these statements vary from district to district, it is common practice for an evaluator to rate teachers' performance on these criteria.
Uses of the Data Collected	The data collected is given to the teacher.	Information written on the district-adopted forms are usually distributed to the teacher, to the district for placement in the employee's personnel file and another copy is retained by the building principal.
Topics Covered	Learning, classroom interaction, instruction, student performance, curriculum adherence, individual student behavior, teachers' behavior and skills, etc.	In addition, may include such performances as punctuality, willingness to participate in extra-curricular and professional activities, personal characteristics, professional attitudes and growth, etc.
Value Judgments	The teacher evaluates his or her own performance according to the criteria that were set out in the planning conference.	Within the word "evaluation" is "value." Teacher performance is rated by evaluations such as Outstanding, Adequate, or Needs to Improve.
The Role of the Observer	The teacher informs the coach of what to look for and what feedback information would be desired and helpful.	Equipped with the criteria from the district's evaluation system, the observer knows what to look for before entering the classroom. Evaluators are often trained in techniques of observing classroom instruction so that they can detect indicators of excellence or inadequacies in the specified performance criteria.
Empowerment	The power to coach is bestowed by the teacher. They "allow" themselves to be coached because of the respect, the helpfulness, and the leadership qualities of the coach.	The power to evaluate is bestowed by the Board of Trustees and the State or Province. It is a line staff authority position.

Cognitive Coaching: A Foundation for Renaissance Schools, by A.L. Costa and R.J. Garmston. ©1994 Christopher-Gordon.

engages freely in the coaching relationship. Clearly, coaching is a powerful strategy for growth.

As defined by Costa and Garmston (1994), the coaching process consists of four phases. Phase One is the planning conference, during which time the teacher clarifies lesson goals and objectives, shares anticipated teaching strategies and decisions, identifies data to be collected on student achievement, and identifies the data the coach is to collect during the teaching. Phase Two is the lesson. During the teaching the coach gathers the data identified in Phase One. Phases Three and Four constitute the reflecting conference. Phase Three, reflecting, asks the teacher to share impressions and to critique the lesson, identifying the data used to arrive at these conclusions. In Phase Four, the applying phase, the coach has the teacher identify teacher learnings and implications for future lessons, as well as reflecting on the coaching process.

The four phases of the coaching process have been dramatically simplified in the discussion above. Coaching requires study and training to be effective. A coach should make a careful study of Costa's and Garmston's book, as well as other resources, before beginning the process. A bibliography of coaching resources is found in Appendix C.

A Research-Driven Model for Inservice Education

So what does all of this say to us about the nature of effective inservice education? Several implications for the design and conduct of inservice activities surface in this review of the literature. The implications for a Research-Driven Model for Inservice Education are described below.

- Change is meaningful when it is dictated by need recognized through practice and research. Staff development efforts should begin with a needs assessment. The Levels of Use questionnaire appears to be a powerful needs assessment tool. The K-W-L Strategy is also helpful.

- Change occurs best when it is driven by a solid understanding of the knowledge base. Staff development efforts should develop understandings of this knowledge base. Study groups with open, non-judgmental dialogue support this learning in a school culture that taps the creative energy of the staff, values creativity, and makes it safe for staff to propose and act on new ideas.

- Because all change is ultimately directed at creating better learning environments for students, staff development efforts should include an evaluation component.

- Staff development training should include theory, demonstration, practice, and coaching. Innovations live or die by the amount and quality of assistance that their users receive once the change process is underway.

- Inservice in the tenets and practices of whole language should be consistent with these tenets. Staff development practices should be participant-centered, move learners from the known to the unknown, and provide opportunities for teachers to try out new learnings in risk-free environments.

- District-level monetary and conceptual support are essential for effective, sustained change in schools.

Let's turn now to the elements of the Research-Driven Model of Inservice Education as it applies to staff development in assessment and evaluation. This model is offered as a *starting point* for planning inservice training, not as *the plan* for all inservice training in assessment and evaluation. Unique school district, school, administrator, teacher, and learner needs will dictate modifications in the model.

Element One: Needs Assessment

There are many avenues by which an educational leader could assess the learning needs of a group of staff development participants. The strategy illustrated here is the "Levels of Use of an Innovation in Classrooms" (LoU) as recommended in the literature by Baker (1992). Figure 13.2 illustrates an LoU survey drawn from twelve of the thirteen principles outlined in Chapter 3. The example asks teachers to comment on the level of use in their classrooms. The form could be modified to ask about levels of use within the school.

Another form of assessing needs is to have inservice participants complete a K-W-L statement. Here the K stands for "what I know about this topic at this time," the W stands for "what I want to know about this topic," and the L, written after a period of study and reflection, stands for "what I have learned." While the K-W-L strategy is usually done as a small-group sharing or brainstorming, it can be useful to have each teacher complete the K and W portions as a form of needs

Figure 13.2 Levels of Use of the Principles of Assessment and Evaluation

Instructions: We are determining faculty needs and interest in inservice topics. Assessment and evaluation is becoming ever more critical as we change instructional strategies. There are thirteen principles of assessment and evaluation listed below. Under each one is a scale describing levels of use in your classroom. Please place an X above the point on the scale that you think most accurately reflects the level of use of that principle in your classroom.

Principle One: Assessment and evaluation activities are conducted first and foremost for the benefit of the individual learner.

non-use	orientation	preparation	stages of use: place a check beside the
(not done	(you are now	(you are getting	best description of your use:
at all)	learning about it)	ready to do it)	____ mechanical use (just mastering tasks involved)
			____ routine use (use is stable, not making many changes)
			____ refinement (making it better for students)
			____ integration (working with my colleagues to make it better for students)
			____ renewal (evaluating, looking at new ideas, setting new goals)

Principle Two: Assessment and evaluation strategies honor the wholeness of language.

non-use	orientation	preparation	stages of use: place a check beside the
(not done	(you are now	(you are getting	best description of your use:
at all)	learning about it)	ready to do it)	____ mechanical use (just mastering tasks involved)
			____ routine use (use is stable, not making many changes)
			____ refinement (making it better for students)
			____ integration (working with my colleagues to make it better for students)
			____ renewal (evaluating, looking at new ideas, setting new goals)

Principle Three: Reading and writing are viewed as processes.

non-use	orientation	preparation	stages of use: place a check beside the
(not done	(you are now	(you are getting	best description of your use:
at all)	learning about it)	ready to do it)	____ mechanical use (just mastering tasks involved)
			____ routine use (use is stable, not making many changes)
			____ refinement (making it better for students)
			____ integration (working with my colleagues to make it better for students)
			____ renewal (evaluating, looking at new ideas, setting new goals)

Principle Four: Teacher intuition is a valuable assessment and evaluation tool.

non-use (not done at all)	orientation (you are now learning about it)	preparation (you are getting ready to do it)	stages of use: place a check beside the best description of your use:
			____ mechanical use (just mastering tasks involved)
			____ routine use (use is stable, not making many changes)
			____ refinement (making it better for students)
			____ integration (working with my colleagues to make it better for students)
			____ renewal (evaluating, looking at new ideas, setting new goals)

Principle Five: Teacher observation is at the center of assessment and evaluation.

non-use (not done at all)	orientation (you are now learning about it)	preparation (you are getting ready to do it)	stages of use: place a check beside the best description of your use:
			____ mechanical use (just mastering tasks involved)
			____ routine use (use is stable, not making many changes)
			____ refinement (making it better for students)
			____ integration (working with my colleagues to make it better for students)
			____ renewal (evaluating, looking at new ideas, setting new goals)

Principle Six: Assessment and evaluation in reading must reflect what we know about the reading process.

non-use (not done at all)	orientation (you are now learning about it)	preparation (you are getting ready to do it)	stages of use: place a check beside the best description of your use:
			____ mechanical use (just mastering tasks involved)
			____ routine use (use is stable, not making many changes)
			____ refinement (making it better for students)
			____ integration (working with my colleagues to make it better for students)
			____ renewal (evaluating, looking at new ideas, setting new goals)

Principle Seven: Assessment and evaluation in writing must reflect what we know about the writing process.

non-use (not done at all)	orientation (you are now learning about it)	preparation (you are getting ready to do it)	stages of use: place a check beside the best description of your use:
			____ mechanical use (just mastering tasks involved)
			____ routine use (use is stable, not making many changes)
			____ refinement (making it better for students)
			____ integration (working with my colleagues to make it better for students)
			____ renewal (evaluating, looking at new ideas, setting new goals)

Note: Principle Eight is not included on this form.

Principle Nine: Assessment and evaluation instruments are varied and literacy is assessed in a variety of contexts.

non-use (not done at all)	orientation (you are now learning about it)	preparation (you are getting ready to do it)	stages of use: place a check beside the best description of your use:
			____ mechanical use (just mastering tasks involved)
			____ routine use (use is stable, not making many changes)
			____ refinement (making it better for students)
			____ integration (working with my colleagues to make it better for students)
			____ renewal (evaluating, looking at new ideas, setting new goals)

Principle Ten: Assessment and evaluation are integral parts of instruction.

non-use (not done at all)	orientation (you are now learning about it)	preparation (you are getting ready to do it)	stages of use: place a check beside the best description of your use:
			____ mechanical use (just mastering tasks involved)
			____ routine use (use is stable, not making many changes)
			____ refinement (making it better for students)
			____ integration (working with my colleagues to make it better for students)
			____ renewal (evaluating, looking at new ideas, setting new goals)

Principle Eleven: Assessment and evaluation strategies are developmentally and culturally appropriate.

non-use (not done at all)	orientation (you are now learning about it)	preparation (you are getting ready to do it)	stages of use: place a check beside the best description of your use:
			____ mechanical use (just mastering tasks involved)
			____ routine use (use is stable, not making many changes)
			____ refinement (making it better for students)
			____ integration (working with my colleagues to make it better for students)
			____ renewal (evaluating, looking at new ideas, setting new goals)

Principle Twelve: Assessment and evaluation occur continuously.

non-use (not done at all)	orientation (you are now learning about it)	preparation (you are getting ready to do it)	stages of use: place a check beside the best description of your use:
			____ mechanical use (just mastering tasks involved)
			____ routine use (use is stable, not making many changes)
			____ refinement (making it better for students)
			____ integration (working with my colleagues to make it better for students)
			____ renewal (evaluating, looking at new ideas, setting new goals)

Principle Thirteen: Assessment and evaluation reveal children's strengths.

non-use (not done at all)	orientation (you are now learning about it)	preparation (you are getting ready to do it)	stages of use: place a check beside the best description of your use:
			____ mechanical use (just mastering tasks involved)
			____ routine use (use is stable, not making many changes)
			____ refinement (making it better for students)
			____ integration (working with my colleagues to make it better for students)
			____ renewal (evaluating, looking at new ideas, setting new goals)

Figure 13.3   A K-W-L Needs Assessment Form

Instructions: Please use this form to identify the topics you would most like to see addressed in inservice training on assessment and evaluation in student-centered classrooms. Following *Topic* indicate the topic you wish to study. Following *What I Know Now* indicate what you currently know about that topic. Following *What I Want To Know* indicate the question you seek to answer or the problems you wish to solve. Thank you for completing the form. Please use additional forms if necessary.

Name: _____

Topic: _____

What I Know Now:

What I Want To Know:

assessment. Figure 13.3 illustrates a form that could be used for this purpose.

At the end of the staff development experience, the K-W-L form could be returned to participants and they could use the back of the form to record what they have learned.

Element Two: Development of the Knowledge Base

Once the results of the needs assessment have been analyzed, the educational leader can make decisions about the content of the inservice project. Several critical questions need to be answered at this point.

1. What content will form the knowledge base for the inservice training? Who are the best people who can help teachers develop this knowledge base? Are they teachers, curriculum consultants, or other educational leaders working within the district or school? Is there need for an outside consultant? What are the budgetary constraints related to hiring persons to develop the knowledge base?

2. What is the best delivery system for the kinds of knowledge to be developed through the inservice? Would teachers' needs best be served by creating a series of "round table" discussions of professional readings? Would it be best to arrange early dismissal so that there would be several hours available for input from a consultant or resident expert? Should teachers be sent to visit model classrooms or programs?

3. How can study groups be formed? Should they be grouped by grade level or across grade levels? Should they be within-school or across schools? How often shall they meet? When will they meet? Will time be taken from regular faculty or staff meetings for study groups? Will they meet before or after school? What are the budgetary implications here? How will they be led? How will parents be involved in this effort? Will there be a reporting system for their work? If so, to whom will they report, how will they report, and why will they report? How can we assure or support transfer from the study groups to classroom practice?

4. Are changes needed in the culture of the school before innovation will be accepted and study groups can be functioning? What changes are needed and how will they

happen? Is the culture of the school collegial? Is the atmosphere non-judgmental? Will teachers be able to enter into dialogue about the knowledge base with creative energy, openness to new ideas, and willingness to take risks? If not, how can this be changed? Appendix A lists resources for developing the knowledge base in assessment and evaluation.

Element Three: Designing Inservice Training

Inservice training should be designed to incorporate the basic tenets of whole language instruction for children. Staff development practices should be participant-centered. Learners should move from the known to the unknown, and they should have opportunities to try out new ideas in risk-free environments. Several critical questions must be answered in building in this element of the Research-Driven Model for Inservice Education.

1. Will the LoU and K-W-L needs assessment adequately focus the inservice on the participants' needs or are there other ways in which the inservice can be made more participant-centered?

2. Are there ways to build in choice for the learner?

3. How can teachers be encouraged to try out new ideas in the classroom?

4. Should the consultant(s) or other knowledge-base experts work side by side with teachers in classrooms following presentations?

5. Should exit slips be used that focus on a presentation and classroom follow-up? Figure 13.4 is an example of an inservice exit slip that would be completed as participants complete a training session. It focuses on the learnings from the sessions as well as the next steps to be taken in the classroom.

Element Four: Theory, Demonstration, Practice and Coaching

Answering the questions posed under Element Two will help the educational leader decide how the theory is to be presented. Typically this is a combination of study groups formed to examine the professional

Figure 13.4   Inservice Exit Slip

Name: _____ Date: _____

Inservice Session Attended: _____

Important Things I Learned in This Session

What I'm Going to Try in My Classroom Next

literature and presentations offered by experts. An element often missing from inservice training is demonstration. However, the research is clear that demonstrations help teachers better prepare for their own practice of an innovation. Several questions must be addressed about demonstrations:

1. Who will conduct the demonstrations?

2. Will the staff development participant be transported to a classroom to witness the demonstration, or will the students be brought to the inservice?

3. If students are brought from their classroom, what problems of authenticity must be addressed?

4. How many demonstrations will be necessary before teachers are comfortable enough to try to practice an innovation themselves?

5. Should the demonstrations be conducted by an expert in the individual classrooms of participants?

6. What are the time, management, and budgetary implications related to demonstrations?

With regard to practice, decisions must be made about how teachers will have time for adequate reflection after practice, ways to plan to modify practice after reflection, and ways to revisit the theory after practice.

The next consideration in this element is the matter of coaching. A myriad of questions must be addressed by the educational leader planning to implement a coaching process. Among them are

1. How will coaches be identified?

2. Should criteria be drawn up for selecting coaches?

3. Who will make the selections?

4. How will coaches be trained?

5. Will training be developed as part of the knowledge base for the inservice or will it be separate? Appendix B lists references for coaching.

Element Five: Evaluation Component

Staff development efforts should have an evaluation component. This evaluation component may have two aspects: one looks at the

Figure 13.5   Staff Development Process Evaluation Instrument

1. List the five most important things you learned during this staff development process and indicate how you plan to use this knowledge in your classroom.

2. What were the most helpful aspects of the inservice for you?

3. What were the least helpful aspects of the inservice for you?

4. What questions do you have that have been left unanswered as a result of this inservice effort?

5. How will you find answers to the questions you listed in #4?

satisfaction of participants with the training; the other looks at the effects of the training on the learning of children. In looking at the satisfaction of the participants, educational leaders should probably design an evaluation instrument created especially to meet the unique needs and questions growing out of a particular inservice. A "generic" staff development evaluation is illustrated in Figure 13.5. It is offered as a starting point for designing an instrument.

The second aspect of evaluating the staff development effort is much more complex than examining the satisfaction of the participants. Looking at the effect of the inservice on the learning of children requires the implementation of a research process. Some schools bring in outside evaluators. Others design very complex (and sometimes cumbersome) quantitative research projects. Increasingly, teachers are seeing themselves as researchers. Teacher researchers often engage in rather informal qualitative research.

We have previously addressed the concept of the intuitive teacher carefully observing the work of children as a viable means of setting learning goals, expectations, for students. The concept of the teacher researcher is gaining wider acceptance within the literacy profession. While teachers should certainly not be the only researchers at work, the role of the teacher as researcher is a previously untapped source of important information about the teaching/learning process.

Patterson, Stansell and Lee (1990) have described the power of teacher research as follows:

> ...teachers can move beyond kidwatching to do systematic research in their classrooms. We argue that teachers' research can inform specific instructional decisions, but we also explore the potential for these research findings to influence teachers' personal theories and our collective theoretical understandings. Teacher research promises to offer teachers a tool for professional development and a vehicle for gaining power in the profession and in policy-making arenas. (p. vii)

Appendix C is a bibliography of resources about teachers as researchers.

Questions to address regarding the evaluation component include:

1. For whom is the evaluation to be done?

2. What questions should be answered as a result of the evaluation effort?

3. What is to be done with the data resulting from the evaluation?

4. What kind of data are desired or required in this evaluation effort?

5. Do the answers to the questions above suggest the need for an outside evaluator, qualitative research design, quantitative research design, or teacher research?

Element Six: Monetary and Conceptual Support

District-level monetary and conceptual support are essential for effective, sustained change in schools. Many of us engaged in staff development know the futility of the "expert consultant" who flies into a city to conduct an hour or three of inservice training for the elementary teachers in a school or district. Without the monetary and conceptual support of the district administrators, school boards and councils — with sustained effort as described in this model — these efforts have little, if any, effect. But the individual building principal or district language arts supervisor cannot do it alone. Effective inservice training requires time, commitment, and money combined with thoughtful, careful, participant-centered instruction.

Effective inservice education is the key to change. The Research-driven Model for Inservice Education lays the groundwork for this kind of effective staff development.

References

Anderson, G.S. (1993, March). A survey of teacher's transition from skills to whole language. A paper presented at the Annual Meeting of the National Council of Teachers of English, Richmond, VA.

Baker, E.J. (1992, January). Does inservice make a difference? A way to measure whether teachers are using what they learn in inservice. A paper presented at the Annual Meeting of the Washington Association of Supervision and Curriculum Development, Seattle.

Costa, A.L. & Garmston, R.J. (1994). *Cognitive coaching: A foundation for Renaissance schools.* Norwood, MA: Christopher-Gordon.

Hord, S., Rutherford, W., Hulin-Austin, L., & Hall, G.E. (1987). *Taking charge of change.* Alexandria, VA: Association for Supervision and Curriculum Development.

Huberman M., & Miles, M. (1984). *Innovation up close.* New York: Plenum.

Joyce, B., & Showers, B. (1980). Training ourselves to teach: The messages of research. *Educational Leadership, 37,* 379–385.

Joyce, B., & Showers, B. (1982). The coaching of teaching. *Educational Leadership, 40,* 4–10.

Joyce, B., & Showers, B. (1983). *Power in staff development through research on training.* Reston, VA: Association for Supervision and Curriculum Development.

Joyce, B., & Showers, B. (1988). *Student achievement through staff development.* New York: Longman.

Joyce, B., Bennett, B., & Rolheiser-Bennett, C. (1990). The self-educating teacher: Empowering teachers through research. In Joyce, B. (Ed.), *Changing school culture through staff development.* Alexandria, VA: Association for Supervision and Curriculum Development.

Mell, B., & Mell, C. (1990). An experience in anchorage: Trials, errors and successes. In Joyce, B. (Ed.), *Changing school culture through staff development.* Alexandria, VA: Association for Supervision and Curriculum Development.

Moss, B. (1992). Planning effective whole language staff development programs: A guide for staff developers. *Reading Horizons, 32,* 299–315.

Ogle, D. (1986). K-W-L: A teaching model that develops active reading of expository text. *The Reading Teacher, 39,* 564–570.

Pahl, M.M., & Monson, R.J. (1992). In search of whole language: Transforming curriculum and instruction. *Journal of Reading, 35,* 518–524.

Patterson, L., Stansell, J.C., & Lee, S. (1990). *Teacher research: From promise to power.* Katonah, NY: Richard C. Owen Publishers, Inc.

Seller, W. (1993). New images for the principal's role in professional development. *Journal of Staff Development, 14,* 22–26.

Shanker, A. (1990). Staff development and the restructured school. In Joyce, B. (Ed.), *Changing school culture through staff development.* Alexandria, VA: Association for Supervision and Curriculum Development.

Showers, B. (1990). Aiming for superior classroom instruction for all children: A comprehensive staff development model. *Remedial and Special Education, 11,* 35–39.

Siedow, M.D. (1985). Inservice education for content area teachers: Some basic principles. In M.D. Siedow, D.M. Memory, & P.S. Bristow (Eds.), *Inservice education for content area teachers.* Newark, DE: International Reading Association.

Wollman-Bonilla, J. (1991). Shouting from the tops of buildings: Teachers as learners and change in schools. *Language Arts, 68,* 114–120.

Epilogue

Applying the Research-Driven Model of Inservice Education

Bill Harp

In this epilogue we will examine one way in which the Research-Driven Model of Inservice Education may be applied to key concepts drawn from Chapter One. It is hoped that this example will serve as a starting point in planning for inservice education.

From Chapter One — The Mythology of Whole Language

One of the key concepts presented in Chapter One was that the concept of whole language is shrouded in mythology. This mythology is the result of misinterpretation and misunderstanding of the nature of whole language instruction. How might the Inservice Model look if dispelling some of this mythology was the knowledge base outcome for inservice training?

Element One: Needs Assessment

Here the point of a needs assessment would be to determine the degree of understanding teachers have about myths selected from those outlined in Chapter One. The K-L format is appropriate here. Figure E.1 illustrates the K-L format needs assessment applied to selected myths of whole language assessment and evaluation.

Figure E.1   K-L Needs Assessment
The Myths of Whole Language Assessment and Evaluation

Teacher's Name _____

Date _____

Directions: When we think about whole language instruction, particularly assessment and evaluation in whole language, we realize there are several myths subscribed to by some teachers. Below are listed some of these myths. Under each myth statement you are asked to write what you know about the myth and what you would like to learn.

Myth One: Whole language teachers don't test; they don't really know what kids are learning.

What I Now Know:

What I Want to Learn:

Myth Two: Children in whole language classrooms do not do well on norm-referenced tests.

What I Now Know:

What I Want to Learn:

Myth Three: Whole language instruction requires that you do portfolio assessment, which is nothing more than collecting work samples.

What I Now Know:

What I Want to Learn:

Myth Four: Whole language teachers don't know whether or not children have comprehended because they don't ask comprehension questions.

What I Now Know:

What I Want to Learn:

Element Two: Development of the Knowledge Base

Step One: Analyze the needs assessment data to determine the myths about which teachers want more knowledge. For purposes of illustration, let's suppose that the needs assessment resulted in the following concepts being identified for study during the inservice:

- Running records are a form of miscue analysis about which teachers want more information. They are comfortable with evaluation strategies in writing, but want more information about evaluating the child's use of the cueing systems and the reading process.

- Teachers want to learn more about portfolios as a form of evaluation. They are comfortable with collecting contents for the portfolios, but are not happy with their ability to analyze the data, evaluate it, and make instructional decisions.

- Teachers are happy with the results of having children retell as a measure of comprehension, but they want more information about ways to develop comprehension ability. They feel that asking comprehension questions per se is outmoded, but are not sure what to put in the place of comprehension questions.

Step Two: Once the content — the knowledge base — to be developed through inservice education has been identified, a series of questions must be addressed.

1. Who is the best person (or persons) to develop this knowledge base with teachers? Can we draw on district personnel or do we need to go outside? What are the budgetary constraints here?

2. What is the best delivery system for the kinds of knowledge to be developed? Should early dismissal be arranged to create a large block of instructional time?

3. How can study groups be formed? Should they be formed by grade level or across grade levels?

4. Are changes needed in the culture of the school before innovation will be accepted and study groups can be functioning?

Other key questions are listed on pages 316 and 317 of Chapter Thirteen. For the sake of illustration, let's assume the decision was made to treat each of the three concepts identified above as separate workshop topics. The first topic to be dealt with is the third one listed in Step One above. How might the questions listed above be answered in light of this inservice topic: *ways to develop comprehension ability.*

1. *Who is the best person (or persons) to develop this knowledge base with teachers?* As a person responsible for inservice education, you consider your strengths in light of the outcomes for the workshop. You then consider other district personnel who might lead the workshop. Finally, you decide that an outside consultant who has recently published in this area would be the best choice of workshop leader. *Can we draw on district personnel or do we need to go outside?* Outside. *What are the budgetary constraints here?* The district can support the costs of travel, an honorarium, and lodging for the workshop.

2. *What is the best delivery system for the kinds of knowledge to be developed?* A presentation by an expert followed up with study groups. *Should early dismissal be arranged to create a large block of instructional time?* Dismiss at noon so that a workshop can be conducted from 12:30 until 3:30.

3. *How can study groups be formed?* Study groups will be formed that require participation by all who attend the afternoon workshop. *Should they be formed by grade level or across grade levels?* Study groups will be formed by grade-level brackets (K; 1 & 2; 3 & 4; 5 & 6).

4. *Are changes needed in the culture of the school before innovation will be accepted and study groups can be functioning?* The culture of the school supports change, especially when that change has been identified by teachers as a need. One fifth grade teacher who says she is going to retire, but hasn't made that official, will need to be encouraged to participate. The building principal will discuss the inservice with her, ask for her participation, and begin a "plan of assistance" process if cooperation is not forthcoming.

Step Three: Theory, demonstration, practice, and coaching. Decisions have been made to have an outside consultant conduct a three-hour workshop on improving comprehension ability. Teachers will be placed in study groups prior to this workshop and will begin professional reading and dialogue. Some possible readings are listed below.

Bibliography for Study Teams
Improving Comprehension

Baker, L., & Brown, A. L. (1984). Cognitive monitoring in reading. In J. Flood (Ed.), *Understanding Reading Comprehension.* Newark, DE: International Reading Association, pp. 21–44.

Fitzgerald. J., & Spiegel, D.L (1983). Enhancing children's reading comprehension through instruction in narrative structure. *Journal of Reading Behavior, 15,* 1–17.

Fitzgerald, J., Spiegel, D.L., & Webb, T.B. (1985). Development of children's knowledge of story structure and content. *Journal of Educational Research, 79,* 101–108.

Goodman, K.S. (1967). Reading: A psycholinguistic guessing game. *Journal of the Reading Specialist, 4,* 126–135.

Harp, B. (1993). *Bringing children to literacy: Classrooms at work.* Norwood, MA: Christopher-Gordon Publishers, Inc.

Mooney, M. E. (1990). *Reading to, with and by children.* Katonah, NY: Richard C. Owen Publishers, Inc.

Peterson, R., & Eeds, M. (1990). *Grand conversations: Literature groups in action.* New York: Scholastic, Inc.

The consultant has objected to including demonstrations with children during the workshop because she does not know the children and therefore the demonstration cannot be authentic in terms of meeting the needs of the children. The decision has been made to use videotapes of strategy demonstrations made by the consultant in other settings. The consultant, who is always uncomfortable about coming into a school, doing a presentation, and then leaving, has agreed to work an additional morning with grade-level leaders on developing strategies so that these persons can work in classrooms with teachers.

The plan for a hypothetical workshop on comprehension follows. The plan is explained in the following six parts, which are identified by Roman numerals.

   I.   Reviewing the Needs Assessment and Writing Goals

  II.   Workshop Topics

 III.   Exploring Understandings and Classroom Applications

  IV.   Planning for Practice

   V.   Using Peer Coaching

  VI.   The Evaluation Component

Workshop Part I. Reviewing the Needs Assessment and Writing Goals

Participants are asked to sit together in study teams and are given the K-L Needs Assessment sheet they prepared earlier. They are asked to review both the "What I now know" statements and their "What I want to learn" statements. They are asked to write three specific learning goals they have for this workshop.

Workshop Part II. Workshop Topics

The workshop presentation by the consultant covers the following topics (adapted from Harp and Brewer, 1991):

✳ The Goals of Comprehension Instruction ✳

1. Readers will be able to monitor their creation of meaning during the reading act and take necessary corrective action.

2. Readers will be able to establish their own purposes for reading a selection and then choose the most appropriate reading strategies.

3. Readers will be able to adjust their reading rate to fit their purposes for reading the selection.

4. Readers will draw on their schemata to interact with the ideas of the writer. They will construct meaning from this interaction.

5. Readers will recognize when comprehension has failed, will then read on, reread, or consult an expert source (book or person), and will apply the most efficient corrective strategy.

6. Readers will ask for help when the comprehension process has faltered.

✳ Direct Instruction in Comprehension ✳

Comprehension can be taught by continually bringing the reading process to a conscious level, by modeling interaction with print for children, and by arranging instructional strategies that help them develop metacomprehension abilities. Pearson and Johnson (p. 4, 1978) listed the following things we can do to *teach* comprehension:

1. Model comprehension processes for students.

2. Provide cues to help them understand what they are reading.

3. Guide discussion to help children know what they know.

4. Ask pointed, penetrating, or directional questions; offer feedback.

5. Generate useful independent practice activities.

6. Help expand and clarify children's vocabularies.

7. Teach children how to handle various formats (charts, graphs, tables).

8. Offer guidance about how to study a text.

✳ Guided Reading as a Way of Developing Metacomprehension Ability ✳

Guided reading is a strategy in which the teacher works with an individual or small group (usually a group) and guides them through segments of a text by focusing on the use of background knowledge, the reading process, and other skills or strategies the children may need.

A form of guided reading known as the Guided Metacomprehension Strategy (GMS) is based on an understanding of the most up-to-date information about the reading process. The focus of the GMS is to help readers learn to monitor their own creation of meaning and their use of the reading process.

Guided Metacomprehension Strategy

1. **Schemata awareness.** Focus: drawing on the reader's schemata to assist in relating the text to his or her background experiences.

   A. Tell readers the topic or theme of the selection. Probe their background experiences and knowledge about the topic or theme.

   B. Ask them to think about three questions: (1) What do I know about the topic? (2) What experiences have I had with the topic? (3) What will I need to remember from my experience as I read?

   C. **Important:** Engage them in thought about the purposes for reading the text — for information, for entertainment, to be persuaded, etc. Purpose depends on the nature of the text; for example, the purpose of reading an expository piece on Egypt would be very different from the purpose of reading a poem.

2. **Prediction making.** Focus: drawing on available clues, the reader makes predictions about the story.

   A. Give readers clues — the title, a picture, a sample sentence or paragraph, an incident.

   B. Get predictions. Ask, "What do you think will happen in this story?" Be sure to get a prediction, or at least concurrence with another child's prediction, from each child in the group. (Note: Do not try this prediction strategy with children who have already read the story. It will not work!) As children are making predictions, point out to them the ways in which they are drawing on their background knowledge in the process. Underscore this important schemata-reading link.

3. **Silent reading.** Assign specified pages. You decide the most interesting way to segment the selection.

4. **Discussion and oral rereading.** Focus: proving or disproving predictions.

    A. Ask, "Which of our predictions can we prove? Which ones were not proven?" Ask, "Can you read aloud the part that proves or makes us change our predictions?"

    B. This is a good time for questions about story structure. (Where are we in the plot? Who are the central characters? What is the conflict? Where does the story take place?)

5. **Prediction making**

    A. Invite reflection on the story so far; it is now a clue to what will follow.

    B. Ask, "What do you think will happen next?" We suggest that you note students' predictions on a pad of paper or the chalkboard so that you do not accidentally overlook a prediction.

6. **Silent reading.** Assign further specified pages.

7. **Continuing to conclusion.** Recycle through Steps 4, 5, and 6 as many times as necessary to complete the story.

8. **Bringing reading to a conscious level.** Focus One: helping readers think about how they used the reading process. This step could be used at various points of discussion throughout the selection as well as at the end of the reading.

    A. Ask readers to retell as much as they can remember about the story.

    B. Ask readers questions about how they dealt with the reading process:

        (1) How did you learn from the story?

        (2) What parts of the story were easy to read? Why? Difficult? Why?

        (3) How did you overcome difficulties you had with the text?

        (4) What did you do when you came to a part that was not making sense?

        (5) What did you do when you came to words you did not know?

Focus Two: helping readers think about their response to the text. This is done by asking questions that focus readers' attention on their personal response to the text: Did anything particularly interest you? Frighten you? Surprise you? Make you think? What information do you want to be sure to remember from this text? Have you ever felt like the characters in the story felt? How is your thinking changed as a result of reading this text (or this section of the text)?

9. **Concept development.** Focus: broadening understandings of important concepts.
   A. Evaluate the retellings and discussion in terms of students' understandings of important concepts.
   B. Students' understandings can be broadened and deepened by modeling, drawing, explaining, demonstrating, examining, and acting.

✳ Developing Understanding of Vocabulary ✳

To address the issue of vocabulary development, we discuss the strategies used by teachers to help children understand word meanings when they read. The steps we follow are fairly common across reading programs:

1. Show the children a sentence containing the word, printed on a card or the chalkboard. It is helpful to underline the word. Presenting the word in a sentence permits children to make use of multiple cues.

2. Ask: "Who can read this sentence?" If no one responds, read the sentence to the children.

3. Ask. "Who can tell us what this underlined word means?" If no one responds, tell the children the meaning of the word.

4. Say: "Listen, and I will use the word in another sentence." Note that the definition given in Step 3 and the sentence used in Step 4 should be consistent with the meaning of the word as used in the reading selection.

5. Ask: "Who can use this word in a sentence of your own?" Listen to several volunteers.

6. Discuss the meaning of the word with the group. Discussions of word meanings are important because through the discussion children begin to "own" the word.

✳ Using Structured Overviews ✳

A structured overview is a way of presenting vocabulary terms that shows the interrelationships among the terms. It is best used when presenting information to students as a part of a unit of instruction in one of the content areas (such as social studies, science, or health). Using an overhead projector or the chalkboard, you place the terms on a diagram as you present them, in order to show their relationship to each other.

✳ Understanding Question-Answer Relationships ✳

Of greater importance than readers being able to *answer* questions about a text is their ability to analyze the *sources of information available* for answering questions about a text. Raphael (1982, 1986) proposed the study of QARs. QARs stands for Question-Answer Relationships. She argued that helping readers understand the mental operations involved in answering questions would promote a deeper understanding of the relationships between the question, the text, and the background knowledge of the reader. QARs improve readers' ability to answer questions about text by teaching them how to find information they need.

In studying question-answer relationships, readers come to understand that one source of question-answering information is the text itself. Recall kinds of questions are *right there* in the text. The answer is easy to find. Other questions can be answered by searching the text carefully for cues to the answer. Raphael called this method a *think-and-search* strategy. The answer is in the story, but a little harder to find. You would never find the words in the questions and the words in the answer in the same sentence. Readers have to search the text and think about relationships among pieces of information found there. Let's use *Ira Sleeps Over* here as an aid to understanding these two kinds of information sources. *Right there* answers are explicitly in the text. "What was the name of Ira's next door neighbor?" *Think-and-search* answers are implicitly in the text, but they have to be thought about and searched out. "How did Ira feel as he was trying to decide whether or not to take his bear to Reggie's house?"

In studying QARs readers come to understand that a second source of information for answering questions about texts is the head of the reader. Questions that are very broad, and not text implicit or explicit, signal to the reader that "I am on my own." The answer won't be told by words in the story. You must find the answer in your head.

Understanding that this question is an *on my own* question guides the reader in tapping the appropriate information source. "Was it right or fair for Ira's sister to treat him the way she did?" is an example of an *on my own* kind of question.

✳ Discussing Texts by Responding to Questions ✳

You can deepen and refine children's comprehension of text by carefully planned discussions following the reading of a selection. Sometimes it makes sense to ask questions at junctures in the guided reading activity. Usually the QAR should be examined in answering questions. Vacca, Vacca, and Gove (1991, p. 96) have identified three types of questions that should be asked at key points in the discussion to keep children actively engaged in the discussion: (1) preliminary questions to identify a problem or issue; (2) a question or two to clarify or redirect the discussion; and (3) a final question or two that tie together loose ends or establish a premise for further discussion.

Workshop Part III. Exploring Understanding and Classroom Applications

As the workshop consultant presents the knowledge base outlined above, participants are frequently put into dialogue groups to explore their understandings and classroom applications of the ideas presented. The presentation also includes videotaped classroom demonstrations of the use of the Guided Metacomprehension Strategy, structured overviews, and exploration of Question-Answer Relationships.

Workshop Part IV. Planning for Practice

After the knowledge base has been presented and participants have had many experiences discussing it, they are asked to return to the sheet on which they wrote their three goals for participating in the workshop. They are then asked to write two things: first, a description of the extent to which each goal was met; and second, what aspects of the workshop they plan to put into practice first. An alternative to this procedure would be the use of the Exit Slip illustrated in Figure 13.4. The staff development organizers will then use these statements about practice to decide how best to use the consultant's time the next day in helping teachers implement this practice.

Workshop Part V. Using Peer Coaching

The next task is to implement a peer coaching plan. This includes deciding how coaches will be selected and trained and when and how teachers will be trained in the coaching process.

Pam Robbins (1991), in an Association for Supervision and Curriculum Development publication, outlined seven guidelines for peer coaching. These will influence the instructional leaders' decisions about implementing the peer coaching plan. The guidelines are:

- Examine all the facts about peer coaching and then compare them with your site characteristics before you determine whether peer coaching is right for you.

- Identify what peer coaching is and is not.

- Develop a clear understanding of the different forms of peer coaching.

- Provide time for questions and answers.

- Solicit teacher input regarding the possible features of a site-based peer coaching program.

- Identify the preconditions for change and the cultural variables that will affect the success or failure of peer coaching at your site.

- Analyze the support available for peer coaching. (Robbins, 1991, pp. 16–19)

Two titles are purchased for the teachers who decided to enter into peer coaching arrangements. Drawn from Appendix C, they are: A. L. Costa and R. J. Garmston, *Cognitive Coaching: A Foundation for Renaissance Schools* (Norwood MA: Christopher-Gordon Publishers, Inc., 1994), and P. Robbins, *How to Plan and Implement a Peer Coaching Program* (Alexandria, VA: Association for Supervision and Curriculum Development, 1991).

A plan covering three weeks of after-school meetings is devised to permit teachers to read the materials listed above and come together to dialogue about the coaching process and to troubleshoot their initial efforts at peer coaching. During this period three videotapes are rented from ASCD to facilitate the process. They are entitled: *Opening Doors: An Introduction to Peer Coaching; Another Set of Eyes: Techniques for Classroom Observation;* and *Another Set of Eyes: Conferencing Skills.*

Workshop Part VI. The Evaluation Component

The final step in planning the comprehension inservice is to devise an evaluation component. This should look both at the satisfaction of the participants with the inservice and the effects on children in classrooms.

Participant Satisfaction

Figure 13-5 illustrated a staff development evaluation instrument which could be used for the comprehension workshop or could be used as a model for customizing this workshop.

Effects on Classroom Instruction

Here is the opportunity to focus on the teacher as researcher. If teachers have been conducting classroom research, they could be asked to collaborate in the design of a research project to test the impact of changes in comprehension instruction. If classroom research is new, following the implementation of a coaching model, study teams could focus on the teacher as researcher drawing from the resources in Appendix B. Then a plan to research the effects of changes in comprehension instruction could be designed and implemented. For example, as part of introducing the Guided Metacomprehension Strategy into classrooms, teachers could begin to have children in grades two through five or six write retellings of the stories they read. These retellings could then be evaluated in terms of amount of detail, inferences draw about the selection, inclusion of plot structure, or other criteria established by the teachers.

✳ The Educational Leader's Inservice Planning Checklist ✳

The staff development effort outlined above is one illustration of how the Research-Driven Inservice Education Model may be applied. Many of the questions answered hypothetically in the illustration must be addressed in planning inservice experiences. The inservice planning checklist in Figure E.2 will assist the educational leader in working through the model.

Figure E.2   Inservice Planning Checklist

___ A needs assessment has been conducted to determine the degree to which teachers want or have implemented the innovation or improvement under consideration.

___ Based on an analysis of the needs assessment, the content for the inservice has been identified. The outcomes of the staff development experience have been stated.

___ Teachers or other possible participants have been involved in deciding the content of the inservice education effort.

___ Budgetary implications for the workshop have been identified and the inservice staff has been planned in light of the budgetary limits.

___ The best "delivery system" for the inservice has been planned in light of the content to be presented.

___ The person or persons who will deliver the content of the inservice have been identified.

___ The inservice delivery system will be participant-centered, and will allow participants to move from the known to the unknown in their learning.

___ Plans have been made for participants to have choices as learners.

___ Exit slips have been designed and plans have been made for their use.

___ Plans have been made for participants to try out new ideas in classrooms.

___ Time arrangements and travel arrangements have been made for participants' visits to classroom demonstration sites.

___ Consideration has been given to having inservice leader(s) follow-up by working with participants in classrooms.

___ Plans for the creation and/or facilitation of study groups have been made, including acquiring the necessary reading/reference material.

___ Consideration has been given to the involvement of parents in the study groups.

___ Plans have been formulated for study groups to report on their work and/or apply the results of their study in classrooms.

___ The culture of the school(s) has been studied in terms of support for study groups and innovation. Necessary changes have been identified and planned.

___ Plans have been designed for the implementation/facilitation of the coaching process.

    ___ It is known how coaches will be identified.
    ___ It is known how coaches will be trained.
    ___ It is known how teachers will be trained in the coaching process.
    ___ Resources for training and implementation have been identified.
    ___ Plans have been made for maintaining the coaching process.
    ___ Budgetary challenges of the coaching process have been met.

___ Conceptual and financial support for the central office have been secured.

___ An evaluation plan is in place that examines participant satisfaction in the inservice education effort.

___ An evaluation plan is in place for examining the effects of the inservice effort in terms of pupil achievement or changes in classroom practice.

___ Consideration has been given to the role of teacher research in the evaluation plan.

___ Plans have been made for using evaluation data when they are available.

References

Harp, B., & Brewer, J.A. (1991). *Reading and writing: Teaching for the connections.* Fort Worth, TX: Harcourt Brace Jovanovich, Inc.

Pearson, R.D., & Johnson, D.D. (1978). *Teaching reading comprehension.* New York: Holt, Rinehart & Winston.

Raphael, T.E. (1982). Question-Answering strategies for children. *The Reading Teacher, 36,* 186–191.

Raphael, T.E. (1986). Teaching question-answer relationships, revisited. *The Reading Teacher, 39,* 616–622.

Robbins, P. *How to plan and implement a peer coaching program.* Alexandria, VA: Association for Supervision and Curriculum Development.

Vacca, J.A., Vacca, R.T., & Gove, M.K. (1991). *Reading and learning to read.* New York: HarperCollins Publishers.

Appendix A

Selected Readings in Assessment and Evaluation

Almasi, J. F. (1993). *Literacy: Issues and practices.* Yearbook of the State of Maryland Reading Association Council. Volume 10. ERIC document ED 356465.

Atwell, N. (1988). Making the grade: Evaluation writing in conference. In T. Newkirk & N. Atwell (Eds.), *Understanding writing* (pp. 236–244). Portsmouth, NH: Heinemann.

Bembridge, T. (1992). A MAP for reading assessment. *Educational Leadership, 49*(8): 46–48.

Beverstock, C., Bintz, W., Copenhaver, J., & Farley, T. (1989, December 1). Exploring freewrites as assessment: Insights and patterns. Paper presented at the National Reading Conference, Austin, Texas.

Bird, L. (1989). The art of teaching: Evaluation and revision. In K. Goodman, Y. Goodman, & W. Hood (Eds.), *The whole language evaluation book.* Porstmouth, NH: Heinemann Educational Books.

Cambourne, B. (1985). Assessment in reading: The drunkard's search. In L. Unsworth (Ed.), *Reading: An Australian perspective* (pp. 165–172). Melbourne, Australia: Thomas Nelson.

Cambourne, B. & Turbill, J. (1990). Assessment in whole language classrooms: Theory into practice. *The Elementary School Journal, 90*(3), 337–349.

Clay, M. (1990). Research current: What is and what might be in evaluation. *Language Arts, 67*(3), 288–298.

Cooper, C. R. & Odell, L. (1977). *Evaluating writing: Describing, measuring, judging.* Urbana, IL: National Council of Teachers of English.

Cooper, J. D. (1993). *Literacy: Helping children construct meaning.* 2nd ed. Burlington, MA: Houghton Mifflin.

Costa, A. (1989). Re-assessing assessment. *Educational Leadership, 46,* 2.

Durkin, D. (1987). Testing in the kindergarten. *The Reading Teacher,* 40(8), 766–770.

Goodman, K. S., Bird, L. B., & Goodman, Y. M. (1992). *The whole language catalog supplement on authentic assessment.* Chicago, Il: Macmillan/McGraw-Hill.

Goodman, K. S., Goodman, Y. M., & Hood, W. J. (1989). *The whole language evaluation book.* Portsmouth, NH: Heinemann.

Goodman, Y. (1989). Evaluation of students. In K. Goodman, Y. Goodman, & J. W. Hood (Eds.), *The whole language evaluation book.* Portsmouth, NH: Heinemann Educational Books.

Goodman, Y. (1978). Kidwatching: An alternative to testing. *Journal of National Elementary Principals,* 57(4), 41–45.

Grindler, M. C. & Stratton, B. D. (1992). Whole language assessment. *Reading Improvement,* 29(4), 262–264.

Guba, E. & Lincoln, Y. (1981). *Effective evaluation.* Beverly Hills, CA: Sage.

Gutknecht, B. (1992). Learning about language learners: The case for informal assessment in the whole language classroom. *Reading Improvement,* 29(4), 210–219.

Jaggar, H. & Smith-Burke, T. (Eds.). (1985). *Observing the language learner.* Urbana, IL: International Reading Association/National Council of Teachers of English.

Johnston, P. (1987). Teachers as evaluation experts. *The Reading Teacher,* 40(8), 744–748.

Jongsma, K. S. (1989). Portfolio assessment. *The Reading Teacher,* 43(3), 264–265.

Mathews, J. K. (1990). From computer management to portfolio assessment. *The Reading Teacher,* 43(6), 420–421.

Myers, J. W. (1993). *Making sense of whole language.* Fastback 346. Bloomington, IN: Phi Delta Kappa.

Paratore, J. R. & Indrisano, R. (1987). Intervention assessment of reading comprehension. *The Reading Teacher,* 40(8), 778–783.

Payne, D. (1974). *The assessment of learning: Cognitive and affective.* Lexington, MA: D.C. Heath and Company.

Pearson, P. D. & Valencia, S. (1989). Assessment, accountability, and professional prerogative. Research in literacy: Meaning perspectives. Thirty-sixth Yearbook, National Reading Conference.

Pikulski, J. J. (1989). The assessment of reading: A time for change? *The Reading Teacher, 43*(1), 80–81.

Pikulski, J. (1990). The role of tests in a literacy assessment program. *The Reading Teacher, 43*(9), 686–688.

Reif, L. (1990). Finding the value in evaluation: Self-assessment in a middle school classroom. *Educational Leadership, 47,* 24–29.

Reimer, B. L. & Warshow, L. (1989). Questions we ask of ourselves and our students. *The Reading Teacher, 42*(8), 596–606.

Richman, C. (1990). Evaluating the whole language learner. *The California Reader, 23*(4), 4–5.

Salvia, J. & Ysseldyke, J. E. (1985). *Assessment in special and remedial education* (3rd. ed.). Boston, MA: Houghton Mifflin Co.

Schroeder, L. (1990). Custom tailoring in whole language evaluation. *Journal of the Wisconsin State Reading Assocation, 34*(4), 45–55.

Shepard, L.A. (1989). Why we need better assessments. *Educational Leadership, 46*(1), 4–9.

Simmons, J. (1990). Portfolios as large-scale assessment. *Language Arts, 67*(3), 262–268.

TAWL (Tucsonans Applying Whole Language). (1984). *A Kid-watching guide: Evaluation for whole language calssrooms.* Tucson, AZ: University of Arizona.

Taylor, D. (1990). Teaching without testing: Assessing the complexity of children's literacy learning. *English Education.* February, 4–74.

Valencia, S. W. (1991). New assessment books. *The Reading Teacher, 45*(3), 244–245.

Valencia, S. (1990). A portfolio approach to classroom assessment: The whys, whats, and hows. *The Reading Teacher, 43*(4), 338–340.

Valencia, S. & Pearson, P. D. (1987). Reading assessment: Time for a change. *The Reading Teacher, 40*(8), 726–732.

Valencia, S. Pearson, P. D., Peters, C., & Wixon, K. (1989). Theory and practice in a statewide reading assessment: Closing the gap. *Educational Leadership, 46*(7), 57–63.

Watson, D. (Ed.). (1987). Shared evaluation In *Ideas and insights: Language arts for elementary children.* pp. 218–219. Urbana, IL: National Council of Teaching of English.

Wisconsin State Reading Association. (1990). *Toward an ecological assessment of reading progress.* Schofield, Wisconsin: WSRA.

Wixon, K., Peters, C., Weber, E., & Roeber, E. (1987). New directions in statewide reading assessment. *The Reading Teacher, 40*(8), 749–754.

Wolf, D. (1989). Portfolio assessment: Sampling student work. *Educational Leadership, 47*(7), 35–39.

Wolf, D. (1987, December/January). Opening up assessment. *Educational Leadership, 45*(4), 24–29.

Appendix B

Selected Readings on Coaching

Barth, R. (1990). *Improving schools from within.* San Francisco: Jossey-Bass, Inc.

Brandt, R. S. (1987). On teachers coaching teachers: A conversation with Bruce Joyce. *Educational Leadership, 44*(5), 12–17.

Church, S. M. (1994). Is whole language really warm and fuzzy? *The Reader Teacher, 47*(5), 362–369.

Costa, A. L. & Garmston, R. J. (1994). *Cognitive coaching: A foundation for Renaissance schools.* Norwood, MA: Christopher-Gordon Publishers, Inc.

Cox, C. L. (1991). A process for developing professionalism, achieving instructional excellence, and improving student learning. *Threshold in Education, 17*(4), 23–26.

Desrochers, C. G. (1990). Teacher-directed peer coaching as a follow-up to staff development. *Journal of Staff Development, 11*(2), 6–10.

Fullan, M. (1990). Staff development, innovation and institutional development. In *Changing school culture through staff development,* Joyce B. (Ed.). Alexandria, VA: Association for Supervision and Curriculum Development.

Garmston, R. (1987). How administrators support peer coaching. *Educational Leadership, 44*(50), 18–28.

Grimmett, P. P. (1987). The role of district supervisors in the implementation of peer coaching. *Journal of Curriculum and Supervision, 3*(1), 3–28.

Hargreaves, A. & Dawe, R. (1990). Paths of professional development: Contrived collegiality, collaborative culture, and the case of peer coaching. *Teaching and Teacher Education, 6*(3), 227–241.

Joyce, B. & Showers, B. (1987). Low-cost arrangements for peer coaching. *Journal of Staff Development, 8*(1): 22–24.

Laurel, E. G. (1991). Employing peer coaching to support teachers. *Teacher Education and Practice, 6*(2): 79–82.

Leggert, D. & Hoyle, S. (1987). Peer coaching: One district's experience in using teachers as staff developers. *Journal of Staff Development, 8*(1), 16–20.

Little, J. W. (1985). Teachers as teacher advisers: The delicacy of collegial leadership. *Educational Leadership, 43,* 34–36.

Neubert, G. A. (1988). *Improving teaching through coaching.* Fastback 277. Bloomington, IN: Phi Delta Kappa.

Nolan, J. F. & Hillkirk, K. (1991). The effects of a reflective coaching project for veteran teachers. *Journal of Curriculum and Supervision, 7*(1), 62–76.

Phillips, M. D. & Glickman, C. D. (1991). Peer coaching: Developmental approach to enhancing teacher thinking. *Journal of Staff Development, 12*(2), 20–25.

Raney, P. & Robbins, P. (1989). Professional growth and support through peer coaching. *Educational Leadership, 46*(8), 35–38.

Robbins, P. (1991). *How to plan and implement a peer coaching program.* Alexandria, VA: Association for Supervision and Curriculum Development.

Sparks, D. (1990). An interview with Robert Garmston. *Journal of Staff Development, 11*(2), 12–15.

Appendix C

Selected Readings on Teachers as Researchers

Anzul, M. & Ely, M. (1988). Halls of mirrors: The introduction of the reflective mode. *Language Arts, 65*(7), 675–687.

Biery C. ()1993). When all the right parts don't run the engine: A teacher-researcher project reflects on practice. *Language Arts, 70*(1), 12–17.

Bissex, G. (1986). On becoming teacher experts: What's a teacher-researcher? *Language Arts, 63*(5), 482–484.

Chall, J. S. (1986). The teacher as scholar. *The Reading Teacher, 39*(8), 792–797.

Glesne, C. E. (1991). Yet another role? The teacher as researcher. *Action in Teacher Education, 13*(1), 7–13.

Johnson, B. (1993). *Teacher as researcher. ERIC digest.* Washington, D.C.: ERIC Clearinghouse on Teacher Education.

Kutz, E. (1992). Teacher research: Myths and realities. *Language Arts, 69*(3), 193–197.

Lytle, S. L. & Cochran-Smith, M. (1992). Teacher research as a way of knowing. *Harvard Educational Review, 62*(4), 447–474.

McKernan, J. (1988). Teacher as researcher: Paradigm and praxis. *Contemporary Education, 59*(3), 154–158.

Olson, M. W. (1990a). *Opening the door to classroom research.* Newark, DE: International Reading Association.

Olson, M. W. (1990b). Teachers who question are teachers who learn (research into practice). *Reading Psychology, 11*(3), 277–282.

Otto, W. (1992). How things are (not!) Views and reviews. *Journal of Reading, 36*(3), 234–237.

Powell, J. H. (1992). Empowerment through collegial study groups. *Contemporary Education, 63*(4), 281–284.

Strickland, D. S. (1988). The teacher as researcher: Toward the extended professional. *Language Arts, 65*(8): 754–764.

Contributors

Bill Harp is Professor of Language Arts and Literacy in the College of Education, University of Massachusetts at Lowell. Bill has been appointed to the International Reading Association's Issues in Literacy Assessment. The committee will collect resources concerning assessment worldwide, monitor the progress of and review emerging U.S. standards documents, and survey literacy assessment practices.

Bill received his Ed.D. from the University of Oregon. His writing draws on his experience as an elementary school teacher, a principal, and university professor. He is coauthor, with Dr. Jo Ann Brewer, of *Reading and Writing: Teaching for the Connections, Second Edition* (1995), published by Harcourt Brace, and editor of *Bringing Children to Literacy: Classrooms at Work* (1993), also published by Christopher-Gordon.

John E. Bertrand is Associate Professor of Educational Administration at Tennessee State University in Nashville, Tennessee. A graduate of The Ohio State University with a Ph.D. in policy and leadership, he has eleven years experience as a public school teacher, including three years as director of an alternative program for troubled youth within his school system. His interest in holistic, integrated educational philosophy and teaching be-

gan following a short time teaching in a British informal school and seminars at Exeter University in Devon. He has participated in three research projects on whole language and is the author of a number of articles and chapters in the field.

William P. Bintz is a doctoral candidate in the Language Education Department, School of Education, Indiana University, Bloomington, Indiana. In 1988, he was a Visiting Lecturer in Language Education at the Armidale College of Advanced Education in Armidale, New South Wales, Australia. In 1990 he was awarded a Spencer Dissertation Year Fellowship for Research related to education from the Woodrow Wilson National Fellowship Foundation. At present, he teaches secondary education courses at Western Kentucky University in Bowling Green, Kentucky.

Maggie Castillo holds her M.A. in reading education. She is a Multi-Age Classroom Teacher at the Sedona School in Sedona, Arizona, and is particularly interested in a multi-age classroom curriculum with literature-based instruction.

C. Jean Church is the Elementary Curriculum Coordinator for the Vigo County School District in Terre Haute, Indiana. She received her Ph.D. from Indiana State University. She is currently investigating the process of change in teachers and principals and also spends a great deal of time in classrooms with teachers observing literacy development.

Ward Cockrum received his Ph.D. in curriculum and instruction from Arizona State University. He is an Associate Professor at Northern Arizona University, and President of the Arizona Reading Association.

Jerome C. Harste, Professor of Language Education at Indiana University, has been an elementary school teacher, a Peace Corps Volunteer, and a Board Member of the International Reading Association (1988–1990). He has also chaired NCTE's Commission on Reading and has served as President of the National Reading Conference and the National Conference on Research in English. He is currently President of the Whole Language Umbrella.

Janice Henson is a doctoral candidate at the University of Missouri at Columbia. She has taught in the elementary grades as well as at the college level.

Dorothy F. King is a Senior Research Associate for Research and Training Associates, Inc., Overland Park, Kansas, and serves as a field-based consultant for Rural Technical Assistance Center, Office of Indian Education Programs. She received her Ed.D. from the University of Missouri.

S. Jeanne Reardon teaches primary grades in the Montgomery County Public Schools, Maryland. She received her A.B. from Oberlin College and has done graduate work at George Peabody College, Vanderbilt University and the University of Maryland. Her areas of special interest include writing, children's literature and classroom research.

Yvonne Siu-Runyan is Associate Professor of Literacy at the University of Northern Colorado where she teaches undergraduate and graduate courses in literacy development. She is currently editor of *The Colorado Communicator* and is a member of the Publications Review Board for The International Reading Association. She has taught grades kindergarten through grade 12 in Hawaii, Michigan, Colorado, Ohio, and California and has also been District Reading Specialist and Language Arts Coordinator for Boulder Valley Schools. She has spoken widely and written chapters in books and articles about whole language instruction, integration, writing and reading instruction, and children's literature. She was a founding executive board member for the Whole Language Umbrella, an International Confederation of Teachers.

Hilary Sumner Gahagan received her M.S. in Special Education from the University of Oregon. She is currently Learning Disabilities Specialist in the Beaverton, Oregon schools. Her current research includes Portfolio Supported Inclusion of Special Education Studies in the regular classroom and Attention Deficit Hyperactivity Disorder.

Dorothy J. Watson is Professor of Education at the University of Missouri at Columbia. She is a former president of the Whole Language Umbrella and has authored or coauthored several books, including *Ideas and Insights* (NCTE, 1987) and *Whole Language: Inquiring Voices* (Scholastic, 1988).

Index